Popes and Politics

BY JUSTUS GEORGE LAWLER

Towards a Living Tradition

The Christian Imagination

The Catholic Dimension in Higher Education

The Christian Image

Nuclear War: The Ethic, the Rhetoric, the Reality

The Range of Commitment

Celestial Pantomime: Poetic Structures of Transcendence

Speak That We May Know

Hopkins Re-Constructed

Popes and Politics

POPES
AND
POLITICS

Reform, Resentment,
and the Holocaust

Justus George Lawler

continuum
NEW YORK • LONDON

2004
.

The Continuum International Publishing Group Inc
15 East 26 Street, New York, NY 10010

The Continuum International Publishing Group Ltd
The Tower Building, 11 York Road, London SE1 7NX

Printed in the United States of America

Library of Congress Cataloging-in-Publication Data

Lawler, Justus George.
     Popes and politics : reform, resentment, and the Holocaust / Justus George
Lawler.
        p.   cm.
     Includes bibliographical references and index.
     ISBN 0-8264-1385-4   ISBN 0-8264-1657-8 (pbk)
     1. Papacy—History—20th century.   2. Catholic Church—History—20th
century.   3. Catholic Church—Political activity—History—20th century.
1. Title.
     BX1390 .L39   2002
     262'.13'0904—dc21   2001052730

"Resentment and animosity succeed in the minds of the many when they find their worldly wisdom quite at fault. They accuse the Church of craft. But, in truth, it is her very vastness, her manifold constituents, her complicated structure, which gives her this semblance, whenever she wears it, of feebleness, vacillation, subtleness, or dissimulation. She advances, retires, goes to and fro, passes to the right or left, bides her time, by a spontaneous, not a deliberate action. It is the divinely appointed method of her coping with the world's power."

John Henry Newman

"There is bound to be formed a solid right that is determined to live in a world that no longer exists. There is bound to be formed a scattered left, captivated by now this, now that new development, exploring now this, and now that new possibility. But what will count is a perhaps not numerous center, big enough to be at home in both the old and the new, painstaking enough to work out one by one the transitions to be made, strong enough to refuse half-measures and insist on complete solutions even though it has to wait."

Bernard J. F. Lonergan

In Memory

Yves M.-J. Congar, OP, who in 1958 after a period of spiritual exile in Strasbourg counseled a young author on Catholic higher education: "Un chercheur intellectuel ne peut pas travailler sous le fouet. Où en sommes-nous? . . . . Il est impossible d'avoir une pensée créatrice sans liberté de recherche, sans une certaine fraîcheur de regard."

Henri de Lubac, SJ, who in Chicago seven years later after reading the Modernist issue of *Continuum,* also counseled that, "jamais, dans aucune temps . . . should there be a question of abandoning the fundamental thrust of the Modernist impulse to spiritual and intellectual renewal which the second Vatican Council is bringing to a conclusion."

Contents

Foreword

A FOREWORD BY definition is a forewarning, an announcement of what is going on in the pages that follow.

Popes and Politics begins by presenting evidence which cumulatively proves that a surprisingly large number of recent authors on the papacy have been guilty of obfuscations and distortions which result in a disastrously flawed view of Catholicism both in itself and in its relation to contemporary tragic events, the most important of which is the Holocaust. Whether such books are written out of devotion to the papacy, as with Ralph McInerny or Margherita Marchione, or out of antagonism to it, they do little to satisfy legitimate public need for genuine insight and understanding, and much to satisfy their authors' personal need for venting sentiments either of loyalty or of animosity over matters relating to the condition of the modern church. But since the devout defenders muster few historical or theological arguments, the first part of *Popes and Politics* focuses primarily on what Harold Bloom in another context calls "the school of resentment," a group that includes among others James Carroll, John Cornwell, Michael Phayer, Garry Wills, and Susan Zuccotti.

Popes and Politics shows that what these latter critics are doing to the church is what the church historically did to the Jewish people—methodically scapegoating an imaginary enemy. This exercise in sanctimony, which purports to be the result of historical research carried out under the banner of "honesty," has had two unfortunate consequences. It minimizes the impact of authentic reformers from the past to purge Catholicism of its historical deadweight and, because of its vehemence and its dissimulations, it inhibits dedicated reformers of the present from moving the church fully and effectively into the twenty-first century.

Among these reformers is John Paul II who, though this book is critical of his preoccupation with centralizing authority in the church, has nevertheless strenuously sought to radically improve relations outside the church: relations with the international community, with the Jewish community, and with estranged Christian communities. It is a thesis of this book that the angry voices in the church, which are only recently speaking out on the problems emerging from the period of the first and second Vatican Councils, are tardily exploiting those problems primarily as a way to attack the papacy. Thus when Pius XII is criticized for actions during the second World War, it often masks the implicit indictment of his successors. Even the Holocaust becomes a club to be wielded in that cause.

The beginning chapters are a detailed analysis of the skewed research and conclusions of various denigrators of the modern papacy. The remaining chapters are an affirmation of the principles of authentic reform found in such earlier Catholics as Newman, Acton, Rosmini, de Lamennais, and in such contemporary Catholics as Congar, de Lubac, Häring, Maritain, The book concludes with practical proposals for the institutional and personal renovation of Catholicism in the present age.

Concerning such things as format and structure, the following offer some guidelines. In the first introductory chapter, as a way of easing into the controversial sections that follow, I treat more or less globally as a single group the criticisms of the authors to whom I am responding—they and their observations will become clearly recognizable as the book develops. In that same chapter the unnamed "psychologist of religion" whom I quote on "taste," is Cardinal Newman. References to articles and books without attribution both in the body of the text and in the notes are by the present writer. Where they are needed for rhetorical emphasis, I have supplied all the italics. Passages originally italicized in a work which I am quoting or citing will be indicated as such. Since the notes throughout are clarifications or confirmations of topics in the body of the text, I have used footnotes rather than endnotes.

Similarly, in order to avoid appendices, in a few footnotes I have included detailed material and bibliographic references. Because these footnotes are closely related to the larger themes in the text, while also allowing brief excursions into ancillary subjects, my hope is that they will not be omitted by the reader. The guiding principle here is to "fill every rift with gold," as Keats, tyro upstart, wrote to Shelley, celebrated cosmopolitan. (I hope the reader will be rewarded.) In the first few chapters which focus at length on specific books, in order to avoid unbroken listings of page numbers with "ibids." or "op. cits." in the footnotes, I have omitted that apparatus altogether and included mainly explanatory materials. In the final chapters, which cover a wide and varied range of references, I use the more conventional format.

Being without academic affiliation for the first time in forty years of writing and publishing I have learned to treasure more than in the accessible past, the wonderful services of skilled librarians, particularly my Jagiellonian philologist colleague, not only a reverent custodian but a lover of literature, Ursula Zyzik, who discovered or retrieved for this exurban boondoctor scores of books, articles, and other texts from virtually all over what used to be called the "four corners of the globe." Locally, the heritage of Andrew Carnegie is still alive, and I am grateful to the reference librarians in St. Charles. Also, kudoi to Jamie Manson for compatibilizing—or whatever the term—my relatively archaic and obsolescent-at-creation word processing technology with its "updated" progeny. Frank Oveis, long-time associate and friend, read the entire text and, as he has done for so many authors, discovered errors that simply evaded my closest scrutiny—illustrating that old saw about the folly of lawyers who have themselves as clients. . . .

I appreciate also the editors who used some of the material that appears here: in England, for a short excerpt, the editor of *The Month;* and, for a more substantial section, the editor of *The Downside Review,* Dom Dunstan O'Keefe, affable successor to Illtyd Trethowan, and confrere of Dom Sebastian Moore, ever vital exemplar of Newman's "elbowroom for the mind" who will forgive my animadversions on the innominable mythopoeist of scapegoat theory. And while on the U.K., I must express appreciation again—on this twenty-fifth anniversary of his death—to the superior of the Edgbaston Oratory, Stephen Dessain, for his hospitality decades ago while researching Newman, whom he subsequently "nominated" for sainthood: the fruits of that half year in Birmingham are evident in every thing I have written since. In this country, *U.S. Catholic Historian* editor, Christopher Kauffman, whose historical range—from ministry to the dying in the great plagues of the late Middle Ages; from the Gallicanizing bishops who created the American church; and to the lay order affectionately known as the "Knights," whose largesse sustains the Holy See—expresses the variety of graced thought, word, and deed that this book extols as illustrating the spirit of Catholicity. Finally, the three youths in the fiery furnace of contemporary American life whose ebullience never ceases to delight: Tom, George, and Rich; the last a primatologist—proving the apple doesn't fall far from the tree of knowledge, as we share a mutual interest in chimpanzees and archbishops. I anticipate from all, the now conventionalized snorts about sparkless risible puns.

Lastly, some "allusionary" debts must be acknowledged: to Joseph Blenkinsopp for "Via col Vento in Vaticano," to Harold Bloom for "Jansenist mumps," to John Meagher for computer euphemisms, and to Charles Talar for Umberto Eco and the Knights Templar.

JUSTUS GEORGE LAWLER
October 2, 2001
Feast of the Poetry of Guardian Angels

1

GAINING PERSPECTIVE

"About a Little Book"

> "Quel ton!" he exclaimed on
> reading the Bible. "Quel effroyable ton!
> Ah, Madame, how unfortunate that the
> Holy Spirit should have so little taste."
>
> *The Maréchale de Luxembourg*

The biblical scholar, Alfred Loisy was excommunicated by Pius X in 1908 for, among other offenses, writing an allegedly heretical book on the gospel and the church, a book which was published in 1902 during the reign of Leo XIII—who had, however, *refused* to condemn its author. As the reader shall see, one of the themes of the present book on popes and politics is the dramatic shift in defining religious policy and in exercising religious authority that frequently occurred with the election of a new successor to the "Chair of Peter." In the memory of many adult Catholics, the transition from Pius XII to John XXIII was such a catalytic event; so too—though more gradual and less dramatic—was the transition from Paul VI to John Paul II. To think of the church which these various pontiffs headed as sharing in the presumably unchanging character of the eternal would not only be against all experience; it would be against the very nature of an institution founded on incarnation, on the "wondrous interchange," the *admirabile commercium* of the eternal and the temporal. The church is by definition an institution *in* history and *with* a history.

Loisy's *L'Evangile et l'Eglise* was placed on the index, along with four of his other books, among them a volume of letters which not only defended his book on the gospel and the church, but which also was in effect a manifesto proclaiming the freedom of the Catholic scholar to pursue scientific biblical research. The name of that volume is the title to this introduction, *Autour d'un petit livre*. I thus employ the old image that I shall use several times subsequently of comparing something of major importance with something of relative insignificance. *Popes and Politics* is a little book in scope and in intended impact, unlike both Loisy's *Gospel and the Church* and the volume of letters with the seemingly modest title, "petit," that he wrote in defense of the earlier book. It is even possible that anticipating condemnation, Abbé Loisy was alluding to another reformist predecessor, Abbé de Lamennais, author of *Paroles d'un croyant* (Words of a Believer), which was condemned by Gregory XVI as a "book little in size but immense in perversity." De Lamennais was also subsequently excommunicated.

The use of the word "little" here is motivated by the same intent and has the same significance as the word "accidental" in such contexts as Anne Tyler's novel about "the accidental tourist," or the computer-simulated game, "the accidental war." Both words suggest something modest and provisional which is situated in the hazy area between disinterestedness and earnestness; their effect is thus to express neutrality and yet also to entail a moderate but serious undertaking—in this case one having to do with popes and politics.

— I —

This is not a book that I planned on writing. Its immediate predecessors were works of literary criticism that had no direct social or political relevance, save in the highly restricted sense of Cardinal Newman's commonplace that if you make people think in secular matters you will make them think in matters of religion—and conversely: which is merely to say that all the areas in the cycle of learning are interrelated. Those earlier books did not even have an implicit message—a subtext as it's now called—in any way related to public affairs. And to the degree they had a methodology, it was to a large extent derived from the one school of criticism that was conventionally dismissed as being indifferent to the social, historical, and even to the cultural background of the art work: the much maligned, though now moderately resurgent, New Criticism.

Hence the "accidental" nature of this book. Though it is a personal work in the obvious sense of representing a personal point of view, it is not a personal work in the sense of being motivated by any ax to grind, or by any antagonist sentiment toward the various writers of whom I am, admittedly, highly critical and even disparaging. After roughly a quarter of a century and many hundreds of printed pages of greater or lesser import, so far as I can remember none of the names of authors whom I criticize in this book have appeared in anything I have published. As to the "why" of this book, any description of the process and motivation of its writing would be as banal as an analysis of the most quotidian of activities, the mowing of a lawn, the washing of a car, whatever. The simple fact is that I merely read out of curiosity one of these books on Catholicism, which led to reading another and then in turn to many others—some of which through the same happenstance procedure will put in an appearance in the pages that follow.

What gradually struck me about the various works I ended up criticizing in detail—and about others I criticize only in passing—were certain traits common in a greater or lesser degree to all of them. There was first a strident tone, an ease about condemning, often vehemently, whatever a given author wanted to oppose. One's attention is concentrated—to put it in the mildly ironic language of Dr. Johnson—at reading that a recent pope publicly told a "deliberate lie"; that attention became more sharply focused when the accuser attempted to prove his point by a deliberate distortion.[1] There was also not just the occasional glimmer of bias,

---

[1] Of course, context is everything. It is tolerable—when verifiable—for an Alfred Delp, S.J., murdered by the Nazis, to draw a comparison between himself and John the Baptist *and* Herod and Pius XII. Such rhetoric is acceptable from a martyr in a prison cell. It is less acceptable when voiced by an academician writing a polemic in a library.

but the flaring, repetitive manifestation of it; as though the writer, hitherto in the dark about some matter, had undergone an incandescent transformation, rays of which she was intellectually unable to repress. As to the repetitiveness, one often ended up feeling like Lewis Carroll's beaver among the snark hunters: "But it fairly lost heart, and outgrabe in despair, / When the third repetition occurred."

Similarly, on reading another writer about "the priestly caste" "playacting" at mass, with "some magic words to say" in "the sacral language, Latin, [which] had more efficacy because the faithful did not understand it"—this priestly caste wearing "ornate vestments" from a "distant culture no longer alive"[2] to distinguish it "from the ordinary mortals outside the communion rail": on reading this kind of thing, one was tempted to cry out with Newman to Kingsley, "Why, man, you are writing a romance!"—in fact a romance or novel whose hero might have been the most radical of Protestant reformers, Thomas Müntzer, who in a comparable fulmination described the Eucharist as "a painted puppet conjured up by priestly incantation." (Though, when one read in this same author that, "hedge after hedge was added to isolate the physical reality of the eucharistic host," one at least may have had an intimation of what the apostle's cryptic "two-hedged sward" might signify.)

All of the above description had to have been written about the mass as celebrated in the church after the reforms of the second Vatican Council, since it was published in the year 2000. The following is by the same author, writing thirty years earlier on the

---

[2] This is a Protestant notion from the days of Calvin and Knox, and is in line with such other reformative acts as stripping the altars, whitewashing the walls, and smashing stained glass windows and statues. It is interesting that after Vatican II when Catholics were literally divesting themselves of priestly robes rich in religious significance through design and color, Protestant ministers were seeking a sense of ritual and solemnity by adopting the dress and colors of academic gowns. What was driven out of the churches in the name of evangelical simplicity was welcomed back in the name of university or seminary loyalties—with ornate vestments that had little symbolic significance. (At academic convocations, one assumes that this Catholic author/professor at a Methodist institution democratically wears street attire.)

Tridentine mass which had been prevalent until the late sixties: "The Mass became a hierarchic dance arranged around the host, bowings, blessings, kneelings, liftings, displayings and hidings of it. . . . a light disk balanced on the tongue by the priest, then lifted to the palate by the tongue, there to stick, hard and alien . . . , plastic dew fallen from heaven. . . . The hosts were hard currency, negotiable stuff of salvation . . . , and each capable of purchasing a soul." Same author, same language—but two different forms of worship. Apart from the fact that Catholics with a memory will find both paragraphs as hard to swallow as the author's imaginary host, there remains the paradox that a reformist author remains as embittered after liturgical reforms as before them—which puts into question whether *any* improvements in Catholic life and worship would ever for him be adequate.[3]

Of course all ritual acts, from a medieval mystery play, to the "Magic Flute," to the opening of Parliament,[4] tend to succumb to perfunctoriness and routine. But regardless of the encrusted detritus accumulated over the centuries or the decades, the mass never became the travesty described above. It entailed a shekinah, a "real presence" dependent on consecration (whether or not with congregational intent), and it maintained continuity with that "presence" literally from time immemorial. So, it was difficult to account for an attitude toward the heart of the liturgy, the mass, that treated it with the raillery of a stand-up comedian, not with the reverence owed something sacred, however falteringly and inadequately achieved. Again, a factor that concentrated the mind.

---

[3] For this writer everything emanating from Rome—whether reform or reversal, whether post-Trent or post-Vatican II—entails a self-protective conspiracy. Thus: "Vatican officials feared change in the liturgy for a very real and practical reason. If you take away the magical aura from the Mass, the existence of a priestly caste with ritual purity is hard to justify."

[4] It is a *British* Catholic, undoubtedly at some time or other observer of the ostentatious grandiosity of parliamentary openings and other regal pageants in London, who manages to make of such spectacles *in Rome* a sign of sin and delusion: ". . . the wearing of robes and the use of outmoded titles—Excellency, Eminence, Grace, Lord—tokens of a mental split. . . . In such a 'hidden' state of mind, it is easy to fool oneself into believing one is holy, to disguise evil for good."

Moreover, the notion that Catholic worship before Vatican II remained virtually identical with that of today contradicts the experience of anyone witness to both—except perhaps amnesiac reformers.[5]

There was also a problem with factual errors, not all that unusual in studies of grand historic sweep, and certainly not unusual in any work about the kinds of controversial issues suggested by my title and by the titles of several of the books I will assess. But when the error seemed to have had as purpose the glorification of the author as a living—and therefore incontrovertible—witness, then one instinctively began to doubt or question innumerable other utterances that might be made. A shadow is cast over an entire book by such self-exaltation as the following which related to "the Vatican" connecting "the image of Pius XII as a saint" with its efforts to prove Catholic opposition to Nazism: *"As a boy, I saw* how this worked. In a letter to the bishops of Bavaria in August 1945, Pius XII praised 'those millions of Catholics' . . . , who had resisted Nazism."* Unfortunately, this author making his own dubious "connection," had earlier told the reader, "I was born in 1943, the year before the jurist Raphael Lemkin coined the word 'genocide'." So, at the age of two our witness *saw* how the Vatican "worked" its multifarious wiles. Perhaps, one is tempted to suggest, someone should have coined the word, "vericide."[6]

Authors who focus unremittingly on hierarchic and clerical antisemitism often seemed dismissive of the spirit or letter of the following by a Protestant scholar, "The tirades against the [Catholic] clergy have to be taken with a grain of salt. The accusations

---

[5] This is hardly to suggest that the post-Vatican II liturgy represented some ideal in worship. In its reaction to the Tridentine service, it often went to extremes of vulgarization and faddishness that were in their way as impairing as what they replaced. But in no fashion could they be described as having about them "a magical aura." Cf. Thomas Day, *Why Catholics Can't Sing: The Culture of Catholicism and the Triumph of Bad Taste* (New York, 1992).

[6] In *The Decay of Lying* Oscar Wilde speaks of an author who "had once the makings of a perfectly magnificent liar . . . [but who now] when he does tell us anything marvelous, feels bound to invent a personal reminiscence and put it in a footnote as a kind of cowardly corroboration."— a prophetic judgment about many of this author's "inventions," several of which as we shall see are in footnotes; but not this one: it is bare faced in the text—though not bold faced.

of lechery, usury, and oppression were virtually identical with those hurled against the Jews. In both cases the objects of criticism are being scapegoated. People projected on to the clergy their own unresolved personal problems as well as society's structural crises." This is not by a defender of papacy much less a condoner of prejudice, but by a balanced interpreter of primary historical data, Peter Matheson, in *The Imaginative World of the Reformation* (Edinburgh, 2000). Nor do our Catholic authors take anything with a grain of salt, as every esoteric oddity of practice or doctrine is ferreted out to prove such things as that "in a new form of idolatry, the Pope becomes a substitute for the Spirit," Mary becomes "semi-deified"; and by the time of the Reformation she becomes the "idol-goddess."

Several authors' errors were so manifold that one was compelled to conclude that they just simply hadn't done the research that their detailed annotations were intended to validate. Or, in other instances, the errors were so egregious that one was driven to conclude that to escape detection and thus censure, a given author was relying on an electronically produced verbal smokescreen, was relying on the sheer volume of wordage being generated;[7] or possibly on a previously earned reputation for diligent research; or, as a last resort, on the flagging attention of the reader when encountering such repetitive excesses. In many cases the notes were as inaccurate as the text, and the indexes were frustratingly useless.

Finally, and also stemming from that irrepressible bias previously mentioned, were the errors in interpretation. Their frequent recurrence suggested an unrestrained prejudice manifesting itself in almost automatic rhetorical twitches, or involuntary argumentative shudders, like a kind of out-of-control compulsion beyond the reasoned guidance of its author/victim. Thus one writer began a paragraph on the subject of the church in Italy being "comfortable with recent Fascist measures against the Jews." She then introduced "a report" which supplies "additional

---

[7] This verbal flood, the result of too facile an access to word processing, results as we shall see in what is almost a silly con game with the innocent reader.

evidence" for this "comfortableness." After a lengthy exposition, she concluded the paragraph by noting, "The report, *of course,* is not *evidence* of Vatican approval. . . ." For this psychological affliction a clinical term has been coined, *pseudologia fantastica.*

Frequently, the possibly involuntary tweak is seemingly trivial, a mere matter of nuance like a verbal grimace, maybe just an implicit elision of a phrase or two subtly to suggest falsity or at least ambiguity—like that obnoxious, universal, and often compulsive automatic hand gesture signifying quotation marks—*or,* as in the very quotation above, the construction of author/reader complicity in coming to an inevitable point of agreement by the seemingly casual insertion of "of course." Much of this spin when looked at discretely was almost indiscernible, but when envisaged cumulatively it could tilt the scales of a reader's judgment toward acceptance of what in the end was unmitigated deception. And, *of course,* as one read more and more and got more and more vexed, one had to say, Enough!—and so we have little books like this.

— II —

The book begins with a wide ranging discussion of works pro and con about the papacy, and more specifically about Pius XII. It then distinguishes among his various denigrators and supporters. Within both groups there are authors who seem ideologically favorable or unfavorable to the pope, and there are historians who share one or the other of those two views, but presumably write from a balanced and objective point of view. I dismiss briefly the ideologues favorable to the pope, since they are unquestionably not only motivated by piety but writing works of piety that do not meet even the lowest standard of analytic theological and/or historical research. The ideologues antagonistic to the pope and implicitly or explicitly to the church, though usually writing from a Catholic perspective, I examine in detail, and point out factual errors and interpretive biases. (For what it is worth, I was utterly unprepared for the enormity of such bias and errors.) As to the historians who one assumed had come to their particular position without any *a priori* assumptions—so far as that is possible—and based their conclusions on the inexorable logic of facts discovered by dedicated study, the surprising element was that they, too, turned out to be manipulators of data, and little different from their ideological counterparts. The one well-researched book favorable to Pius, though not written by a "professional" historian, I treat briefly but with ungrudging admiration.

Chapters two and three are severe critiques of errors of fact and interpretation in several books on the papacy covering roughly the period of the last two centuries. Because of its central importance chapter four considers the Holocaust, particularly in its relation to Pius XII. There I point out the flawed arguments of his "hanging judges," while emphasizing the difficulty of coming to any definitive viewpoint about his role. Chapter five puts much of the preceding treatment into the context of the last two centuries of confrontation between the center and the periphery, that is, between papacy and curia—"the church teaching"—and the reformers or insurgents from the ranks of "the church taught." The final two chapters while drawing on historical illustrations mainly from the nineteenth and twentieth centuries are studies respectively in the personal and the institutional dimension of reform in the church of today.

The overall perspective of the book is one of cautious optimism. Any reading of history, even by the most bigoted anti-Catholic or anti-Romanist, makes clear that the state of the present church is purer than the church at the end of the Dark Ages, purer than during the Babylonian Captivity, purer than during the high Renaissance, purer than during the reign of Pius IX. And even the most prejudiced historian would have to say that the evils embodied in the church have been less apparent as each new age dawned, so that what would have been tolerated during the reign of Leo X would have been abominated during the reign of Pius IX, and what was tolerated during the reign of Pius IX was in fact abominated by John XXIII.

As for the reign of John Paul II, its achievements have been many, particularly as evidenced in the definitive repudiation of age-old antisemitism, in the frequent denunciation of weapons of mass destruction resulting in total war, in ecumenical overtures to other religious bodies, in the rehabilitation of such Catholic theologians as Congar, de Lubac, and von Balthasar; and in his vigorous and consistent condemnation of capital punishment.[8] On the other hand, there has been an almost ruthless preoccupation with conformity even on open and unresolved issues; and with centrality of governance even in relation to national bishops conferences. Regarding the former, the words of Cardinal Newman during the reign of Pius IX—and to be frequently cited in the pages that follow—offer a pertinent analysis of causes and consequences: "There was true private judgment in the primitive and medieval schools,—there are no schools now, no private judgment (in the religious sense of the phrase), no freedom, that is, of opinion. That is, no exercise of the intellect. No, the system goes on by the tradition of the intellect of former times." Regarding the second issue, governance, the words of Cardinal Manning—several years after Vatican I where he had been a leader of the pro-infallibilist party—are pertinent to the present excessive centralization enforced by the Roman curia. Manning said it resulted in "a Catholic presbyterianism" which reduced "the episcopal college to only the pope's vicariate": also a text that will recur in the pages that follow.

The "cautious optimism" of which I speak is based on the historical data summarized above. For several of the denigrators of

---

[8] According to the dictum, judge a person by his enemies as well as by his friends, one might look at the internet links: "Religion > Christianity > Catholics > Not in Communion with Rome." The last entry will lead to scores of organizations in varying degrees of opposition to John Paul II. These may appear to be negligible fringe groups, but there numbers are not insignificant, particularly the Society of St. Pius X, though the latter is but a shadow of the Sodalitium Pianum, the Society of St. Pius V, a pan-European secret society which during the Modernist crisis denounced archbishops, theologians, intellectuals in general for not being "integral" Catholics—which meant for the most part not being sympathetic to heresy hunts and monarchists. The present admirers of St. Pius X (whose canonization was delayed while the secret society which flourished during his reign was investigated) attack John Paul II himself as being a heretic, a philosemite, an ecumenist, and above all, a defender *of Vatican II.* It is noteworthy also that whereas formerly, discontented Catholics looked for redress from a future council, in the twenty-first century they look for redress in the past, by calling up as models the heritage of Pius X and Pius V.

papacy and church whom I will criticize ("our authors"), John XXIII is both a hero, and an inimitable exception. But the reform of Catholicism from Leo XIII on is an exception; its reform from the Council of Trent on is an exception; its reform from the Council of Constance on is an exception; its reform from Hildebrand on is an exception. Ultimately the Incarnation is an exception, history is an exception. Spirit emerging out of the primordial planetary mass is an exception.

There is no rule for relating insurrection and resurrection, renewal and reversal, reformation and counter-reformation. In some instances, perhaps as in the reign of Pius IX, the periphery is condemned by the center; in others, perhaps as with the Council of Constance, the center is condemned by the periphery. Whether one conceives this process as a kind of Hegelian dialectic (with Bernard Häring), as a Spenglerian cycle of growth/decline (as possibly with Cardinal Suhard), or as Toynbee's historical interchange of stimulus/response—all that matters little. What matters is that "salvation history" is defined as nothing less than the history of exceptions. The existence of a kind of self-regulating principle, a homeostatic principle, which maintains an equilibrium between center and periphery is historically evident. There is in the institutional church, in this mystical/historical body, a kind of immune/suppressive mechanism (called "providence") that comes into play when the equilibrium is threatened.

One might think of the reign of Innocent III as the beginning of the infection known as the imperial papacy, and the counterbalance to that centralizing impetus in the emergence of the mendicant orders and the universities. Closer to home—and intentionally a more controversial example—is the reign of Pius XII; controversial, because the single lens through which he is now viewed is the Holocaust, which as I indicated above will be subject to scrupulous examination in the chapters that follow. But Pius, in contrast to all his twentieth-century predecessors believed in subsidiarity. He recognized in a fashion unknown since, the important role of national bishops conferences, and he created the majority of the cardinals who elected John XXIII. In the midst of the war he wrote the revolutionary *Divino afflante Spiritu*—known in the land of Loisy as *l'encyclique libératrice*—the charter of biblical study, which in the broadest theological scheme of things was responsible not only for doctrinal renovation in the postwar period but also for the wholesale regeneration of moral theology during the second half of that century. Two years after the war he authored *Mediator Dei*, the first papal encyclical to address liturgical reform. But Pius's own conservative reaction to the reforms he had generated—like his condemnation of advocates of the misnamed "nouvelle théologie"—was as noted above counterbalanced by John Paul II in the elevation of several of them to the cardinalate. This notion of a structure of equilibrium in salvation history is what warrants in the present age a cautious optimism about the future. It cannot be stressed enough that salvation history itself is the chronicle of "exceptions."[9] And as Newman has said: "Heretical questionings have been transmuted by the living power of the Church into salutary truths."

— III —

This book is, then, basically a study of the interplay of periphery and center, of responses and condemnations; condemnations by Rome, but also—and possibly even more so—condemnations of both periphery and center by authentic and would-be reformers.

---

[9] The clearest statement is the concluding chapter of Newman's *Apologia* where he speaks of "Authority and Private Judgment": ". . . it is the vast Catholic body itself, and it only, which affords an arena for both combatants in that awful, never-dying duel. It is necessary for the very life of religion, viewed in its large operations and its history, that the warfare should be incessantly carried on. Every exercise of Infallibility is brought out in act by an intense and varied operation of Reason, both as its ally and as its opponent, and provokes again, when it has done its work, a re-action of Reason against it; and, as in a civil polity the State exists and endures by means of the rivalry and collision, the encroachments and defeats of its constituent parts, so in like manner Catholic Christendom is no simple exhibition of religious absolutism, but presents a continuous picture of Authority and Private Judgment alternately advancing and retreating as the ebb and flow of the tide;—it is a vast assemblage of human beings with wilful intellects and wild passions, brought together into one by the beauty and the Majesty of a Superhuman Power. . . ."

The literature of such condemnations is not a novel genre: though much of it, as Newman said, does read like a novel. Almost from the very beginning Christians were accused by pagans of devouring children and of incestuous unions: both based on legends accruing from dramatic representations (the "romances" or "novels" of that time) of the house of Atreus; in these two instances the banquet of Thyestes, and the marriage of Oedipus. Then occurred the attacks by philosophers like Celsus and Porphyry, followed by that last noble pagan, Julian the Apostate—all countered by such Christians apologists as Origen, Justin Martyr, and Irenaeus. Soon came the Gnostic onslaught of Valentinus and Marcion; then heresiarchs, like Montanus and Novatian, and on into the medieval period when a reformer like St. Peter Damian would decry clerical abuses in *The Gomorrah Book.* This culminated in the Reformation when the focus was as much on beliefs as on their politics, represented by the Peasants War, and the wars among rival princes for both religious and political domination. In the age of secularization, and anticipating the author of *The Sword of Constantine,* Thomas Hobbes, spokesman for the "English Enlightenment," wrote in *Leviathan*: "The papacy is no other than the ghost of the deceased Roman Empire, sitting crowned upon the grave thereof." In the nineteenth century Antonio Rosmini, founder of the religious society, the Institute of Charity, wrote a powerful reformist manifesto called *The Five Wounds of Holy Church.*[10] And, in the early twentieth century, like the early pagans vulgarizing classical tales, the largest publishing venture in North America—literally millions and millions of copies—was engaged in the production of "the little blue books" of Haldeman-Julius which condensed in pocket format three centuries of protestant anti-Romanist and anti-Jesuitical propaganda. (One may

---

[10] Another indication of the fluctuating changes that can be effected by the election of a new pope is that Rosmini's writings—theological, philosophical, political, and pastoral—were the object of much criticism by the Roman curia with two titles briefly on the *Index* during the reign of Pius IX. But during the reign of Leo XIII, again after curial condemnation, they were subject to only the mildest form of censure—as was also true of Leo with regard to Loisy. In the reign of John Paul II, Rosmini, along with the equally suspect Cardinal Newman, was

wonder whether our authors, in their childhood rummaging through the attic on some rainy afternoon, may have discovered, and furtively dared *to read* these subversive little blue books—decried in their parents' day from pulpit and lectern as the pornography of ideas.) But that propaganda, too, was countered by scores of popular works on Catholic apologetics and by widely read pamphlets published by the Knights of Columbus.

What distinguishes the current raft of books critical of all aspects of Catholicism—save what their authors approve—is that several of them are written by authors who profess an unquestioned loyalty to some notion of the importance and value of Catholicism in their lives. They affirm that they are writing as faithful to the essential principles of their church, however broadly or loosely they would define those principles. But one omnipresent theme runs through all their books: the failure of this church to live up to its mandate. One author writes of the church, even up into the reign of John XXIII, as "institutionalized and bureaucratized misanthropy," and writes of Catholics as "taking the weight of its world-hatred for granted." (Being more gifted, he naturally is not numbered among the "takers.")

Invariably left unexamined is precisely how to define that mandate which has not been lived up to. It is not the "gospel mandate" since the gospels are themselves sedimented with the very evil being exposed—for one author, antisemitism. It is not the "mandate of tradition" for the tradition itself is seen as corrupted—but a corruption *of* what, since the origins have themselves been described as tainted? From what pure source, then, could there have been a falling away? It is not the mandate of the body of the faithful ("the church taught," as it was known), since particularly in popular practices, and even in popular devotions, the most revolting aberrations and superstitions had crept in and been fostered—as two of our authors lavishly detail: a relic of Mary's milk, a nail used in the crucifixion, blood libels, various black madonnas, wood splinters from the cross, holy shrouds,

completely rehabilitated. An axiom of the latter, which will also recur in the treatment that follows is "What one pope can do, another can undo."

etc.[11]—not to speak of such papally inspired "deceits" as the dogmas of the Immaculate Conception and the Assumption. Lastly, it is not the mandate of the "church teaching," since if there is one topic *all* agree on it is that the hierarchy—whether local officials or the Roman curia or both—has been primarily responsible for all the evils described, dissected and, in several works, delightedly depicted.

So, given this catalogue of flaws from so many sources and over so many centuries, even from the very beginnings, what is it that these authors remain faithful to? What is it that they find important and valuable to their lives in this corruption-ridden body? If its outward signs are so disfigured, where do they locate its inward grace? And moreover, how can there be such a location at all, if the outward signs *are* the inward grace? As every sacramental theologian from Peter Lombard to Marshall McLuhan recognized, the medium *is* the message. That being so, the question remains: what is the appeal, the hold, of an institution that one lives in while assaulting and demeaning it—indeed, that one makes one's living by such assaulting and demeaning?

One professedly faithful Catholic speaks of "the great truths of faith—the Trinity, the Incarnation, the Mystical Body of Christ"—this latter truth, though implicit in the tradition, was explicit only in the last century, and certainly is not as central as resurrection, whether of Jesus or "of the dead," as the creed says. Another writer, equally as demonstratively faithful, says of the "disciples' notion that after Jesus' death he was still among them": "That *intuition* is what we call Resurrection. . . . To *imagine* Jesus as risen was to expect that soon all would be. . . . His love

---

[11] One author of what may be called a heartbreaking work of staggering length describes as occurring throughout the Christian era various religious hoaxes, aberrations, perversions, superstitions, fakes, etc. Yet he concludes his long historical account—it is indeed the climax of the whole book—with a mawkish and superstition-ridden scene in Hitler's bunker, "a chamber of hell," where he disrupts his offspring's gamboling: " 'No!' I screamed. . . . swooping down on them, grabbing each one by an elbow and dragging them back. . . . My children looked up at me mystified . . . 'This was Hitler's place!' And I led them away." Thus disproving the dictum, "other times, other mores," and confirming Wilde's response to the maudlin expiration of Little Nell.

survived his death—which is what the Resurrection means." But comforting expectations and benevolent teachings are universal in all the great world religions. The one singularly unique trait about the Jesus of the Church *is* belief in the fact of resurrection. So maybe the "great truths of faith" are not really so important. Why not embrace the Buddha, the Tao, selective Hinduism, since any or all of them offer comfort and, to a greater or lesser degree, fulfillment of expectation?[12]

Surely it would be simplistic to suggest that the answer to that question can be found in the mere power of custom. It could not be that mere ethnic, social, and cultural familiarity explains this attachment to so flawed an institution; an attachment that results in the trite—but possibly *actual*—fact that one simply decides to talk most about what one happens to knows best. And because the shocking and the *épatant*—every trafficker in triteness soon discovers—have more consumers than do the nullities and dullities of daily life, and moreover because nothing is more shocking than the spectacle of vice masquerading as virtue, nor more appealing to that vast world of nonbelievers freed from the shackles of religious superstition—then, so would go this relatively naive supposition, all those factors explain the subtle and maybe unwitting seductiveness of ecclesiastical matters among authors who contemn the spirit that animates the very life *within* those matters.

But that is admittedly simplistic—even though we had earlier exhausted the other possible appeals Catholicism might have: the gospel message (contaminated and mythic), the traditions (corrupted), the devotions (exaggerated), the doctrines (incredible), the authority (abusive). So, in the interest of finding something more valid, however subtle—and maybe in the name of Teilhardian complexification—one is driven to conclude that the solution

---

[12] If one took all of the "reformist" doctrinal and devotional demands in the aggregate one would end up with a "church" with no unique revelation of deity; no Nicene creed, no resurrection, no liturgy, no episcopate and priesthood: a church which was neither one, nor apostolic, nor catholic—as to "holy," there is no reference anywhere I can recall to what is called "prayer life." In short, a church that would look very much like a unitarian assembly—and which would have about as much impact on the larger culture.

to the conundrum must come down to something immeasurable and intangible. Perhaps it is merely a phenomenon as universal as a feeling of being at home, or being at ease (through a kind of *otium insanctum*) with an undefined reality whose outward expressions, nevertheless, are often found almost hilariously contemptible—as the comments on liturgy above exemplify. But what then can this *homely* Catholicism be? It can only be something akin to a socio-psychological "drift" or "mood":[13] words necessarily vague and even vaporous; but not entirely unexpected among critics who manage to find something seriously flawed in every other aspect of their church, in its approach to dogma, worship, morals, and above all, governance. And, again, when one seeks the solution to these serious flaws—apart from the faithful standby of returning to some equally primitive, and thus almost undefinable, ke-rygma—one necessarily encounters a slippery paradoxic lingo (like resurrection as "intuition"), and that latter, simply because the gospel itself has been vitiated in its composition and transmission.

Perhaps a more concrete and precise but still not entirely exact term, for the attraction of a church which by all these accounts is in its public manifestations worthy of disdain, would be "style." There is a kind of idealized Catholic style of belief, acceptant but skeptical; a Catholic style of living,[14] unostentatious, but "solid"

---

[13] Again, Newman in the *Apologia* recognized the difficulty of defining the grounds of embracing Catholicism—with a significant reservation: "To that large class of minds, who believe in Christianity after our manner,—in the particular temper, spirit, and light (whatever word is used) in which Catholics believe it. . ." And here he introduces the anchor of those large vaguenesses. He is talking about *dogma*, here about the Immaculate Conception which two of the most cited "reformers," whom I will discuss explicitly, describe as a screen for papal deceit or as a subtle piece of antisemitism.

[14] One critic, occupant of the moral high ground in admiring Dorothy Day, and *certainly* in light of the following remarks even emulating her poverty, ob-serves: "Priests may today be celibate; but—with *some* honorable exceptions—they usually maintain a comfortable life style, especially as compared with the poor they profess to be serving. We all know priests with refined tastes in food and drink, nice cars, expensive *stereos*" (like those comfortable archbishops with their Bösendorfers). This author then tells his readers that when the Jesuit gen-eral commanded "all Jesuits to stop smoking," he was disobeyed. "It was felt to be asking too much" of these men with vows of poverty. Then speaking of smoking bishops at the Council (white smoke over the Vatican? an auto da fé in

and cosmopolitan (it is, after all a global church), a Catholic style of ruling, consultative but decisive. Words like "drift," "mood," "gist," are too colorless and neutral to capture this Catholic sensibility, but "style" stands for *bon ton;* for a trait which is admirable though not demonstrable; which suggests rather than declaims; which indicates a "fit" between the institution and its members, without implying rigidity or any kind of undeviating attachment. In the populist lexicon, its counterpart is "cool."

"Style" is discerned and then determined by what we ordinarily call "good taste," an intuitive recognition of excellence which leads one to shrink from all blemishes, whether institutional or personal, as from a physical disfigurement. (One author in the context of *Humanae Vitae* speaks of Paul VI's "sad sunken eyes in their smudgy Italian sockets"—adding the mandatory commendation that "he was a good and noble man.") Since according to à Kempis it is better to practice a virtue than to define it, I will offer a couple of practical illustrations of the exercise of this "good taste" written by an acute psychologist of religion: "Accordingly, virtue being only one kind of beauty, the principle which determines what is virtuous is, not conscience, but *taste.*" The person of "taste" is "at liberty on his or her principles, to pick and choose out of Christianity what he or she will; he or she discards the theological, the mysterious, the spiritual." "It matters not that, instead of planting the tree, he or she merely crops its flowers. . . ."

Such would seem to be the bond between some of our authors and Catholicism. Whether that is in fact true can only be determined by reading the pages that follow. But first, I note that this

---

the piazza?), he concludes: "They may be estimable men, but they are not convincing as desert fathers." The only commentary this deserves is another of Newman's responses to Kingsley: "So we confessedly have come round to this, *preaching without practising;* the common theme of satirists from Juvenal to Walter Scott." Newman then quotes from Scott's *The Fortunes of Nigel:* "O Geordie, jingling Geordie, it was grand to hear *Baby Charles* laying down the guilt of dissimulation, and Steenie lecturing on the turpitude of incontinence." —a biting piece of personal polemic on Newman's part who was told by a friend that "the prophet of muscular Christianity" (Charles Kingsley) was being referred to "by no other name than Baby Charles." And "it was grand to hear" our author luxuriating in his academic quarters "laying down the guilt of" *stereos* and *smoking.*

"style" may be the scriptural two-edged sword (met earlier in one author's description of eucharistic magic); since from these books, one soon learns that it is a "style" which allows one vigorously, perhaps even sincerely, to attack virtually all aspects of Catholic life and thought. And yet in that undertaking one employs the same invective and slipshod methods, and exercises the same duplicity one professes to be exposing. "Vigor" and "sincerity," are certainly acceptable traits so long as they are not in the service of deception and fraudulence.

— IV —

Paolo Sarpi, a Venetian Servite, and friend of the Doge, was at the beginning of the seventeenth century a vehement opponent of papacy and curia; a stance that was exacerbated when the newly elected pope, Paul V, excommunicated both Doge and Senate, and then placed the entire city under interdict. The pope, a Borghese, and relatively admirable in his personal life, was an upholder of the religious status quo (initiating the Galileo affair), and more concerned with the beautification of Rome (including the completion of St. Peter's) and with personal and family privilege than with theological disputes (taking no position, while definitively ending the public controversy, *De Auxiliis*, about grace and free will). His quarrel with Venice was over traditional privileges which, with Sarpi's support, were being revoked: the exemption of clergy from civil courts, and of church construction from approval by the Venetian government. In addition to religious and political motives, Sarpi had a personal investment in what evolved into a controversy over what might be called "church-state relations."[15] He was recognized as one of the most brilliant debaters

---

[15] The overall issue was the power of the papacy over civil rulers. It was Paul V who canonized Gregory VII, five centuries after the latter's death, as a symbolic gesture of homage to the medieval pope who had consolidated papal over imperial power. In the event, the Doge of Venice, no more than Henry IV ("Paris is worth a Mass") of France, or even James I of England—all of whom Paul crossed—proved willing "to go to Canossa."

of his time and was matched with two equally gifted and possibly more learned opponents, the historian Cardinal Baronius and the theologian Cardinal Bellarmine—who at one time had also barely avoided excommunication, and subsequently was canonized. After considerable deployment of various legal and canonical precedents, as well as much heated rhetoric on both sides, the schism was ended with minor face-saving gestures but little resolution of the specific issues. As is not unusual in ecclesiastical controversies, there were two parties with reciprocally justifiable causes in fierce opposition to one another.

But in the midst of all this, a murderous attack was made upon the person of Fra Paolo Sarpi. Who perpetrated the assassination attempt remains unknown, though Sarpi's cry—which has echoed through the centuries—"Agnosco *stilum* romanae curiae," does not leave his own verdict in doubt. The entire affair now evokes that contemporaneous dramatic genre known as "tragedy of blood," then flourishing in England—where Sarpi had Protestant friends, defenders, and publishers. Since in "real" life, few victims of bloody assault scream out in puns (the attack took place roughly around the time of the writing of *Othello),* the quibble on style/stiletto may also evoke Shakespeare's own fondness for wordplay—even, as Dr. Johnson noted, in the most inappropriate contexts.[16] Sarpi who was know for his friendship with English visitors may have been crying out "Roman dagger" or may have been shouting for vengeance against the "Roman style" of attack—a style he would himself adopt even more outrageously than any curialist in the last two decades of his life.

Rome's "stile" like "Constantine's sword" is also two-edged. It can be the instrument of disclosing the flaws and scandals of the institutional church, and it can be the instrument which lays bare the lies and distortions behind many such disclosures. Sarpi himself, from a moderate critic of the papacy became one of its most

---

[16] The irony is that Shakespeare's alleged violation of dramatic verisimilitude was, in the case of Sarpi, provedly "true to life." Johnson wrote: "Whatever be the dignity or profundity of his disquisition . . . , let but a quibble spring up before him, and he leaves his work unfinished. . . . A quibble was to him the fatal Cleopatra for which he lost the world, and was content to lose it."

embittered and venomous castigators, far out-protestantizing such incensed polemicists as another contemporary, John Milton, who described Paul V as "wearer of the triple crown, borne on men's shoulders, carrying with him his gods made of bread"— much like today's Catholic critics of the papacy and the eucharist.

It is quite possible that Sarpi began his attacks on Roman abuses out of honest anger at their shamelessness and prevalence. At an early age, he had been provincial of the Servites in Venice and Procurator General of the order for three years in Rome where he could certainly have witnessed the corruption of the papal court. Since the curia was the only constant in Rome—the average papal reign during his adult life was less than three years—it would have been the main target of his wrath. And that wrath would certainly have intensified when he was rejected on three different occasions by the "holder of the keys" for episcopal office—aspiration to which, according to Aquinas, was not a sign of worldly ambition, but of a justifiable desire for the "plenitude of the priesthood." Given this rejection, and the intensity of his passion when defending the Venetian republic, climaxing with the murderous attack at the age of 55, it would hardly be surprising if righteous anger turned into black hatred.

This he vented for nearly two decades becoming so abusive and alienated that he was far more guilty of the evils he was denouncing than were their alleged practitioners. Attacking all things Roman, he wrote or inspired innumerable pamphlets and six acrimonious volumes, including *The History of the Council of Trent* which could be published during his lifetime only in James I's England. Even Leopold von Ranke, no defender of the papacy, found the work seriously defective.

The "moral" of the parable is not that old chestnut, *"Qui mange du pape en meurt"* (who eats of the pope dies of the pope), since clearly uncountable political and religious leaders as well as multitudes of reformers and protesters have had a bite at that repast— and flourished. No, the lesson, *if* it must be spelt out again, is that the "stile" is indeed double edged. On the one hand, it is the instrument "of choice" for attacking the church viciously and persistently; on the other, its intrinsic ambivalence means it may rebound on its wielder and destroy him or at least his credibility and reputation. Sarpi proved, both by the vehemence of his invective *and* by the self-destructiveness of his all-consuming hatred, the truth of that other French dictum, "the style is the man." In his rancor toward others, he destroyed himself: "Lo stile è l'uomo."

2

SKEWING CATHOLIC SCHOLARSHIP

The New Papaphobia

> "It became a rule of policy to praise the spirit when you could not defend the deed."
>
> *Lord Acton*

A specter is haunting Europe or, rather, haunting what is still called Western Civilization by that dogged remnant of anti-postmodernists that refuses to believe in such fashionable fictions as "the end of history." But rather than a specter, it is more precisely a spirit redivivus that was unforeseen by those gullible nineteenth-century social prophets whose own collective *nunc dimittis* is now only a fading echo. So rather than failed visionaries like Marx and Engels, we must hearken to a chronicler of history, Lord Macauley, writing around the middle of the nineteenth century and also going against prevailing fashions in his memorable description of an institution long viewed as moribund by his contemporaries. Describing the Church of Rome, Macauley said: "She may still exist in undiminished vigor when some traveler from New Zealand shall, in the midst of a vast solitude, take his stand on a broken arch of London Bridge to sketch the ruins of St. Paul's."

From the eighteenth-century Enlightenment with its social, intellectual, and industrial revolutions up to the period of the great world wars, the papacy had been viewed as at best an archeological relic much like the Hapsburg Empire, and at worst as the last bastion of religious superstition and political reaction. The seal had been embossed on its coffin by Pope Pius IX, around the very time Macauley was writing, in a document repudiating "progress, liberalism, and modern civilization." The universal obloquy since heaped on the papacy—save by a negligible remnant of what were assumed to be the elderly, the ignorant, and the retrograde—can be represented by the chilly exclusion of Benedict XV from any role at Versailles after World War I, and by the utter indifference among the heads of all European governments to the unceasing pleas for peace before and during World War II by Pius XII—who was also excluded, save as occasional mediating agent, from participation in plans for peace.

Nothing in the modern era better symbolized the ineffectuality of the bearer of such exalted titles as Patriarch of the West, Supreme Pontiff, Heir of St. Peter, and Vicar of Christ than the plan by Hitler in 1943 to emulate Napoleon's capture of Pius VII in 1809—even to the dismissive gibe first voiced by Napoleon and later by Stalin, as to how many battalions had the pope. To draw a page from Gibbon on the Holy Roman Empire, this leader of the "one, holy, catholic, and apostolic church" governed a body that was neither *unified* (German Catholics were slaughtering Polish Catholics); nor *holy* (financial scandals were germinating); nor *catholic* (dissident bishops were raising challenges from China to Ukraine); nor *apostolic* (a pedigree long viewed as undermined by historians and biblical scholars).

— I —

So, how then is one to explain that in the last forty years books on the papacy not as religious authority but as political force have been multiplied in every major language (even Japanese) in almost uncountable numbers, particularly and most divisively during the past two decades in the English-speaking world? I mention only a few titles, of which ten were published during the years 1999–2001. *Under His Very Windows: The Vatican and the Holocaust in Italy,* by Susan Zuccotti; *The Catholic Church and the Holocaust,* by

Michael Phayer; *The Italian Refuge: Rescue of Jews during the Holocaust,* edited by, K. Voigt, J. Burgwyn; *History, Religion, Antisemitism,* by Gavin Langmuir; *Vatican Diplomacy and the Jews during the Holocaust,* by John F. Morley; *Three Popes and the Jews,* by Pinchas Lapide; *Hitler's Pope,* by John Cornwell; *Pius XII and the Second World War,* by Pierre Blet; *Controversial Concordats,* edited by Frank J. Coppa; *Papal Sin,* by Garry Wills; *Constantine's Sword,* by James Carroll; *Pope Pius XII: Architect for Peace,* by Margherita Marchione; *Hitler, the War, and the Pope,* by Ronald J. Rychlak; *The Defamation of Pius XII,* by Ralph McInerny; *Pius XII and the Holocaust,* by José M. Sanchez.

The crux of the political issue is clearly the papacy and the Holocaust. But this is the same papacy which political scientists, historians, social commentators, and intellectual observers in general, had dismissed for well over two centuries as a negligible factor in public life. Why then is there now such intense scrutiny of every personality and every document from that controverted period as they relate to the extermination of the Jews? It is argued that archives have been opened, new materials circulated, deeper insights gained. But acknowledging an element of truth to those assumptions, how then explain that the debate is more combustible at this late date, even though the basic positions and even the putatively supportive documents remain nearly identical or at least highly congruent with those disclosed (1965–1980) in the aftermath of Rolf Hochhuth's attack on the pope in his drama, *Der Stellvertreter*?

Among Jewish scholars, one must recognize that there is certainly a continuing passion for truth and for what is commonly (and perhaps naively) called "closure." Among some Catholics, there is probably all of that too; but also it soon becomes apparent among other Catholics that different agenda are here in play. In short, the reason for such renewed ardor and animosity is that this arena has—with exceptions I shall note—largely become the precinct of ideologues. The ideological *denigrators* of the papacy such as James Carroll, John Cornwell, and Garry Wills appear to speak in the language of candor and honesty, and with a view to reform of a corrupt and "deceitful" (Wills' term) ecclesiastical structure.

But in fact they speak in the language of Hobbes' *Leviathan,* as I pointed out in the preceding chapter. The ideological *consecrators,* such as Ralph McInerny and Margherita Marchione are patent apologetes, clearly motivated by piety and loyalty to prevailing church norms and to religious tradition. That the denigrators are generally from the political left, and the consecrators generally from the right only adds to the factious fury. But as is usual in such polarizations, ideologues of the right are generally less persuasive because, at least ostensibly, less intellectually grounded than those of the left. As a result, the analyst of such a controversy must of necessity devote more attention to the latter. Ideas *have* consequences as a conservative observer once noted; whereas piety, loyalty, and traditionalism, like matters *de gustibus,* are not subject to dispute or public debate.

Since the ideological consecrators proffer testimony to the righteousness of their viewpoint rather than exposition or argument to support that viewpoint, they can be dispensed with speedily and briefly. Marchione quotes everyone from Einstein to Ed Koch on the merits of pope and church during the Holocaust, and attributes the denigration of Pius XII to such factors as that "anti-Catholicism is alive and popular today"; "cultural changes that swept over the Western world in the 1960s . . . , religion was mocked, the death of God espoused, passion exalted . . ."; "moral and family values declined." In addition to testimonials, she provides interviews with other partisans, quotations from supportive documents, discusses "Arians" and "non-Arians" as though this were a fourth-century debate, and supplies an "annotated bibliography"—the following excerpt from which indicates the tone, while this preliminary comment indicates the context.

To many non-partisan observers, John F. Morley's work on the Vatican and World War II is one of the most balanced, least tendentious historical studies of the last twenty years. (When one considers the historical studies critical of Pius XII that I analyze next, that will be seen as very high praise.) Nevertheless, in Marchione's bibliographic estimate: "Father Morley's book has become the 'Bible' of anti-Pius XII commentators"; she then quotes an allied critic to the effect that it is: "a grotesque anti-historical and in the end self-defeating incrimination." Not surprisingly, Marchione's potpourri is described as "a sober and documented work," by Ralph McInerny who—only incidentally—regards Morley's book as "providing aid and comfort to enemies of the Church," and who also sees the papacy in the context of "passion exalted and moral values in decline." This is prelude to an unexpected tirade, which quickly degenerates into a foaming frenzy about "the culture of death": "Proponents of abortion do not like hearing it compared to the Holocaust. The Holocaust lasted less than half a dozen years. The scourge of abortion has been going on for more than a quarter of a century. . . . We are all Nazis now."

An illustration of his polemic strategy is evident in his attempt to dismiss Garry Wills' *Papal Sin* on the ground that: "When Lillian Hellman's *Scoundrel Time* appeared in 1976 it had a long fawning thirty-page preface by Garry Wills," who after about five hundred words of condemnation by McInerny is indicted for, in effect, backing the wrong nag in the Hellman-Mary McCarthy sweepstakes.[1] One might have to delve into McInerny's own "memories of a Catholic boyhood" to see the relevance of any of this to *The Defamation of Pius XII*—a work which itself suffers from being merely an extensive paraphrase of two other studies of the pope by, respectively, Pierre Blet and Pinchas Lapide—apologetes both. When McInerny deviates from their works, it is either to indulge in warped polemic to prove that Zionist leaders and organizations (implicitly by contrast to Pope and Holy See) were indifferent to the Holocaust, or to engage in on-stage and off-target cultural pedantry.[2]

---

[1] This plays out in McInerny and fellow first-thingers' embrace of Hans Urs von Balthasar and the *Communio* faction vis-à-vis Wills and fellow last-enders' embrace of James Carroll and the *Concilium* contingent. One can even imagine McInerny greeting Neuhaus with "Oh! you're the imitation me." As that nineteenth-century observer I alluded to in the first sentence of this chapter approximately commented: "The first time as farce, and the second time—. . . . as farce again."

[2] Cardinal Newman did *not* define "what he meant by the liberalism he opposed in an appendix to his *Apologia.*" He defined in the *Apologia*, "what I meant *as a Protestant* by Liberalism"; his definition *as a Catholic* (most of his adult life) was his speech in Rome on accepting the red hat. The treatment of Maurras is

Ronald Rychlak is an attorney—and I presume a formidable one—whose mastery of the relevant literature is impressive. Nor in *Hitler, the War, and the Pope* are there any self-inflating excursuses on his own personal politics or on his nostrums for the moral tribulations of the cosmos. Moreover, though he might be classified as an ideological consecrator, he proves himself to be less biased than the professional and "leftist" historians I shall examine shortly. But there are some minor problems with the book: it is primarily a detailed response to various critiques of Pius, and only secondarily a constructive assessment, even when the response and the assessment do dovetail rather effectively. Second, as the work of a legal scholar it relies on oral witnesses who do not often seem either supported by documents or subject to rigorous adversarial protocol. An example is the acceptance, albeit somewhat hesitantly, of the testimony of Sister Pasqualina, Pius's dedicated assistant and, after his death, ardent defender. Nevertheless, it seems to me as a book by a partisan of Pius to be as honestly and as forthrightly executed as, from a different point of view, is John Morley's *Vatican Diplomacy*.

---

contradictory; moreover the attraction of Maritain to Action Française had less to do with "the tradition of French Catholicism" than with the influence of Père Clérissac. Nor should Professor McInerny, the director of the Jacques Maritain Institute at the University of Notre Dame, assert that Maritain opposed the Falangists because he was "bewitched by propaganda about Guernica *and* the atrocities of Franco." He opposed them because they and their clerical allies appeared to the common people as representing "nothing but imposture" (*The Martyrdom of Spain,* Introduction, [1938]). When France fell, "Marshall Pétain took counsel with the *representative of the Holy See* about the anti-Semitic laws." One assumes, and this appears to be what McInerny believes, that such a representative was attached to the nunciature. But in fact it is the exact opposite: Pétain consulted the *French ambassador to* the Vatican. His report is important, as will be clarified in the discussion of Zuccotti's book below. Again: "Occupied Holland was to show a nobility and courage that contrasts dramatically with what that land has since become." This *non sequitur* may be based on Holland's present-day policy toward euthanasia, indicating its endorsement of "the culture of death"—now reified as a sociological category. —just a minor correction of our self-described "author *to* nearly 100 books": after Holland, one doesn't expect another gratuitous ethnic slur, now *cum* solecism. "Totalitarianism might have the look of *opéra bouffe* in Italy." Not quite: it might have that look in France; but "in Italy," *opera buffa*.

But as I have noted, in addition to ideologues of either stripe, there is also a third party, the historians, who are usually allied with the left, but as professional advocates of objectivity and independence, must appear to be above the fray. This is the first group I shall consider in detail before moving on in the next chapter to the views of their "amateur" companions in arms. What will emerge in the present chapter is the startling phenomenon of slanted and bogus scholarship where one might least expect it; not among the ideologues of the right who are blatantly but negligibly sanctimonious and adulatory, but among the acknowledged professional exponents of candor, honesty, and rectitude. Unfortunately what is lost sight of by ideologues of both categories is the reduction of the greatest crime in history to the status of a mere tactical ploy in an intermural ecclesiastical wrangle over the office and function of the papacy. That this is to hijack the Shoah for Christian purposes—much less noble than the kinds of goals analyzed by Tim Cole's *Selling the Holocaust*—seems to have been lost sight of even by Jewish scholars anxious for "answers" and eager to grasp at any straw of ecumenical reciprocity.

— II —

I begin with Susan Zuccotti's *Under His Very Windows* (the pronoun refers to Pius XII), and will then take up Michael Phayer's *The Catholic Church and the Holocaust,* and will conclude with what by contrast to those two works can only be described as a revolutionary treatment, entailing a radically different approach to the whole range of Holocaust issues: Gulie Ne'eman Arad's *America, Its Jews, and the Rise of Nazism* (Bloomington, 2000), a work not listed among the titles at the beginning of this chapter, since it does not directly relate to the role of Catholics or the Holy See. However, as will become evident at the end of this chapter, it is in its overall perspective utterly different from those other titles, and particularly Zuccotti's and Phayer's.

My concern with the latter two books is less with their general conclusions (though I differ with them strongly), but with the persistent bias they display in reinforcing such conclusions. It is the accumulation of incidental distortions combined with verbal legerdemain that results in provably doctored inferences and that may confirm (Zuccotti's book has been the recipient of the Revson Award for "Jewish-Christian Relations,"and Phayer's has received widespread praise in Catholic journals) the epigraph to this chapter from Lord Acton: "a rule of policy to praise the spirit when you could not defend the deed." Some may praise the drift of Zuccotti's and Phayer's broad-gauge theses; it is less easy to defend the foundation on which they are often established and which reveals what can only be defined as an omnipresent papaphobia—a term resuscitated in the nineteenth century by Coleridge.

Since it is axiomatic among papal critics that modern popes have been obsessively anti-communist while scanting the evils of fascism, Zuccotti in her first chapter discusses these encyclicals of Pius XI: on Hitler's Germany (*Mit brennender Sorge*), on international Communism (*Divini Redemptoris*), and on Mussolini's Italy (*Non abbiamo bisogno*). Of the latter she makes three assertions that are either verbally extravagant or simply false: "Despite claims to the contrary, the pronouncement [the encyclical] cannot be *glorified* as a *sweeping* and courageous condemnation of Fascism." First, "He never uttered the word 'Fascist' . . . he added, clearly enough, 'we have not said that we wish to condemn [second] the party as such.' . . . Nor can *Non abbiamo bisogno* be described as [third] an appeal for democratization and civil rights. . . ." Yet the words "fascismo" and "fascisti" *are* in the encyclical (cf. para. 23 and para. 67); second, "the party as such" is attacked at least twenty times; third, pleas for "a free press" and for "citizens' desire for peace and order" would seem by any reckoning to pertain to "civil rights." As to the alleged failure "to utter" specific "words": that a highly critical socio-religious manifesto, written in Italian and addressed to Italians living in a one-party state could not be discerned as aimed at Mussolini's government evokes the image of some dim-witted onlooker laboriously straining to comprehend the over-worked tautology: is the pope Catholic?

Zuccotti then discusses the encyclical's treatment of the fascist oath which as Pius XI observed, "even little boys and girls are obliged to take . . . which inculcates hatred, violence, and irreverence. . . . Such an oath, as it stands, is unlawful." To which Zuccotti adds without a pause, "unlawful, for in case of conflict between the demands of government and those of natural law *as defined by the Church,* the latter had priority." But it is not the demands of government "as such" but of a government which is "against all truth and justice." Moreover, what constitutes "natural" law is precisely that it is not defined by the Church (if it were, it might loosely be termed "supernatural" law) but by the individual person's own rational faculties. Had Zuccotti deigned to read the entire encyclical she would have seen it make precisely that distinction when it condemns "a 'statolatry' which is no less in contrast with the *natural* rights of the family than it is with the *supernatural* rights of the Church." It might also be observed that the use of the word "statolatry" would seem to be a fairly sweeping and even courageous condemnation of fascism.

After her comment about "natural law as defined by the church" taking priority, she continues: "He [Pius] *suggested* that the difficulty could be overcome if individuals who had already taken *or were required to take* the oath made a mental reservation 'before God, in their own consciences' to recognize *that priority.*" The reader may determine why she provides a paraphrase here rather than the direct quote—which is: "It seems to Us that such a means [to restore tranquility of conscience] for those *who have already received* the membership card [containing the oath] would be to make for themselves before God, in their own consciences, a reservation such as . . . 'in accordance with the duties of a good Christian' with the firm purpose to *declare* also externally such a reservation if the need for it occurred." Thus Pius's "suggestion" that this could apply to those who "were required" to take the oath in the future, is entirely Zuccotti's fabrication. Furthermore, the term "mental reservation"—which the pope does *not* use—in English is a euphemism for equivocation (indeed, the OED, supplies it as a euphemism for "Jesuitry"). Third, the "reservation" is *not* for recognition of "the priority of what the church defines," but for recognition of "the duties of a good Christian." Lastly, and obliterative of the canard here being dredged up—"Papists can lie for the church," as Charles Kingsley's disastrous attack on Cardinal Newman also affirmed—the encyclical insists on a *firm intent to publicly declare* the reservation when necessary.[3]

Of this book to which the heavy-handed sequence above is merely the ponderous Introduction, one jacket blurbist, Michael Berenbaum of the University of Judaism—taking note of Zuccotti's plumbing the depths to which the papacy can sink—observes: "It will only further enhance Zuccotti's reputation for balance, scholarship, and appropriate *gravitas.*"

Concerning *Mit brennender Sorge,* Zuccotti warns the reader that "a careful examination of its contents is in order" because it like the Italian encyclical "is often cited as evidence of Pius XI's courageous stand against Fascist and Nazi regimes." Again, three tendentious claims are proffered. First, the encyclical begins "with a protest against violations of the treaty of 1933 by 'the other contracting party,' *meaning Germany.* [Second] It never used the words 'National Socialist,' and [third] it *rarely even* referred to the Reich government as such." As to the first claim, there is no sinister omission here. In fact, Germany is mentioned five times on the very first page of the encyclical. Second, we are presented with another argument *ex silentio* comparable to Zuccotti's earlier, "He never uttered the word 'Fascist'," since to what "other contracting party"—which is standard legalese—could the encyclical be referring than to Germany's ruling party, the National Socialists? Third, "Reich government" also appears on the very first page of the encyclical.

Then after quoting a lengthy statement from the encyclical praising the Hebrew Bible unrestrainedly, and in language the most orthodox rabbi would endorse, Zuccotti comments: "The Old Testament [*sic*], then, must be taught because it is a credit to Christians rather than to the Jews who wrote it." The gravamen of this argument will escape most readers, since the quotation

---

[3] Through an anomalous lapse Peter Hebblethwaite in *Paul VI: The First Modern Pope* also uses the term "mental reservation," and speaks as though it could relate to some future occasion. He does, however, emphasize the disturbing impact of the encyclical's provisions on the fascists.

makes no implicit or explicit mention either of authorship or of Christians.

After denigrating Pius XI, but only as prelude to calumniating Pius XII, Zuccotti comes to the point of her first chapter: papal indifference to Nazism relative to papal obsession with Communism—a difficult case to make to anyone who has *actually* read *Mit brennender Sorge.* And as one might expect of an author afflicted with *gravitas*, the proof will be quantitative. "Even though papal condemnations of Communism were not *at all* new, *La Civiltà Cattolica* [a journal, randomly anti-Jewish, edited in Rome by Italian Jesuits][4] printed *Divini Redemptoris* in full, in *two* successive issues, along with *two* lengthy articles on the subject. It subsequently printed *Mit brennender Sorge* in a *single* issue, along with *one* article of comment." Not to get caught up in Zuccotti's brand of cliometrics, I would merely note that this difference in coverage might just come from the simple fact that the encyclical on Communism is roughly twice as long (82 numbered paragraphs) as that on Nazism (43 paragraphs). But the more obvious reason—which again evades her—for this gravely special "spatial" difference in coverage is that an encyclical addressed to the universal church in the church's universal language, Latin, is likely to get more attention in an Italian Jesuit journal than an encyclical written in German and explicitly addressed "to the Archbishops and Bishops of Germany."

Zuccotti, having disposed of the encyclicals, then concludes a discussion about the Church in Italy being "comfortable with the recent Fascist measures against the Jews," by noting about such comfortableness that "additional evidence emerged" during the German occupation of France when Marshall Pétain asked his ambassador to the Holy See, Léon Bérard, to determine "the Vatican's attitude toward the new anti-Jewish decrees." The ambassador sent an unusually detailed and desultory report containing among other things, descriptions of medieval practices regarding Jews, quotations from Thomas Aquinas, and ending with the observation that "someone in authority said to me at the Vatican there is

---

[4] Cf. " 'Everyone Has to Tell the Truth': Heidegger and the Jews," by Thomas Sheehan, *Continuum,* Autumn, 1990.

no intention of quarreling over the Jewish statute." Zuccotti, again arguing from silence, says that Cardinal Maglione, the Vatican Secretary of State, "never denied the report or declared that it was inaccurate. . . . The report, *of course,* is not *evidence* of Vatican approval of the *entire* content of the French anti-Jewish legislation. But neither was there any public expression of dissatisfaction." Yet this discussion of the report was initiated by her comment that "additional *evidence* emerged"; now it ends up, after a sequence of insinuations, that the "report, of course, is not evidence." And why the Secretary of State should express *anything* about a report privately communicated to him remains unexplained. The two face-saving phrases for her are *"entire* content," since then she can insinuate, though not too subtly, that *some* of the content indicated Vatican approval of the anti-Jewish legislation, and *"public expression,"* since "public" is not only undefined, in this context it can't be defined: expression *to* what public, and *by* what means? The people of Rome, the people of France (since the report was written for Pétain), in newspapers, radio messages, the aula of St. Peter's?—and expression by whom? the French ambassador, a Vatican functionary, the pope? This tissue of suppositions displays an astonishing reliance on unverified and unverifiable assumptions.

This can all be compared to Rychlak who notes that the distinguished Jesuit theologian, Henri de Lubac, devoted two chapters to the Bérard report in his memoir of the war years, *Christian Resistance to Anti-Semitism,* and supplied reasons for viewing it as a hoax: "If the ambassador had been able to obtain from any personage at all in Rome a reply that was even slightly clear and favorable [to the anti-Jewish laws], he would not have taken so much trouble to 'bring together the elements of a well-founded and complete report' obviously fabricated by himself or by one of his friends." And this internationally renowned scholar—later a cardinal—who a few years after the war was silenced by Pius XII added: ". . . from the very first day . . . the opposition between the orientation of the Vichy government [toward the Jews] and the thought of Pius XII was patent." De Lubac's memoir was first published in 1988 in French, and two years later in English; certainly sufficient time for a scholar like Zuccotti to have taken it into account, particularly since in her *The Holocaust, the French, and the Jews* (1993), she has high praise for de Lubac's efforts to aid Jewish refugees.[5]

I now want to consider another substantive instance of Zuccotti's doctoring her facts—but an instance that will also provide the transition to Phayer's equally questionable alterations. The Capuchin friar Marie-Benoit Peteul—known for his rescue efforts as "le père des Juifs"—was a friend of an Italian Jewish banker, Angelo Donati, who himself had long been active in helping the refugees. In the summer of 1943 Donati developed a bold and ingenious plan to save more Jews. Aided by Father Marie-Benoit, Donati met in the Vatican with representatives of the Italian, British, and American governments with a view to transporting by ship some forty thousand Jews to safety in North Africa. According to official US diplomatic records, the project was aborted because the consensus of the American and British officials, both in Rome and in their respective capitals, was that the undertaking could not be carried out given the imminence of the armistice which would

---

[5] James Carroll in *Constantine's Sword* (p. 542) introduces the Bérard hoax into a discussion of Edith Stein: "Because of the world into which she was thrust, she was forced out of the supersessionist mold. That said, it is also important to acknowledge that many of Sister Benedicta's earlier assumptions about the guilt of her 'unbelieving people' reflected Christian religious antisemitism." The footnote between the first and second sentences reads: "An example of the prevailing attitude is the report from Vichy's Vatican ambassador, Léon Bérard, referred to above." But the "reference" is to another footnote that doesn't mention the doubts attached to the "report," that Maglione criticized Vichy's "exaggerated conclusions" from it, and referred to its alleged subject, the *Statut des juifs,* as an "unfortunate law." Since I treat Carroll only as a subordinate participant in these discussions of the papacy, this may be the place to mention briefly his methodology which is, quite simply, to assemble quotations from books in the general area being treated, and then insert references to them wherever more or less relevant—here *less* since there is no connection with Stein and Holland, and Bérard and Vichy, except of course the ubiquitous theme of Catholics and antisemitism. A nontendentious treatment of the "report," though before de Lubac's memoir, is *Vichy France and the Jews* by Michael R. Marrus and Robert O. Paxton, (New York, 1981), where it is treated as an inconclusive "curious exchange" exploited by the Vichy government.

place all of Italy under German military control. The Italian representative himself blamed the failure of the project on General Eisenhower who was believed to have broken the pledge to postpone announcing the armistice until the refugee ships were out of port. In fact, though the armistice was signed on September 3, it was announced only on September 8.

Subsequently Father Robert Graham, an editor of the official papal documents (and therefore suspect as a creature of the Vatican, or as described by Phayer, "a Vatican operative"), observed that the plan "was easily seen as *unrealizable* in time of war." Immediately following this quotation Zuccotti detonates a curious *non sequitur:* Are we, then, to believe that it received no Vatican support because it was so *preposterous?"* After a couple of sentences of annotated irrelevancies, she resumes: "The plan was not unrealizable because of *the war* but because of *the lack of time* [to which Graham would have said, *per me fa lo stesso,* "to me it's the same thing"] and, *perhaps,* good will." That transitional "perhaps" elides into the realm of the ethical, i.e., of the Holy See: "Vatican officials seem to have been, *again,* highly conservative; unwilling to risk the loss of *prestige* that a failure might have entailed, and much too ready to decide that a difficult project was an impossible one."

However, it was the American, British, and Italian representatives exclusively who made *that* decision which had nothing whatever to do with "Vatican officials," much less with some specious "loss of prestige." As I said, the armistice was formally announced by Eisenhower on September 8. But that latter is the date *Zuccotti herself* gives for the Vatican's being *informed* of the details of the project, "exactly the kind of project that causes conservative bureaucrats to hesitate." In another inexplicable *non sequitur* a hundred pages earlier, in a different context, she notes that the armistice *"inadvertently* led to the German occupation of Italy and the onset of Jewish deportations." But it wasn't "inadvertent": it *was* predictable; it was *predicted;* and it occurred. Hence the urgency for action on the Donati overture. Moreover, it is self-defeating (and self-contradictory) for Zuccotti to then say: "Officials at the Vatican Secretariat of State were informed of the Donati plan *before* the armistice rendered it impossible," since in fact, the "informing" and the "announcing" were on the same day—this entirely apart from the sheer impossibility of transporting thousands of people, not in a matter of hours but even in a matter of days or weeks. But clearly from all this discussion the villain of the piece is the Vatican which, in fact, had nothing to do with the success or failure of the project.

One cannot but feel a touch of pathos when one reads *all* of the above in the light of Zuccotti's 1993 book on the holocaust in France. In that book Pius XI's leadership during the period from the late twenties to the early thirties in improving relations with Jews is praised; and *Mit brennender Sorge*, "a protest against atheistic Nazi confrontations with the Church," is quoted in confirmation of that improvement. In the earlier book of nearly 400 pages, the name, "Pacelli" or "Pius XII," who in *Under His Very Windows* is the triple-crowned phantom hovering over despairing victims: in that earlier book, the name never *once* occurs. The Donati plan (seen above as virtually sabotaged by the Secretariat of State) is discussed in the earlier book with no mention whatever of anything connected with the Holy See, save the single observation that Père Benoit "introduced Donati to influential individuals at the Vatican" who happened to be the representatives of the American, British, and Italian governments. The Bérard "report," with its implications of papally inspired antisemitism (although written at the request, and by a representative, of the Vichy French government) is *nowhere* discussed in Zuccotti's earlier book on "the holocaust, the French, and the Jews."

Lastly, and most paradoxically, while in *Under His Very Windows* the entire world of Vatican officialdom is depicted as knowledgeable in 1941 of the Nazi concentration camps and, less than a year later, of the beginning of the extermination process, in *The Holocaust, the French, and the Jews* virtually no one—social workers, members of Jewish or Christian agencies, officials of the Free French government, church leaders whether Catholic or Protestant—seemed to know of or believe in the existence of the death camps. Zuccotti here is all magnanimity, generously forbearing, and detailed (pp. 145–54) in her condonation of this nescience and incredulity.[6] The Communist press tried to expose the gassing of Jews in October, 1942, but it "had already made sweeping allegations of other types of atrocities, and [its] credibility was low." Of Protestant churchmen we are told: "... *like government and religious leaders throughout the world* with partial knowledge of the mass murders being committed in the east [they] did not necessarily understand emotionally what they knew intellectually. That failure of imagination ..., continued until the *end of the war.*"

But it was not just a "failure of *imagination.*" In her earlier book Zuccotti tells the reader that, "The full and unique reality of the Holocaust ... can be comprehended today with the help of thousands of haunting personal testimonies, documents, photographs, and physical remains of gas chambers and killing centers. *During the war it was almost inconceivable.*" However, it was *not* almost inconceivable in the Vatican. There it was a truism, however cunningly concealed. In *Under His Very Windows* we are told: "The summer of 1942 [when the French communist press was ignored because of its "low credibility"] witnessed the deportations to Auschwitz of thousands of Jews from France, Belgium, and the Netherlands, and the onset of systematic selections and gassings at the camp." Because sick and elderly, and not just potential laborers, were being deported the nuncio to France in a note to the papal Secretary of State inferred that extermination was possibly their fate. He added that "the Holy Father has made clear allusions in order to condemn such inhuman persecution" although fear of the extension of such draconian measures "incline him to prudent waiting." Zuccotti's gloss is unfalteringly condemnatory: the

---

[6] In fact, she seems to go beyond neutral objectivity to explain why the Holocaust information was not credible. The Riegner report of August 11, 1942 was accepted in London, Rome, and Washington, but a month later when Cordell Hull denounced to the French ambassador the extermination process, she says: "But again, this was information from opponents of the Third Reich, and thus dismissable as enemy propaganda. Furthermore, Hull's warning, like the earlier Radio Moscow and BBC reports, formed part of a wealth of rumors and assertions, many of which turned out to be as false as the allegations of German atrocities against civilians during the First World War had been. We cannot assume that information proven with hindsight to be correct should have been recognized as such at the time."

nuncio "suspected that people were being deported to their deaths, yet he was willing to *fabricate* papal responses and point out reasons for 'prudent waiting.' His mentality, as well as his writing style, was typical of his colleagues *in Rome*."

Interea, as epic transitionists say, back *in France:* "The postwar testimony of *hundreds of survivors*, many of whom had seen Resistance tracts and heard BBC reports *throughout the war*, reveals similar incomprehension" about the extermination process. Raymond Aron, "with the Free French in London, where information circulated freely," is quoted: ". . . but the gas chambers, the industrial assassination of human beings—I must confess that I did not imagine it, and because I could not imagine it, *I did not know*." The Jewish physician at Drancy had been at the departure camp for Auschwitz until the summer of 1944. Of his experience, he asserted: "I was one of the best informed about the mental state of several dozens of thousands of internees . . . , trying to understand the sense of these events"; it was simply "the exploitation of Jewish manpower by a Germany more and more short of labor . . . , aggravated by the wish to isolate the Jews in an immense and miserable ghetto." And on and on— all in startling contrast to the vitriolic description of the broad range of allegedly precise knowledge, grasped early in the war years and conveyed to his emissaries by the detached and indifferent figure of the pope frigidly gazing down at the swelling ranks of the doomed "under his very windows."

On September 27, 1942, the American representative at the Vatican formally inquired *if* the Holy See "had *any* information to confirm reports" of Jewish massacres. A couple of weeks later,[7] the Secretary of State confirmed "from other sources" the reports, and

---

[7] For a large bureaucracy this would seem gratifyingly expeditious; for Zuccotti this short period is riddled with dilatoriness and suspicious delays. *"Despite* the recent reports [actually only one] from Malvezzi" [September 30], another "via the Polish government in exile [October 3], and Scavizzi [October 7], Vatican officials *declined* Taylor's request for confirmation of reported atrocities. [no date is given for this "decline" nor is there any footnote reference]. *Nine days after* Tittman asked for an answer to Taylor's request, and *three days after* receiving the Scavizzi report, Maglione [Cardinal Secretary of State] replied." —in all less than two weeks to assemble "information to confirm *reports*" of massacres.

added: "It has not yet been possible for the Holy See to check the exactness of such news. As is known, however, it avails itself of every possibility that is offered to ease the suffering of non-Aryans." Again, Zuccotti's gloss: "Apparently, help to 'non-Aryans' did not include cooperation with efforts to learn what was happening to them." But in her earlier book she exoneratingly describes how "the Jewish publishers of *J'accuse* suffered agonies of indecision about whether to print news of gassings" in that same month when, in her later book, she is indicting the Vatican for having "to check the exactness of such news." Moreover, even a *full year* later in the summer of 1943, "the president of the Consistoire [the most important "non-Aryan" organization in France] received a copy of a letter" from one of those "uncooperative and unhelpful" papal offices, the nunciature "in Munich describing the crematoriums and mass execution of Jews"; nevertheless, and entirely absolved by Zuccotti *prima*, the president of the Consistoire (known also as Alliance Israelite Universelle) "still found it *unimaginable....*" Whereas in Italy, in that same summer of 1943, Zuccotti *secunda* tells us that not only were mass execution of Jews imaginable, but "Vatican officials were *perfectly aware* of the fact [that] *millions* of European Jews had been murdered in the Soviet Union and in Poland."

And so the juxtaposition goes back and forth between the benevolence dispensed in the earlier book and the malevolence depicted in the later; between *carte blanche* exoneration for Free French authorities, for acquiescent French Jewish and Christian leaders, for the BBC information sources beamed to France on the one hand, and the unsparing condemnation relating to all things papal and "Roman" on the other. Again, the issue is not whether papacy and Rome deserve to be criticized; the issue is whether this is the kind of scholarship that clarifies or obfuscates; whether, in short, this is history or propaganda.

One final irony. All of these benignly described events and persons in *The Holocaust, the French, and the Jews* appear in that book which was published more than a decade after the completion of the 11 volumes of *Actes et Documents du Saint Siège relatifs à la seconde guerre mondiale*—which is the single most utilized source for

Under His Very Windows. Thus the difference in perspective, from charitably descriptive in the first book to acrimoniously critical in the second, cannot be attributed to a massive infusion of new data.[8] The pathos to which I referred earlier derives not from such a transformation of perspective—which is no one's affair but the author's—but from the reader's experience of an unfathomable sense of psychic dissociation A chasm divides two books on the very same theme and by the very same author, a chasm which seems to be viewed not as unbridgeable but as non-existent: as though the argument of *Under His Very Windows* were merely the logical continuation of the argument of *The Holocaust, the French, and the Jews*. This "dissociation" is what in another context Dr. Johnson characterized as resulting from the "violent yoking together of discordant images." Perhaps, one muses, the startling difference between the two treatments suggests that there is some validity to the notion—otherwise thought vulgar superstition—that a turn of a century *or* of a millennium can precipitate individual or collective metanoia.

— III —

Michael Phayer's initial reference to Father Marie-Benoit is possibly an illustration of "even Homer nods," since it is also based on an argument *ex silentio.* Of Pius XII's audience with Père Benoit, Phayer writes: "He gave Pius a written report on the Jews of France, which included those of the Italian-occupied zone who

---

[8] In her Introduction she informs the reader: "The purpose of this book is to separate fact from fiction, reality from myth, about what the two popes and their principal officials at the Secretariat of State actually *did* [her italics] to help Jews in Italy, the country where they enjoyed the greatest opportunity to be useful. For that purpose, the *Actes et Documents du Saint Siège* are more than adequate. Although much that is unfavorable may have been omitted, it is reasonable to assume that all that is favorable was included." That last sentence is known, acceptably and neutrally, as the expression of a Ricoeurian hermeneutic of suspicion, a valuable corrective particularly for issues relating to minority status. That hermeneutic, particularly among feminists of the second generation, has generally been supplanted by a hermeneutic of empathy.

were being pursued by the Germans. (This document is not contained in the Vatican Collection *Actes et Documents du Saint Siège pendant le IIe Guere Mondiale)."* The misspelling and mistitling are mere carelessness, though the implication here, and more frequently in *Under His Very Windows*, is that "Saint Siège" should be spelled "Saint Sieve" and that documents were intentionally omitted by the editorial board to put a better face on Vatican misdeeds. (Hence, too, Zuccotti's assault above on Father Graham one of the editors: "all priests," as she says in her Introduction, failing to note that, even worse—*all Jesuits*.) But in fact Phayer is simply mistaken: the document with annexes is included in its entirety in *Actes et Documents. . . .* Moreover, John Morley—who, notwithstanding ideologues of the right and historians of the left, never engages in spin in his truly exemplary *Vatican Diplomacy and the Jews*—certifies that Pius was well-disposed to Benoit's requests, that this was reassuring to Jewish leaders, and that the pope expressed surprise at the information because "he would never have thought such conduct possible in France."

What cannot be attributed to any *etiam-Homerus* hermeneutic of generosity is Phayer's observation about the Donati plan requiring consent of the American and British who controlled the Mediterranean—the latter a simple fact; but then Phayer adds: "Donati hoped that the Vatican would allow him to speak to the American and English diplomats to the Holy See, but permission to do this was refused, as we saw in chapter 4." However, in chapter 4 there is no reference at all to Donati (described as a "Franciscan rescuer"), and in fact the latter did communicate in the Vatican with the diplomats. Concerning the allegation of maltreatment of Father Benoit, the reader is told that "his request for an audience with Pope Pius was not granted. (A Vatican official informed him that Pius no longer gave private audiences, but in March he had given one to Margin Slachta . . .)." But throughout that spring Benoit was out of the country. ". . . on July 16, Benoit, accompanied by his religious superior, *finally* saw the pope." But not after the suggested lengthy interval; in fact, Benoit returned *to Rome* late in June, and less than three weeks later had his audience, at which he presented the documents to Pius who responded in the terms of concern cited from Morley above. Again, one is compelled to suggest, this is not quite history as an Acton would have wanted it written.

In another unwarranted effort to cast doubt on *Actes et Documents . . . ,* Phayer observes of the correspondence between the pope and his personal friend, the anti-Nazi bishop of Berlin, Konrad von Preysing, that: "Of his letters to the pope—thirteen of them in fifteen months, eight in 1943 and five in 1944—*only two* have been included in the Vatican's document collection, . . . omissions which suggest that Preysing was pressing Pope Pius to *speak out* about the Europe-wide murder of the Jews." But the fact is that "omissions which suggest" this don't exist. In the 1943 volume alone there are four letters included relating to the persecution of the Jews; three others with excerpts but not quoted in full since they relate less to the Holocaust than to the execution of priests. The editors of *Actes et Documents. . . .* in a footnote referring to another letter state: "Information omitted on the religious life and the bombing of the cathedral of Berlin." One concludes that any omitted letters were personal and not official.

But two far more serious errors than those above relate to events in postwar Germany—on which Phayer's book does make a signal contribution. The first concerns the Catholic philosopher, Jacques Maritain, whom we encountered in McInerny's diatribe, and who was briefly de Gaulle's ambassador to the Vatican. Maritain in two letters pleaded with his friend in the Vatican secretariat, Archbishop Montini (later Pope Paul VI), for a statement on Germany's collective responsibility for the Holocaust. Phayer, again arguing *ex silentio,* writes: "What kind of a hearing Montini was able to get for Maritain's thoughts is *unknown.* It appears, however, that *the pontiff* rejected them *explicitly* when he raised the bishops of Berlin, Cologne, and Münster to the cardinalate early in 1946, *to indicate* to the world his high esteem for the German church." But it doesn't so "appear" explicitly or even implicitly since Maritain's letters were written in July and August, and the consistory creating the cardinals took place six months *earlier* on February 18, 1946. Not only is this warped chronology a blatant attempt to attack the pope on the grounds of indifference to justice, but it also renews the "canonical" cliché of Pius's critics that he was blindly partial to all things German.

Nor does Phayer hesitate to stigmatize—as he piles Pelion on Ossa—the bishops of Berlin, Cologne, and Münster who were clearly being honored primarily for their vigorous opposition to Nazism. Phayer himself had earlier noted: *"No other* German bishop spoke as pointedly [against Nazi policies] as Preysing [of Berlin] and Frings [of Cologne]."* (Of the bishop of Münster, more shortly.) Moreover, as to Pius's making cardinals in order to "indicate" his high esteem for favored countries, it should be noted that at the same consistory the three French prelates elevated with the strong backing of de Gaulle were known opponents of the Vichy regime: Petit de Julleville of Rouen, Roques of Rennes, and Saliège of Toulouse. Finally, it should be emphasized that Pius had declined to offer the purple to the Berlin wartime Nuncio, Cesare Orsenigo, whom Phayer describes, a bit ham-fistedly, as a "pro-German, pro-Nazi, antisemite fascist who would have no trouble adjusting to the Nazi regime in Berlin [in short according to ideologues of the left, a man after the pope's own heart] . . . and who hankered after a cardinal's hat." The "hankering" is not overstatement; and after the consistory Orsenigo—as Herodotus might have moralized—"died of a broken heart."

As to the third German cardinal, von Galen of Münster, *all* references to him by Phayer up to the postwar period mention *only* his universally admired courageous denunciation of the Nazi compulsory euthanasia program. This is curious since any historian of that era would have certainly mentioned that von Galen, though a bishop only one year, sponsored and prefaced a book attacking the Nazi bible of racism, Alfred Rosenberg's *The Myth of the Twentieth Century*. The bishop's supportive *imprimi potest* resulted in the critique selling more than 200,000 copies in the period *shortly after* Hitler had come to power. In 1935 and 1936 after Rosenberg himself ventured to Münster, the bishop again denounced Nazi racism. Nor is there any mention in Phayer of the fact, found even in popular short accounts like the *Encyclopaedia Britannica,* that after von Galen's barrage of sermons attacking the euthanasia scheme,

Hitler's aide, Bormann, was dissuaded by Goebbels (who antici-pated propaganda embarrassments) from pursuing the bishop's execution "until after the final victory."

Goebbels had in mind the massive and unprecedented public demonstrations against the regime (also not mentioned by Phayer) that followed on the bishop's demands that crosses be re-placed in schools, and that the other "cross," the swastika, not appear on any religious building or at any religious ceremony. Fur-thermore, Goebbels' propaganda ministry is also recorded as not-ing that action against von Galen—who had supported the attack on the "atheist" Soviet Union—would turn the bishop into a mar-tyr and create opposition to the war not only "in Münster, but in all of Westphalia." Nor does Phayer tell the reader that the pope wrote von Galen that his anti-Nazi stand had inspired Pius's 1942 Christmas condemnation of the Holocaust; nor that in the follow-ing year, after this long series of public anti-Nazi confrontations, von Galen was honored with the title Assistant at the Pontifical Throne. Finally, and most astonishingly for a book titled "The Catholic Church and the Holocaust," there is no mention of the tragic fact that as a result of the failed assassination attempt on his life, Hitler by his own personal order had the bishop impris-oned in the concentration camp at Sachsenhausen where he re-mained until the end of the war.

What obviously doesn't now have to be mentioned is that all three prelates were made cardinals not—as these conspiracy theo-ries masking as history would suggest—to counter some utterly irrelevant letters from Maritain, or not because of Pius's "predilec-tion for Germans"; but because—like their brother bishops in France—of their "open and courageous" (Pius to von Galen) oppo-sition to the Nazi regime.

But the matter of Phayer's oddly parsimonious treatment of von Galen remains to be explained. So many omissions of central events in the life of one of the most outspoken critics of Nazism are only with difficulty justifiable as oversights or scholarly lapses. Neither should anyone be surprised, certainly not by this phase of our consideration of these various books attacking the role of the

Holy See, that one can relate this distorted treatment to their unrelenting leitmotiv of subornation by the papacy. Though it takes more than a "bystander's" detachment to attack a death-camp survivor, if the ideological prize is the further ventilation of papaphobia—then, why not? The plot—in the narrative, not the conspiratorial sense—played out in a matter of less than a year, roughly from the Allied occupation (Münster was in the British zone) to the bishop's death in March of 1946, a month after being made a cardinal. Von Galen who had opposed the Versailles treaty, then the Third Reich, now opposed the British occupation as well as the Nuremberg trials (this latter, perhaps, the "moral" basis of Phayer's biographical erasures) with their initial assumption of Germany's collective guilt—though they were opposed by scores of British jurists, as well as by such Americans as William O. Douglas and Learned Hand.

True to his episcopal motto *nec laudibus, nec timore*—roughly, "neither for praise, nor out of fear"—the bishop proved such a scourge to the British that, like victors throughout history vaunting their power, they even tried to prevent his journey to Rome for the papal consistory. His criticism of the occupation force was not a mere matter of pique or resentment; though his complaints do not differ greatly, say, from those of Okinawans toward the American military today. He complained to the British officers about undisciplined soldiers, increased crime, the violation of military curfew, and destruction of property. On a more significant level, he consistently spoke out against the allied assumption of "collective guilt" on the part of all Germans. But the issue here is not the validity of that assumption, nor the licitness of the Nuremberg trials (which, however flawed, did attempt to bring criminal leaders to account), and certainly not the bishop's complaints about the unruliness of the occupation troops.[9]

---

[9] Phayer's facile assumption that "collective guilt" (a notion Pius criticized in *Nessuno Certamente,* his 1944 Christmas address) is a self-evident basis for censure or condemnation can be put in a less geographically and chronologically remote context by consideration of such ever more serious issues as reparations for indigenous peoples and for African-Americans. But who specifically is to pay the unquestionably justifiable compensation; to whom is it to be paid; and who

The only issue here is Phayer's reading of the bishop's "diatribe" (Phayer's term) "attacking the Nuremberg 'show trials'," and its alleged consequences—a "reading" which again entails juggled chronology as well as a plot, now, in the conspiratorial sense. Phayer after noting that the German bishops' Fulda conference "had unequivocally said that those who engaged in atrocities must be brought to justice," then states that "only months later German Catholic bishops began to plead for leniency for those who had engaged personally in the Holocaust." The footnote to this references *U.S. War Crimes Trial Program in Germany* (1989), by Frank M. Buscher, one of Phayer's students. But the discussion on those pages refers only to "the end of 1946" and a sermon by Cardinal Frings on New Year's Eve of 1947 (and the rest of the book covers a period of ten years after the war). So rather than "only months later," we have events of a year and a half, and a full decade later. Phayer continues immediately: "The reason for the bishops' reversal can be traced to *Rome.* Just months [actually nine months] after the Fulda statement, Bishop Clemens August Graf von Galen . . . published an address in which he sharply attacked the Nuremberg 'show trials'." *But* he also attacked the notion of collective guilt, *and* the Allied occupation authorities. (Rhetoricians might also want to note in the above paragraph a familiar tactic: on the previous page it had been simply "Bishop von Galen"; now we get the full name and a panoply of titles, after the fashion of Democrats in the seventies syllabicating "President Richard Milhous Nixon.")

Phayer continues: *"Abruptly* after church leaders found out about von Galen's attack, they distanced themselves from OMGUS [Occupational Military Government—United States]

---

determines the answers to both questions? But certainly no "collective guilt" devolves on, say, citizens of the West coast for the internment—Roosevelt once slipped and said "concentration"—camps where over 100,000 Japanese-Americans were held? But that leaves unanswered the question whether a payment by the government of twenty thousand dollars forty years later to the survivors, along with a presidential apology, was just or even adequate recompense? As Pius implied in his Christmas address, "collective guilt" is elusive, elastic, and in the end unjust; like capital punishment it offers only a sham sense of that fictive entity, "closure."

authorities. . . . *Of course*, the fact that von Galen's tract came out *in Rome* signaled the bishops that *the Holy See opposed* punishment of German war criminals. Given the green light *from Rome*, German bishops began a long and largely successful campaign to free imprisoned criminals. . . ." Three times in this short quotation the sinister Roman provenance is mentioned. (Another principle of rhetoric *and* metaphysics is that the most unvarnished proof is not only the most elegant, it is usually the most effective—less is more; or as the Franciscan metaphysician would have had it: "provenances" should not be multiplied *sine necessitate*.) The reason the "diatribe" did not come out in the bishop's episcopal see, Münster, is that an attack on the British occupation authorities could hardly have been published in the British occupied zone. But why Rome? Simply because the bishop had been there a few weeks before at the consistory.[10]

But again, the issue is not whether the bishops did or did not do what is here (somewhat exaggeratedly) affirmed: "campaign to free imprisoned criminals." The issue regarding the bishops is: "why?" Did they do it because von Galen (hitherto a heroically independent figure) was acting as tool of the always deceitful papacy? Did they do it because of the persuasive power of a document that appeared in March, the very month von Galen died, and that presumably was circulated immediately throughout the German episcopate, convincing the entire hierarchy to "reverse" a long-standing position? Moreover, there is the view of Phayer's associate, Frank Buscher, that, "When it came to opposing Allied trials of war criminals, the two major religious hierarchies in Germany shared identical views. The issue, like few others, united

---

[10] To further taint the *dramatis personae* of this Bishop of Rome-Bishop of Münster axis, Phayer says that von Galen "made the outrageous claim that the prisons of the [British] occupational authority were worse than the Nazi concentration camps. . . ." To which Phayer in a note adds: "To provide an 'out' for this assertion, Galen referred to an anonymous English newspaper writer who had made the comparison." Anonymous he apparently was not, since article, newspaper, date, and author are supplied—along with a more benign interpretation— by Suzanne Leschinski's "Kardinal von Galen in der Nachkriegzeit," in Joachim Kuropka, ed., *Clemens August Graf von Galen: Neue Forschungen* [but not so new as to be unavailable to Phayer], 1992.

Catholic and Protestant clergymen." Are we to believe the Protestant clergy were also influenced by the impetus and inspiration of the long-dead von Galen—he of course, even from the grave, being responsive to the "green light from Rome"? I think any unbiased reader would say that one doesn't have to be a David Hume to dissolve this whole *post hoc ergo* fabrication of causality whereby the bishop of Münster, in the month before his death, moves the entire German hierarchy from a posture of sympathy and cooperation with the occupation forces to one of active opposition.

Nor, one is morally obliged to add, does it do honor to the profession of history to obliterate a record of heroism on the part of von Galen in order to taint him with antagonism toward an occupying power and a legal proceeding—the Nuremberg trial—that, however ostensibly well-intentioned, were disorganized, indiscriminate, and conflicted almost from the start. Von Galen was one of the few genuine and consistent opposition heroes of the Hitler period—albeit a man of conservative and patriotic bent.

At least as damaging to Phayer's credibility as the "three cardinals" incident is his treatment of (the always villainous) Pius on matters relating to noncombatant immunity and the bombing of civilian centers. The reason these are crucial is that a case could be made, as I tentatively shall in chapter four, that if the pope's repeated denunciation of destroying non-strategic urban areas—which violated the traditional Catholic just-war doctrine as well as the Geneva Conventions—was ignored, might not a similar fate have met any repeated denunciations of what led to the Holocaust? Again, however supremely important Holocaust condemnations are, *that* is a matter to be postponed to a *later* phase of this discussion. Phayer's assessment of Pius's alleged preoccupation with the bombing of Rome introduces the *present* issue: "The problem facing Pius XII was that he had failed to condemn the German bombing of England *during 1940 and 1941*, but then spoke out against *the bombing of civilians* when the Allies gained aerial superiority." Pius also "made a serious tactical mistake," by "expressing sympathy for Germany's bombed-out churches after not having regretted the Nazi destruction of Coventry." Again, we have Pius's alleged philo-germanic inclinations raised to a canon of interpretation.

But in fact Pius spoke out against the destruction of civilian centers from the very beginning of hostilities. In 1939, less than a week after the ten-day bombing of Warsaw the pope said, "We cling especially to the hope that civilian populations will be preserved from all direct military operations." Three months later in his Christmas message: "Among such crimes. . . . We must include the unlawful use of destructive weapons against noncombatants and refugees, against old men and women and children." On March 24, 1940: "More than once, to Our great distress, the laws which bind civilized peoples together have been violated; most lamentably, undefended cities, country towns and villages have been terrorized by bombing, destroyed by fire, and thrown down in ruins. Unarmed citizens, even the sick, helpless old people and innocent children have been visited with death." On June 2, 1940: "Nor do we think it right to refuse to express Our sorrow in seeing how the treatment of noncombatants. . . . is far from being in conformity with humane standards." On April 13, 1941: ". . . the ruthless struggle has at times assumed forms which can be described as atrocious . . . , the sufferings of civilian populations, defenseless women and children, the sick and aged. . . ." On June 29, 1941: "There is a decadence of the spirit of justice . . . , human bodies are torn by bombs or by machine-gun fire; wounded and sick fill hospitals." On December 24, 1941, two months after the last bombing raid on Coventry which unlike London was a manufacturing city: "We think of the mental and physical pain, death and destruction which air warfare has inflicted upon cities, populations, and industrial centers." Clearly Pius did not "fail to condemn the German bombing . . . during 1940 and 1941"—nor is it surprising that he continued to condemn all such bombing in the following years, particularly if one takes into account that in 1943 alone the allies dropped 200,000 tons of bombs on Germany, whereas the Luftwaffe dropped 2,000 tons on England. So, once again the professional historians—to put it kindly—have distorted facts to support personal prejudices.

— IV —

At the beginning of this chapter I made a crude but functional distinction between the ideological denigrators of the papacy and the ideological consecrators, and noted that generally the first group is akin to the liberal left, while the second, to the conservative right—admitting the fuzziness of all such labels. I also noted that because of the intellectual poverty of the second group of ideologues, I have devoted only minimal attention to them: piety, fidelity, loyalty, etc., are virtues, but they are not a critical or rational stance, however intrinsically admirable, and indeed essential to any polity they may be. I also observed that what I called the "professional historians" are generally allied with the first grouping, but not in any way as rigidly or as programmatically. From what I have sketched above, that may sound like a dubious encomium to the professoriate, since I have concentrated on some very seriously skewed scholarship. But the difference between the "professional historians" and the "ideological denigrators" is that the former are concerned primarily with methodology, the latter, with goals. Of course there are shaded areas, but it probably still remains true that the historians are concerned with disclosing the facts as they see them, however influenced by social, economic, and other biases. The denigrators are concerned with disclosing many of the same facts but mainly with a view to some external agenda, loosely defined as reform of the church, collegiality, democratization, gender parity, freedom of expression whether in the pew or in the academy, etc.. These goals are possibly of concern to some historians, but their attainment is at best a by-product of their research, not its objective.

If I criticized the historians above for professional lapses which might generously be described as either derived from the exhilaration of hunting down clues based only on heuristic intuitions, or derived from the truism that "even Homer nods," I will, on the other hand, be condemning in the next two chapters those I have termed "ideological denigrators" for not merely skewing, but actually corrupting, their research to reach a pre-ordained conclusion.

Here a personal note—though I shrink from anything that smacks of the memoirist—may be called for. John Cornwell in *Hitler's Pope* professes to have begun the book with a view to disproving Hochhuth's mean-spirited depiction of Pius XII. That is possibly a dubious assertion since his previous "papal" book, *A Thief in the Night: The Mysterious Death of John Paul I,* sustains the arc of attention by holding out to the reader throughout its narration the tantalizing prospect of a Vatican murder—until that arc collapses in a tardy exposé of the Vatican banking scandal, which even the catchy title never hints at. (There may have been no truth-in-advertising regulations in Thatcherian England.) Nevertheless, he claims that it was only after he was engaged deeply in his own research into Pius XII—just as research into a murder led to a reversal of his original intent—that he was *driven* to conclude that the pope was indeed the punctilious, self-centered (though "humble"), diplomacy-obsessed human being that Cornwell's readers can readily recognize.

On first examining Zuccotti and Phayer, I was aware of their bias, but since they had gained my sympathy both as serious scholars (one of whom I had published) and as welcome contrasts to obviously eulogistic defenders of Pius, I found myself unwilling to abandon that view, and even willing to contemplate some exculpatory dialectics that would leave them untarnished. My initial argument—which I abandoned utterly as I read and analyzed their work more closely—was that they were fulfilling the role every researcher is familiar with (again, witness Cornwell): that of the scholar as sleuth. This is a role that readers of PI ("Private Investigator"; formerly, just plain "Detective") fiction are accustomed to. The latter is also the genre—so I was going to suggest—that determines the mood of these books, as clue after clue is pursued to validate what appears originally to be the slimmest suspicion, until finally the ardor which possesses the author, by an almost intangible contagion influences the reader to also embrace what becomes clearer as the "trial" reaches its end: a conclusion of "guilty as charged."

What happens, I tried to persuade myself, is that such authors being hunters (ostensibly of the truth), get caught up in the exhilaration of the chase which then so possesses them that marshaling their data towards a discovery of guilt becomes not only a means to vindicate their research but also to convince themselves of serving the cause of truth. I even contemplated citing Cardinal Newman's Dublin lecture, "Literature," where he described the satisfaction experienced by the gifted writer who, self-mesmerized by his own rhetoric or mastery of argumentation, delights in setting off pyrotechnic displays of skill, whether of discovery or of refutation. He compared the experience to that of the giant wielding his club not out of aggressive boisterousness but out of the sheer joy of the exercise. (One might well think of the verbal overkill in the thirty-nine "blots" of Newman's—subsequently wisely excised—indictment of poor Kingsley.) So, too—I almost had myself convinced—with critics such as I have discussed in whom the scholarly complexus of impulses and emotions, of drives to achieve and triumph, is a humane and humanistic passion and, at least initially, admirable and guiltless. It is in any case, I told myself, entirely different from the motivation of what Harold Bloom identifies as "the school of resentment" (some of whose members I will discuss in the next two chapters), which arbitrarily manufactures adversaries in order to settle imagined scores, or to cicatrize old psychic wounds, or hubristically to indulge in the *Schadenfreude* of vilification.

Alas, it just didn't wash. As I read more and more, the temptation to exonerate these perpetrators of scholarly errors grew weaker and weaker. Good people, noble spirits even, have had their reputations sullied. And regardless of what those perpetrators imagine in the precincts of their own conscience, it must be said that no matter how—in the larger cause of liberal thought, even of legitimate reform of abuses—they think themselves justified: I do not. They may even in the sketching of the overall picture prove to be right. But if in the details they are distorting truth, that sketch will be right only by the fortuity of unanticipated chance, not by the persuasiveness of their argument.

— V —

The reason for their failure is that their goal has been to satisfy an *a priori* assumption, i.e., the Holy See was derelict both on humane and religious grounds in its obligation to "save" the Jews. This was their own, perhaps honestly reached, allegation which they then set out to prove. And in that effort and with that methodology—short of deliberate distortions which we have seen are manifold—they are representative of a large body, in fact the largest body of professional historians examining the Holocaust. If one looks at the titles which I cited at the beginning of this chapter, they bear a remarkable similarity to the following representative list relating, now, not to the papacy and the Holocaust but to the American Jewish community and the Holocaust: *While Six Million Died; No Haven for the Oppressed; The Abandonment of the Jews; The Jews Were Expendable; The Sacred and the Doomed;* and *The Deafening Silence*—the latter two presaging or echoing the titles of books indicting the papacy.

Lord Acton in a letter to Mary Gladstone warned her of the pitfalls awaiting any historian who finds facile parallels between situations and events that superficially may appear to have something in common, but which on investigation are clearly lacking in significant similarities. But one cannot look at those titles and not hear a ring of familiarity, and given their common theme, the Holocaust, there is no doubt that they can cast some light on issues that transcend the purely American or even the purely national. Students of both the American Jewish community and the papacy, and indeed of the Holocaust in general have, in the words of one historian, Henry Feingold, written what "are as much cries of pain as they are serious history." Michael Marrus speaks of "a strong tendency . . . to condemn rather than to explain," while Feingold adds that the "indictment against the witnesses [or "bystanders"] is as predictable as it is irresistible." The most recent contributor to this "revisionist" approach summarizes the crucial differences as follows:[11]

---

[11] All quotations and those that follow are from Gulie Ne'eman Arad's

The extent of the tragedy and the failure to reduce it, let alone prevent it, inspires a tacit moral-psychological posture that renders the bystanders as guilty until proven innocent. Furthermore, with the end result known, rescue becomes the indisputable expectation and the six million victims reinforce an intuitive-ethical inclination to evaluate the results of the American Jewish leaders' actions as a function of the sufferers' needs and not of the bystanders' means. Such an analysis is based on the fanciful notion that American Jews should have totally identified with the plight of their European co-religionists in the belief that unequivocal altruism, itself based on an idealized vision of kinship solidarity, could have overcome any objective or subjective obstacles to a determined will to help. This is a deeply felt moral-emotional argument. But it is also deeply flawed.

Now I am certainly not going to suggest one simply substitute "papacy" for "American Jews," or "fellow human beings" for "European co-religionists," to make the parallel more effective. But it should be clear that an entirely different perspective from that of papal critics whom I will examine shortly or whom I discussed earlier, particularly Zuccotti and Phayer, is here being envisioned with regard to the Holocaust.

If Lord Acton were living today, he would certainly have warned his protégée about another abuse of the historian's art, the facile adoption of academic slogans or clichés as explanatory devices for complex realities. Certainly he would have found offensive the rampant invocation for every conceivable social change, however trivial, of the already exhausted phrase "paradigm shift." Rather than describing some historic transitional sequence of perspectives, the term has been almost eviscerated of any real meaning by its application to everything from new styles of dress to new brands of breakfast cereal, from haute couture to oat meal. So true is this, that even sloganized ironies like the exhausted, "brother can you paradigm," elicit only a dismissive shrug. And

---

America, Its Jews, and the Rise of Nazism (Bloomington, 2000). She is a student of Saul Friedländer, and is now associated loosely with the Israeli New Historians whom we shall encounter in chapter four.

that represents a great misfortune, because beyond all its abuse by cliché mongers, it remains the best term to encapsulate the kinds of embryonic effort the quotations above adumbrate: a revolution in redescription.

The authors that Arad has cited are among those that are "initiating" this shift. The earlier paradigm of what may be called "judgmental" scholarship has an honorable lineage, certainly in the modern era beginning with that historian I have been citing, Lord Acton. And I should make clear that what appears here is not an embrace or an endorsement of this newer perspective, but merely an acknowledgment of its existence and its importance. Thus in the chapters to come I shall be writing in the more or less "standard" fashion, and that not merely because I am responding to critics who have adopted that mode in their historical narratives, but also because in the long run I have more trust in the persuasiveness of a judicial, adversarial approach—so long as it is not based on doctored data.

Nevertheless, I am convinced this shift is not just another fashionable quest for "difference"; nor, as with many revisionary tactics, merely an attempt to rejuvenate an enervated discipline (like Civil War studies); nor, finally, an effort to introduce novel approaches into traditional fields (like that urbane sprawl known as "culture studies"). This is literally a shift in the patterns and templates and taxonomy whereby one may get a new "handle," a new "purchase" on an elusive and over-interpreted subject. It cannot be ignored, and it is relevant to what I have already criticized in this chapter. Before taking up the precise illustrations of this shift, another effort at definition is called for:[12]

> Among historians the desire to dispel the ambiguity that surrounded the early perceptions of the Nazi regime is not entirely innocent. Not least because of the cataclysmic aftermath, we tend to expect "knowledge" and "understanding" to coincide. Hence, the question "What did they know?"—they being the victims *and* the witnesses—has never been a purely scholarly question. Indeed, in

---

[12] Arad., p. 109.

its updated version— "Had they known more, could they have done more?"—the query is even more loaded. . . . In the existing historiography this assumption often leads to judgment instead of critical analysis of the period, particularly regarding the behavior of the witnesses and the issue of rescue. The implication is that lack of information exonerated inaction, or, conversely, availability of facts can serve as grounds for condemnation if action did not result.

Around the time that John Morley wrote his study of the papacy and the Holocaust, another American scholar, a gentile, David S. Wyman, wrote a comparably balanced study titled *The Abandonment of the Jews: America and the Holocaust* (New York, 1985). This was a creative contribution to a growing literature on the topic which concluded to the failure of American officials, specifically of Roosevelt and the State Department as well as leaders of Jewish organizations, to take the necessary steps to save hundreds of thousands of European Jews. The parallel which hardly needs spelling out would be the alleged failure of the pope as well as of Vatican officials to take comparable steps: in the case of America, bombing the death camps and access to them; in the case of the papacy, condemning publicly the extermination of Jews. (A reader may note that in the first case, it is a question of an action, a deed; in the second, it is a question of a statement, a proclamation; yet Pius's failure has not merely marred his image, it has over the last few decades virtually destroyed it, while that of Roosevelt has been progressively burnished.) And as with the papacy, several historians, some quoted above, attacked Wyman for writing a moral tract not a historical analysis.

Arad who clearly knows all the literature refers to Wyman's work only in a bibliographical note, and writes with no polemical intent. Nevertheless, her "reading" of events concentrates on what might be called "thick redescription." In late summer 1943 when the totality of the extermination struck the leaders of American Jewish organizations, some of them expressed regrets at their failure to speak out. This failure was attributed to the fact that they had not "been ready enough to shake the bond of so-called amicability in order to lay our troubles upon the conscience of our Christian neighbors and fellow citizens." Arad comments that "this kind of catharsis so late in the day, however sincere, was still of little real consequence. If we prefer to attain an understanding rather than reach a judgment, then analyzing individual or group behavior on the basis of an idealized vision of human nature, where the exception is expected to be the rule, is of little avail. American Jews were thoroughly normal fallible human beings" (p. 220). This may sound exonerative, defensive, even pollyannish, but it may very well simply be an analysis of the humanity common to everyone regardless of place in society, regardless of status as victim or witness.

Arad also cites, as did Wyman and others, such instances of failure or betrayal as the State Department's delaying Gerhard Riegner's message—received also in London and in Rome—about the planned "final solution" from reaching Rabbi Wise, the major Jewish leader: delayed because of the "fantastic nature of the allegations." Only ten weeks later was Wise allowed to disclose the contents of the message to the press, and to seek the long postponed audience with Roosevelt which finally, five months after Riegner's message, was granted. (Does this not sound like the makings of a Zuccotti-style plot?)[13] Meanwhile, a New York officer of the World Jewish Congress was expressing outrage not about the *contents* of a report that Jews from all German occupied countries were being murdered, but about the fact that the report was *released*: "We don't really need to convince ourselves that Hitler is capable of anything, and if we want to convince others, we must be sure that we have *evidence of some value.*" When Rabbi Wise finally met Roosevelt in December and requested a statement from the president about conditions in Europe, Roosevelt authorized the re-issuance of a July statement "without any change in wording" and "which had not specifically emphasized *Nazi crimes against Jews.*"

---

[13] It does, and it is. Cf. p. 51 *supra* and her discussion of events surrounding communications beginning September 27, 1942 by the State Department to the Vatican.

The first thought that comes to mind is how similar are all ruling agencies, not because of structures of deceit but simply because of what might be described as structures of bureaucracy. Of these various betrayals, particularly by Roosevelt, the contrast between Arad's perspective and that of zealots attacking the papacy can only be described as *stark*. Speaking of her own inability to understand the continuing esteem of Jewish leaders for Roosevelt, she writes: ". . . probably few would contest the wisdom of American Jews in embracing their nation's interest. Rather more difficult to accept is their deep affection for the 'chief' who had done so little to help them lessen the tragedy of their European counterparts." Then true to her search for understanding *not* judging, and rather than elaborating on the monstrosity of White House functionaries, including their leader—an elaboration that could have colored her narrative from the beginning as it colored that of Pius's critics—she continues immediately: "But that too can be grasped when we acknowledge that despite what they had endured in America, they were eternally grateful, especially during the difficult times of the 1930's, for the protection their adopted country gave them from a far worse fate" (p. 221).

Perhaps on my part an irenic gesture at this point in the exposition would be to suggest some kind of merging of paradigms: a fusion of the judgmental and the empathetic—more or less after the fashion of Milton (again, to compare great things to small) who employed the Ptolemaic system when it suited him, and at other times the Copernican. However, it would be easy to act on such a combination or variation of approaches, if it weren't for the multiple distortions employed by the "adjudicators." The next chapter will illustrate precisely how difficult that will be in the light of even more historical falsifications than those exposed above. A shift shouldn't mean shiftlessness: lies and deceptions are not components of any workable paradigm.

3

SQUINTING AT HISTORY
The Rhetoric of Stigmatization

> "Neither before nor after the Second Vatican Council did I write and publish everything that was on my mind. But I took a great deal of pain not to write anything I believed to be false."
>
> *Father Häring*

F irst among the ideological denigrators—a group which includes both James Carroll and, again, John Cornwell—is Garry Wills in several studies beginning with *Bare Ruined Choirs* and culminating in *Papal Sin: Structures of Deceit*—on which I will focus. "Focus" is the precise term, because unlike my treatment of the "professional scholars" above, I will concentrate in this chapter not so much on factual errors, but on Wills' self-imposed blinders which lead to a historically distorted vision of Catholicism. In short, I am examining a scholarly methodology which blurs perceptions, and results in what common parlance (as well as the dictionary definition) would call a "cockeyed" view of things.[1] Such factual errors as the following can in some cases be dismissed as the result of ignorance or sloppiness: confusing Mary

---

[1] In an earlier version of one of the chapters of this book (*U.S. Catholic Historian,* Summer, 2000), I wrote: "Garry Wills has over the last twenty-five years or so proved himself to be the Edmund Wilson of American Studies." I cited eight titles by Wilson that illustrated his cosmopolitan interests, and a comparable number by Wills relating to American history. It was a sincere tribute, though it noted another parallel: that between such acerbic and crotchety polemics by Wilson as *The Cold War and the Income Tax* and *Fruits of the MLA*, and by Wills as *Bare Ruined Choirs* and *Politics and Catholic Freedom*. The clear inference was that these

Stuart with Mary Tudor, Luigi Sturzo with John Bosco, Paul VI
with John Paul II, Lord Acton with Richard Simpson, Archbishop
Pecci with Bishop Gerbet, Cardinal Hohenlohe with Bishop Strossmayer (like Bishop Dupanloup here designated "Cardinal"), the
Franco-Austrian with the Franco-Prussian War, the date of the
Lateran Treaty with the date of Mussolini's dictatorial ascen-
dancy; other such errors include the designation of Husserl as the
father of "phenomenalism," of Scheler as a "dissolute Catholic,"
of the revolutions of 1848 as "socialist," and on and on. In chapter
five I will show why too hasty a dismissal of these kinds of
straightforward mistakes is, itself, a mistake.

But for the purposes of present discussion these factual errors
may be regarded as less grievous, if only because they relate to past
events and personalities. But there are lessons to be drawn from the
context of those errors, lessons on how Catholics of the past coped
with the conflict between the demands of the institutional church
and the conscience of the individual believer. That context will be
analyzed in chapter five which—though taking as point of departure Wills' assemblage of perennial complaints and revolutionary
proposals—will constitute the bridge between these first two, intentionally negative, chapters on the methodology of mendacity,
and the concluding, strongly affirmative, chapters on the genuinely
reformative goal of "not the metamorphosis of traditional data but
the deepening of them" (Maurice Blondel to Baron von Hügel).

But in this chapter we are still in the phase of clearing the
ground by shedding the light of historical discernment on issues

---

"eccentric" works seemed to touch some raw nerve, and that in the case of Wills
this might at least partially explain the multitude of dissimulations, not to say
errors and distortions, that scar *Papal Sin*. It will be helpful to see whether his
book on Venice—announced as this present book is going to press—also a cosmopolitan and broad-gauge study, well beyond the relatively parochial ambit of his
American interests, will also be an idiosyncratic entry in his broader oeuvre.

Since having written the above months ago, and in the process of correcting
proofs, I must add that I have now read the Venice book. It is a beautiful and
brilliantly written work. The achievement of a Humanist in the best renaissance
conception—as we would apply that term to an Erasmus or a Dean Colet. This
perhaps makes my inference above all the more relevant.

which relate to the scholarly methodology and intellectual credibility of Wills and others. One reviewer, Tad Szulc in *The Washington Post,* spoke of Wills' "impressive erudition and historical and theological analysis" in terms which suggested that these alleged qualities were such established truisms as not to be subject to examination. Since I am concerned precisely with scholarship or "erudition," I will have to attend to Wills' reliance on second-hand sources, such as *Anti-Judaism in Christian Theology, The Hidden Encyclical of Pius XI, The Kidnapping of Edgardo Mortara, Hitler's Pope, Lead Us Not into Temptation,* "The Saint and the Holocaust" (*The New Yorker),* and other reportage to which he often gives *carte blanche* in order to provide a presumably factual foundation for his narrative, or not infrequently to merely spice it up. One can at least be grateful he has not discovered the masonic lodge revealed in *Via col Vento in Vaticano*—Gone with the Wind in the Vatican— another recent catalogue of papal sin (probably "now a major motion picture coming soon to a cineplex near you": *The Loggia on the Loggia*). Nor, thankfully, has Wills exposed any conspiracies on the part of the Knights Templar—the sure sign, according to Umberto Eco, of an ideological fanatic.

Most of the studies I name above are cited by Wills in his four chapters on antisemitism grouped together under the heading, "Historical Dishonesties." But since such *vulgarisations*, however *haute,* do not provide the intellectual patina he needs to academically legitimate his argument, he is often compelled to fall back either on redundant displays of learning or on elaborate token gestures of having consulted the most recherché of sources. For reasons of brevity in validating that criticism, I will draw initially on those same four chapters to illustrate Wills' own "historical dishonesties" which take the form of obfuscations and dissimulations that run throughout his book, and which ultimately belie his seemingly scholarly perspective. That perspective is so blurred in its approach and so fudging in its exposition that it is reminiscent of the comic creation of the British humorist, J. B. Morton, "Dr. Strabismus"—a latter-day Rube Goldberg—whose fabrications included false teeth for swordfish, a screw for screwing screws into other screws, and similar such devisals. Professor Wills is not as entertaining as Dr. Strabismus but he is certainly as inventive and farfetched.

— I —

In his treatment of the specific charge of deicide brought against the Jews, and relying uncritically on Charlotte Klein's well-intentioned but biased *Anti-Judaism in Christian Theology* to prove that "antisemitism is a modern sin, not just an ancient one," Wills indicts the most influential Catholic theologian of this era. "One of the leading liberal theologians at Vatican II, Karl Rahner, could publish *in the very year of the Council's statement* [*Nostra Aetate*] these words about the Jews: 'We could almost say that a supernatural demonism is exercising its power in the hatred of *this people* against the true kingdom of God'." The term "demonization" has become a commonplace in the ductile language of recent political commentators; but to hear it invoked in its literal sense by a revered theologian, a German at that, and with regard above all to the Jewish people is an affront not merely to ecumenism or interreligious dialogue, but to humanity itself—so surely the quotation is as shocking as Wills insidiously suggests.

But is it? This isolated sentence is taken from Klein who, however, does make clear that anti-Judaism is not to be identified with "the sin of antisemitism" (a distinction *with* a difference), though as I shall note briefly she is also guilty of her own distortions. But it is absolutely unquestionable from the context of the quotation in Klein—though not in Wills—that "this people" is metonymy for "Sanhedrin"—thrice repeated: "The Sanhedrin had already condemned Him to death . . ."; "The mentality of the Sanhedrin . . ."; finally, the paragraph immediately preceding the quotation begins: "The Sanhedrin's death sentence on Jesus . . ." Regardless of the fact that "Sanhedrin" may not be in this instance the precisely accurate ascription, it is to be noted that what is omitted by Klein and therefore also by sedulous Wills is the sentence which follows immediately: "But even here Israel remains the people of God—a people so closely bound to God that its very existence is a divinely willed sign of salvation."

Klein also tendentiously excises the concluding phrases of Rahner's observation relating to Jesus' avowal that he is the Son of God: "In fact, they [again, that pronoun's *only* antecedent is not "the people," but "the Sanhedrin"] misuse it as a pretext to secure the death penalty. . . . Jesus is condemned in the name of good order, national pride, the good of the country, truth, belief in Yahweh." In Klein the quotation ends with a period, not an ellipsis after the word "Yahweh." Indeed, her *whole paragraph* ends there. But in Rahner the sentence continues without break, as in this italicized passage: ". . . truth, belief in Yahweh, *theology and philosophy, beauty and symmetry—really in the name of everything on the face of the earth."* This global catalogue makes abundantly, even ironically clear that as opposed to fundamentalist notions of the universality of Jewish complicity and guilt, the condemnation of Jesus rather than being ethnically or juridically specific is the consequence of every fallen human enterprise and every fallen human being "on the face of the earth."

To further impugn Father Rahner as not just an antisemite, but as one who persisted in his "modern sin" even "in the very year of the Council's statement," Wills has to ignore Rahner's own detailed explanation of the provenance of this book from which he and Klein are quoting, a book which I published first in this country and then in England under the simple title *Spiritual Exercises.* Though Wills, again following Klein, puts "Meditations" in the title—a word which, after having arbitrarily inserted, she then criticizes for entailing some kind of sinister exculpatory strategy: "As a book of meditations and not straightforward theology, this work exercises a more subtle influence and disarms criticism of its assertions." Actually, the first word in the German title which neither Klein nor Wills uses, brings out more clearly the book's provisional nature: *Betrachtungen,* "considerations" or "observations."

But had Wills—as any serious scholar making so rash a charge must perforce do—even casually examined the book itself, he would have found spelt out almost abecedarianly in the Foreword

that this work was composed by seminarians from Rahner's re-
treat reflections for which "there never was a written text";
which were then circulated in a mimeographed version which was
"neither controlled nor edited by the author" who "had nothing
to do with the redaction"; and lastly, which dated from his years
"in Pullach near Munich," i.e.; *twenty years before* "the Council's
statement." Perhaps this explains the clearly disingenuous if
not craftily ambivalent, "Rahner *could publish* in the very year . . ."—
rather than what one might expect, the plain and unvarnished:
"Rahner wrote," or "Rahner maintained. . . ." It is difficult to explain Wills' ignoring such a tessellation unless, consumed by the
zeal of his papaphobist crusade, he now perchance subscribes to
the tenets of that obscure anabaptist sect—in fact known as the
Abecedarians—which preached salvation through the rejection of
reading.

Finally, and explicitly with regard to the term "deicide," *four
years before* the conciliar decree, Rahner lamented the "indescrib-
able wrong" of Christian persecution of Jews "for the pseudo-
theological reason that they were 'deicides'." This is from the 1965
fifth edition of the Rahner-Vorgrimler *Theological Dictionary* where
the authors' Preface notes "with some satisfaction that nothing
whatever needs to be changed because of the Council." Wills may
be excused for not knowing this widely read work—though such
nescience, again, doesn't exactly suggest scholarly scrupulousness
but rather a practice of picking and choosing among whatever
statements, whether accurately contextualized or not, he imagines will bolster his argument. However, he cannot be excused for
not even looking at the book, *Spiritual Exercises*, from which he
professes to be quoting in order to condemn *tout court* a justly es-
teemed priest and theologian.

A similarly fudging equivocation is even more blatant in my
next illustration, also derived by Wills entirely from Charlotte
Klein, but here rigged to appear as the result of his own scholarship. We now have to do not with a distinguished theologian but
an equally renowned biblical scholar. Immediately following the
chronologically warped quotation from Rahner, Wills with a fris-
son of the bombast of his earlier *Bare Ruined Choirs* clamorously

bursts out: *"More astonishingly* [one can almost overhear, *zut alors!*—remembering, however, that "un oeil qui dit *zut*" says simply, "to squint"], the priest who edited the *Revue Biblique* (Pierre Benoit) *brought out* this accusation *three years after* the Council's decree: 'The religious authority of the Jewish people took on itself the actual responsibility for the crucifixion. Israel closed itself off from the light that was offered it, from the expansion of view demanded of it. . . . That refusal has continued down through the ages, to this very day. . . . Every Jew suffers from the ruin undergone by his people when it refused Him at the decisive moment of its history'." But this quotation, all of which appears with correct attribution though slightly different wording in Klein, is now cited by Wills as though representing his own original research from "Pierre Benoit, O.P., *Exégèse et théologie,* Vol. 3 (Editions du Cerf, 1968), p. 420." However, had this been the fruit of his own research, he could not have overlooked the fact that though the book was indeed published in 1968, "three years ["astonishingly"] after the Council's decree," the essay in question begins with a footnote giving the year of publication as before *Nostra Aetate*.

Now I am not *here* disturbed so much by the perverse implications of these mutilated quotations, though "historical honesties" demand that one should note that Benoit—as Klein acknowledges but Wills does not—makes this statement in the light of "l'histoire du salut" and that he then adds, ". . . the Christian must remember that every sinner in his own way is responsible for the death of Christ." What is of primary concern now is neither Wills' decontextualizations nor his more odious scholarly defalcations, but his pervasive and "deceitful" tactic of fudging. Either there is no original research and all is derived from Klein (but why then not credit her with an *"op. cit."* or an *"ibid."*¿), or Wills, following her lead and consulting the French work, saw the date of the original article and rather than state the obvious, "Pierre Benoit wrote," or "affirmed," or "declared," instead to cover his tracks, asserts as ambivalently and as "dishonestly" as he did with Rahner, "Pierre Benoit *brought out* this accusation . . . ," etc. So much for this aspect of Garry Wills' confectionary scholarship—in the context of which I would personally recommend as prophylaxis against fudging, Margret Rey's *Curious George Goes to a Chocolate Factory.*

But why this effort to contaminate with the virus of antisemitism two of the noblest spirits in the history of contemporary scholarship, and in the case of Father Rahner, the most creative and respected Catholic theologian of at least the last four centuries? It is, as I have said from the beginning, the anti-papal blinders and the hubristic overreaching that result in trying to prove a case by any and every means at hand; in short, by what is called in our journalistic and litigious era "prosecutorial abuse."

Another illustration of such fudging, now in the realm of what has come to be called "fuzzy math," is the treatment of the penultimate conciliar vote on *Nostra Aetate.* Deriving his data entirely from Msgr. John Oesterreicher's commentary on the decree, Wills observes accurately that those who voted that the Jews should be blamed for the death of Christ numbered 188, while those who in effect voted that the Jews should be rejected or accursed by God numbered 245. Then once again he goes into full fustian flight: "But it is astounding [an emotion experienced by this author also in the case of Pere Benoit] that even the weakened form of the statement, unaccompanied by any recognition of past persecution or any expression of sorrow and repentance, could *still* be rejected by *hundreds* of Catholic bishops." Only by a calculated miscalculation would 188 suggest "hundreds," certainly not out of a total of 2072.

As to the 245 figure, Wills deceptively ignores what Oesterreicher clearly brings out, that this relatively large number was the result of extensive lobbying for a *negative* vote by those who wanted an *even stronger* "form of the statement," one which would explicitly underline the evil of the accusation of "deicide." Nor does Wills mention anywhere the pressure from bishops in the Arab world, including the four Patriarchs of the Near East who were fearful of anything that might appear to their flocks, much less to their governments, as an accommodation with the Israelis. "But it *is* astounding" that he doesn't provide the figures for the final tally on the day of the proclamation of *Nostra Aetate:* 2312 votes in favor; 88 against. Where then are "the hundreds of Catholic bishops" who rejected "the statement"?[2]

Now, a brief excursus on the "methodology"of embezzling references that has already been encountered regarding Père Benoit. Several pages before his discussion of the balloting, Msgr. Oesterreicher in a footnote quotes an article by Charles Journet on the non-traditional character of the term "deicide." Journet, for much of his career a professor of theology at Fribourg and later a Cardinal, had cited Augustine on the crucifixion as being not "deicidal," but "homicidal," and supplied the reference: *"Enarrat. In Ps.,* 61, 5: *PL,* XXXVI. 791." Wills paraphrases the quotation and without acknowledging Journet or Oesterreicher—again, not even the gesture of an *"op. cit."*—proffers as the result, presumably, of his own discovery of the text in Migne, the plain citation: "Augustine, *Explaining the Psalms* 61. 5 (PL 36. 791)." *Q.E.D.*

Another example of fudging the numbers occurs in Wills' treatment of the Vatican document, vigorously endorsed by John Paul II, "We Remember: A Reflection on the *Shoah."* Wills writes regarding the notion that Jews are "responsible for killing Christ": "That view is still powerful, despite the assurance in *We Remember* that the church has denied its legitimacy. The ADL study [Quinley and Glock, *Anti-Semitism in America*] found even *after that* official denial, that 11 percent of Catholics still agreed with this statement: 'The reason Jews have so much trouble is because God is punishing them for rejecting Jesus'." But the book, *Anti-Semitism in America,* was published in 1979, not *"after* that official denial" but two decades *before*, as even Wills should have known, since his

---

[2] James Carroll is less deceptive but, typically, more dramaturgical: "Indiscretions, intrigues, near-eastern misunderstandings and fears [Edward Said's "orientalism"?], especially of a political nature, all became entangled. In addition to this, there was what could be called 'Christian obstinacy,' a certain inability to understand, found among some Christians at the Council. They were mentally unprepared for the topic." Both the numerical distortion and the descriptive spin are intended to illustrate the endemic antisemitism of Catholics even into the early 1960's—though as I shall point out it would be another thirty years before Carroll and Wills would treat the issue in any detail.

endnote indicates the date of the Quinley and Glock book. However, what he doesn't even hint at is that the treatment in Quinley and Glock was simply a summary of Glock and Stark, *Christian Beliefs and Anti-Semitism*, which had been published in the Spring of *1966*, and summarized by both authors—as well as by Oscar Cohen, director of the Anti-Defamation League—in an issue of *Continuum* the following Autumn. Had Wills deigned to look at any of these first-hand treatments, he could not but have noticed that the actual research was done in 1963: two years before *Nostra Aetate* and *thirty-five* years before "We Remember."

After having referred to that later statement only, Wills' concluding *non sequitur* might generously be described as brazenly disjunctive: "History is not altered by a single decree, especially one that comes out of the blue, as Vatican II's did." *But* this whole discussion had nothing to do with Vatican II; it had been exclusively focused on "We Remember."[3] Nor could anyone fairly assert that John Paul's many efforts at reconciliation, culminating in "We Remember," came—to employ Wills' sprightly imagery— "out of the blue." All of this makes abundantly clear that for Wills, even if the lying papacy should perchance appear to do what he vociferously professes to favor, then it would do so either too begrudgingly, or too inadequately, or too tardily to satisfy whatever arbitrary or newly designed criteria he can manufacture—and if even by his flexible or fluctuating standards he couldn't make a case for such putative deceptions, cunctations, defections, then garbled language or calumnious asseverations or filched scholarship or (as we shall see) deliberate mistranslations, will have to do. Lastly, for this catch-as-catch-can redactor of *l'Improvvisatore Romano*, there is always chronology (or just plain addition and subtraction) that can be juggled.

One final, and at this stage, predictable omission relating to "deicide." Relying now on *The Hidden Encyclical of Pius XI,* a work of exemplary scholarship occasionally in the service of a fragile thesis, Wills refers to "the words of the Pope himself [Pius XI],

---

[3] "That view is still powerful, despite the assurance in *We Remember* that the church has denied its legitimacy."

calling Jews the ones who killed Christ" in the "decree suppressing the Friends of Israel." But these words are *nowhere* to be found in that decree of the Holy Office, though their gist is evident from an article on the decree in *Nouvelle Revue théologique* which is summarized in *The Hidden Encyclical*. The article does refer to "Israel's participation in Christ's death" but, though hardly a model of irenicism, it also affirms that "no one wants to make 'deicide' a sort of 'original sin' borne by every Jew today." And the authors of *The Hidden Encyclical* make their own the words of the *NRT* article: "Nonetheless, in 1928 the Holy Office had indeed expressed 'one of the most explicit condemnations of anti-Semitism that Rome has pronounced up to this time'." Also, neither to be overlooked nor immoderately exaggerated, is the condemnation two years before of the antisemitic and inchoately fascist Action Française.[4] All this gives the lie to admittedly overdue acts of repentance and reconciliation coming "out of the blue" six or seven decades after Pius XI.

— II —

Il faut, dans l'Eglise, des prophètes, said Cardinal Congar. There are those who have viewed *Papal Sin* as such a prophetic work, particularly with its insistent refrain of attacking "dishonesty." Three

---

[4] It is worth noting here that was also the occasion for Maritain's writing *Primauté du spirituel* (E.T., *The Things that Are Not Caesar's*) in which he makes the observation concerning members of the organization that "nothing is so unreasonable [for those] called upon to obey, as to go and ransack history for a collection of precedents of mistakes made by authority"—or for "non-precedents," as with more recent ransackers. Apart from its present-day relevance, there is little doubt that Maritain had in mind among others Georges Bernanos who, though he had broken with Charles Maurras, was vehement in his attacks on the Holy See for inserting itself in French "political" affairs. A royalist in politics (and a Port Royalist in spirituality) and thus a Gallicanist in religion, Bernanos was like Léon Bloy passionately anti-clerical—as few can fail to note in de Torcy, the central figure in *The Diary of a Country Priest*. The year of the condemnation of the Action Française was also the year of Bernanos' *Sous le Soleil de Satan,* a title which mockingly echoes what is for many the *Commedia* of the twentieth century, Claudel's *Le Soulier de satin*—that latter in its baroque exuberance being the antithesis of Bernanos' intensely Augustinian severities.

main section titles are: "Historical Dishonesties," "Doctrinal Dishonesties," and "The Honesty Issue." Under the last title, one of
the subheads is "The Age of Truth," meaning the nineteenth and
twentieth centuries. But should not there be a section devoted to
"intellectual honesty," a virtue becoming to all of us heirs of so
blessed an era, and more particularly to heirs of that Saint lauded
in this book, Augustine, who wrote a public retraction of his earlier errors? Wills writes of past Christian *attitudes* "toward Jews":
"The attempt to whitewash [them] is so dishonest in its use of
historical evidence that a man condemns himself in his own eyes
if he tries to claim that he agrees with it." (I suppose, short of Tom
Sawyer, the attempt to whitewash *anything* is dishonest.) But
does the mantle of prophet justify the "dishonest use of historical
evidence" apparent in the discussion earlier, and will a dévoté of
Augustine living in this "age of truth" retract his errors?

Lastly, I would merely point to the many differences in tone
and interpretation in Wills' Introduction to *The Hidden Encyclical*
and in his treatment of the same matters in *Papal Sin*. The latter
is both more shrill and more skewed than the former. Perhaps the
advocates of what biblical students would call *Gattungsgeschichte,*
genre criticism, are on to something. If the clothes make the man,
the genre here dictates the style and the rhetoric. In the end, the
decision to write a philippic rather than an unembellished exposition determines one's place in what is beginning to look more and
more like the papal demolition derby. Currently in the pole position is *Constantine's Sword,* brandished and burnished by James
Carroll, an author whose cutting edge is so severely blunted by
self-indulgent effusions that it puts one in mind—to compare
small things to great—of Cardinal Vaughan's remark on Newman's *Apologia*: "The egotism may be disgusting but it is venial."

In fact, there is now in the literary marketplace a jumble of carping tractates, mélanges, potpourris, hybrid memoirs and low-
brow histories, all on "coming-of-age-and-discovering-the-truth-
about-Catholicism"—with the feminine wing being represented
by Mary Gordon whom both Wills and Carroll cite reverentially.
A new classification may have to be invented, undreamt of by Librarians of Congress or Dewey Decimalists: possibly a catalogue

entry under the rubric, *L'Education Ressentimentale.* In fact, there already exists a designation for most of these authors in our more up-to-date libraries, "creative nonfiction," a category undreamt of by Bennet Cerf in the days of what now must be termed "the pre-postmodern Modern Library." (Some more *au courant* public libraries, to the possible consternation of the ACLU, even have for the ease of their patrons a classification termed, "Christian Mysteries"—but not violative of separation of church and state; not proselytizing books related to the sacramental theology of Dom Odo Casel—just the "Private Investigator" genre for evangelicals.)

Give or take a few years, most of this current crop of carpers was born in the late 1930's or mid 40's, and reached adulthood before the culmination of the conciliar reforms in 1965; while at the height of the Vietnam war half a decade later they would have been voting in national elections for ten years or so. Yet, curiously, few of them at those climactic moments made any extensive public criticism of either the Council's Declaration on Non-Christian Religions (specifically, the section on antisemitism) or on the war. Carroll's conversion to the anti-war cause—among clerics led by the Berrigans—was tardy, and trammeled in his own self-publicized familial entanglements. Wills had attacked the Berrigans and other signers of the Declaration of Conscience opposing the war for "fomenting rebellion"—only in the late seventies to very quietly recant in a collection, aptly titled *Confessions of a Conservative.* As for *Nostra Aetate* and all it represents, Carroll took nearly thirty years to unravel what he saw as its implications. Thus it is understandable that the vehemence of their language *now* would raise questions as to whether such loose and all-embracing condemnations as they are airing represent simply the zeal of the true convert, or whether perhaps they manifest an effort to enlist universally recognized misfortunes in a personal cause—many have suggested resentment at *Humanae Vitae* and anger at the centralism of John Paul II.

Wills' motive, insofar as it can be discerned from habitually hyperbolic and derisive language, would seem at first glance to be some kind of tabloid exposition of every type of ecclesiastical (and human) disorder to be adjudicated in the forum of a public fixated on the scandalous and the shocking. But if, by an act of considerable intellectual ascecis, one abstracts from the exaggerated rhetoric and imagery, one can discern in his book the lineaments of a program which in essence might be called "pastoral." Apart from issues relating to church governance and to antisemitism, the bulk of *Papal Sin* is centered on those ethical issues which for the most part confront the whole of Western society. Those issues mainly relate to individual morality: contraception, celibacy, homosexuality, women's subordination (and in many religious bodies, its odious residuum, ordination), marriage, divorce, pederasty, abortion.[5] As I also noted, there is little in these areas that is uniquely Roman Catholic, or even uniquely religious; they touch on the worlds of commerce, of politics, of the media, etc., as well as of mosque, synagogue, and church. Of course, such issues resonate in the social arena, but only as a consequence of their impact on increasing numbers of individuals. Stripped of the inflammatory language, a good part of Wills' agenda is simply to bring Catholic teaching more in line with Catholic practice, and Catholic practice more in line with the mainstream consensus of American society. In short, to bring "official" teaching about personal morality in line with what might now be called "moral commonsense," and what in the past was called "natural law"—a matter to which we shall return in the last chapter.

As to Carroll—ecdysiast of Freud's family romance in the setting of lace-curtain, Studs-Lonigan Catholicism—his goal appears

---

[5] Both ideologues of the right and the left see these issues not as common points of disagreement and conflict in all advanced nations, and derived from a host of causes, but simply as the result of a conspiracy. On the right, McInerny writes of "hot items on the secular liberal agenda—contraception (and sexual liberation, in general), the supposed plight of women, and clerical celibacy. . . . The subversive role of the *theological caste* was essential in misleading priests and subsequently the faithful. . . . The *treachery* of dissenting theologians is behind the confusion that has come over the faithful in matters sexual." One begins to wonder if this is a debate between Hindu sects when Carroll writes of the "sacerdotal caste" as a medieval remnant, and Wills titles an entire chapter, "the *priestly caste.*" (In the latter two instances, one knows that the juggernaut of Rome is shortly to put in another appearance.) Treatments whether from the left or the right lead into discussions of celibacy, of bishops out of touch with their diocesans, shortage of vocations, gay priests, divorce and remarriage, pederasty, ordination of women, etc.

to be some kind of general council which will, first, embrace all those good things like theological syncretism, pluralism ("of belief and worship"), "the holiness of democracy," feminism, "regional differences" ("that give rise to religious denominations"); and, second, renounce all those bad things like "binary thinking" [6] (as well as trinitarian), Nicaean Christianity, supersessionism, medieval absolutism, "the universalizing pseudoscience of the Enlightenment," the "clerical caste," and lastly every vestige of hatred for Jews and Judaism. (All these wonderful desiderata are bracketed—paradoxically, thoughtlessly?—by quotations from that super-supersessionist, and proponent of the "holiness" of monarchy, T. S. Eliot.) To which one may aver, at least of the last item in this conciliar agenda: so far so good.

But is it far and good enough? I will take up that question shortly. But first, it must be said that, without in any way minimizing the frightful acts committed by Christians and the Christian church against the Jewish people, nevertheless to envisage those acts—as does Carroll—as the ultimate defining point of synagogue and church is to drastically devalue the faith of both, and to ignore their *eternal* mission of universal conciliation. Unless one subscribes to a postmodernist relativism[7] to make the sinfulness—however devastating—of the past two millennia the ineradicable *axis mundi* of Judaism vis-a-vis Christianity is simply to dismiss

---

[6] There is even an index entry for "binary thinking": right between Bible and Birkenau.

[7] The recent book, *Denying History* (2000), by Michael Shermer and Alex Grobman, analyzes the influence of such relativism on those German historians who maintain that the extermination of the Jews was an *ad hoc* improvisation. The resulting disagreement led to what is known as the Historikerstreit which these two authors treat in the broader context of Holocaust deniers and their academic supporters. (I shall look at the "conflict of historians" more closely in the next chapter.) Interestingly, in the present context Shermer and Grobman, along with most historians, would endorse a notion of "objectivity" akin to that of Bishop Butler as revised by Cardinal Newman: "an assemblage of concurring and converging probabilities" sufficient for belief. Newman goes on to say in a sentence the first clause of which may be applied to Pius XII, and the second unquestionably to the Holocaust: ". . . it might be quite as much a matter of duty in given cases and to given persons to have about a fact an opinion of a definite strength and consistency, as in the case of greater or of more numerous probabilities it was a duty to have a certitude."

the future of humankind. It is to take a relatively thin slice of time, and make it an irrevocable template. Now, for a change, current jargon may have a place, since what is here being endorsed by Carroll is precisely a microdimensional "Eurocentric" view of entities that are global, indeed are no less than planetary, in their import. That skimpy perspective finds its stylistic replication in his inability to envision any phenomenon, social, cultural, religious outside the constricted ambit of its impingement on matters related almost exclusively to *him* and *his*. This explains the appalling grotesqueries one discerns, and ultimately the chilling embarrassment one experiences at the ravenous ingestion of all external experience merely for the nourishment of his own ego.[8] For the Psalmist to the Lord, "The zeal of thy house has consumed me," Carroll would substitute, "The zeal of my house has consumed me." This is certainly not to see reality as used to be said, *sub specie aeternitatis*; but *sub specie sui ipsius*. Our age of memoir has begotten an American Catholic "M. Teste."

So, does Carroll's advocacy of a general council on his terms go far enough, and is it good enough? I am reminded of an earlier plea to Pius XII for a council by Father Max Metzger captured by the Gestapo, described by the initially pro-Nazi nuncio Msgr. Orsenigo (whose indifference to the plight of the Jews in August, 1942 sets off the action in Hochhuth's *Der Stellvertreter*) as being guilty of "una eccessiva imprudenza," and finally executed with two other priests and a Protestant minister. A council of peace as the

---

[8] A hermeneutic of compassion allows only the briefest citations: "Note that Josephus's report of activities in the time of Jesus involves a time lag roughly equivalent to that between the Easter Rising of 1916 and my first visit to Ireland in 1969" (p. 635). There is the elaborate correlation of Cardinal Spellman and St. Ambrose with Carroll's mother and St. Monica—all leading ineluctably to the equation of Carroll with St. Augustine: "sons who follow their mothers into piety" (p. 209). Concerning "the Vatican's" connection of "the image of Pius XII as a saint" with its efforts to fabricate Catholic opposition to Nazism, Carroll writes: "*As a boy, I saw* how this worked. In a letter to the bishops of Bavaria, in August 1945, Pius XII praised 'those millions of Catholics' who had resisted Nazism . . ." (p. 531). Earlier (p. 27) he informs the reader: "I was born in 1943, the year before the jurist Raphael Lemkin coined the word 'genocide'." So this diapered infant, eclipsing Jesus in the Temple, *saw* through the ruses of priestcraft at age two.

heroic Metzger saw it would address professedly "religious" questions, particularly those relating to Christian unity. But it would address them in the context of "the very experience of war and its miseries [which] has awakened in many hearts the desire to exert every effort to salvage the human race and to revitalize the debilitated Christianity which has been powerless to influence world affairs. Not until war has plunged all nations into the depths of anguish will the whole world look forward to the great promise of deliverance." Thus reunion of the churches would be a symbolic prelude to a total peace among all nations, rather than the phenomenon of total war that this martyr glimpsed faintly from his prison cell—a phenomenon more clearly understood now in a world of nuclear deterrents, and in the wake of Vietnam and Desert Storm than it was in 1943 in Berlin. But on this issue of the very survival of the planet, it cannot be denied that these much maligned pontiffs have been the most unambiguous of all world leaders.[9]

— III —

The arbitrary selectivity of Wills' adversarial approach is again emphasized by the unexpected deference he shows to a personal acquaintance, the psychoanalytically oriented literary critic, René Girard "with whom I [G.Wills] used to go to Mass when we both taught at Johns Hopkins." Wills reads Girard in the light of the work of the theologian Raymond Schwager, whose *Must There Be Scapegoats?* I published when I was editor at Harper San Francisco. One notes that to the question in Schwager's title—must there be scapegoats?—Wills' answer would have to be in the affirmative.

---

[9] For Pius XII there is the analysis of his immense corpus of writings in René Coste, *Le Problème du droite de guerre dans la pensée de Pie XII* (1962); for John XXIII, there is the encyclical *Pacem in terris* (much derided by various conservative groups); for his successor, the unprecedented address validating the mission of the United Nations, and denouncing weapons of mass destruction; and for *his* successor there have been so many such denunciations as to be literally uncountable.

His entire book witnesses, if not to his convictions—always friable—then to his current emotional mood or prosecutorial strategy, that the pre-eminent and permanent Catholic scapegoats are those vile bodies, the Curia, the Roman dicasteries, and the papacy itself. But Wills latches on to Girard's notion of religious origins in order that he may doughtily criticize what is in fact generally criticized by a majority of contemporary theologians: the obsolete and literalistic notion that—as Wills condenses it—God the Father is someone "whose aggressions need to be bought off. Jesus is not an item of barter in the exchange system set up by sacrifice." The reference is to the soteriological theory of that ardent defender of the papacy, St. Anselm (also one of James Carroll's host of villains), whose deceptive doctrine of cleansing in the blood of the lamb makes him here the proverbial wolf in sheep's clothing, now to be driven from the fold by René Girard; all in confirmation of a metathetic Virgilian tag—Capella lupum sequitur: "the goat follows the wolf." (Or it is not inconceivable that, on his own terms, Girard's foundational notion of mimetic desire engendering lethal antagonisms may be the result of his own rancorous competition with another therapeutic rival: thus lycanthropy engenders Lacanthropy. And the resolution of the two, obviating analysis interminable, will be based on reconceptualizing "burnt offerings" and on recognizing infantile individuation as "eidetic reflection." In short, smoke and mirrors.)

Wills' quotation earlier from Girard is touted as his "most radical assertion." Though if our author would bother—in the midst of the beguiling exercise of dispensing gratuitous indictments for antisemitism—to take such matters with requisite scholarly seriousness, he would find throughout Karl Rahner's writings a far more radical, while also far more traditional and less fanciful, understanding of redemption in its broadest sense than anything in René Girard. As a first step, Wills might want to check out, again, in the Rahner-Vorgrimler *Theological Dictionary* (as well as in the encyclopedic *Sacramentum Mundi*) the carefully and precisely written definitions under such entries as "Death," "Theories of Satisfaction," "Salvation," "Cross," "Sacrifice"; and, lastly, the little tract under the entry, "Protology," with its suggested links to related subjects. This latter will be particularly relevant to Girard's "mimetic" response to a couple of other "radical assertions": that marvel of confabulation, *Moses and Monotheism* by Dr. Freud, and the still long-awaited, *Key to All Mythologies* by Mr. Casaubon.

As a second step, Wills might examine the implications of another vulpine deluder, Duns Scotus, who taught that the election of angels, of Adam and Eve, and *a fortiori,* of Mary was dependent on the merits of Christ but not on the suffering of Calvary. (To appropriate Yeats, "I take this cadence from a man named" Charles Journet, the innominable source of Wills' purloined Augustine passage.) Moreover, Scotus made the keystone of his theology the assumption that even without an Original Sin, Incarnation would have occurred for the glorification of God and of creation. The Anselmian doctrine ought not to be read as though Calvary represented Adam's surrogate, Jesus, satisfying the Father's demand for punishment. The crucifixion was certainly not something willed by God. It was the freely chosen act of evil men. The suffering, death, burial, and "descent into hell" of the Creed represented Christ's total humanness, and his solidarity with all of humanity throughout *all* of history; that is throughout what is called "the common era" and the period before. At the conclusion of this entire critique, Scotus will be central to the discussion of Wills' treatment of Mary, and more specifically of the proclamation by Pius IX—another perennial villain—of the doctrine of the Immaculate Conception. It might be added, cautiously, that for a Lincoln scholar like Wills to deprecate in order to execrate "sacrificial death" is to ignore the import, in the first instance *real* and in the second instance *symbolic,* of the theologically accurate, "Jesus Christ died for the world," and—*mutatis mutandis*—the politically accurate, "Abraham Lincoln died for the country."

But with regard to the specific topic under consideration, the capriciousness of Wills' accusatory capers (all cognates of the omnipresent Girardian "scapegoat"), it must be pointed out that in Rahner the Hebrew Bible is viewed with reverence as a font of true revelation and not with the supersessionism of Girard who treats it merely as a disposable prologue to the New Testament. He thus displays an antijudaism that would certainly have been included in Charlotte Klein's compendium, were it not for Girard's undisguised ignorance of or indifference to Christian theology whether past or present—blinders that seem also to have afflicted his admirers. Of the theological and biblical scholars, Rahner and Benoit, Wills insouciantly tells the reader that their writings prove they are guilty of "the sin of antisemitism." Of the theorist of mythopoeia, Girard (who is repeatedly compared to . . . ¿ not Adler, not Frazer, not Freud, but *St. Augustine)*, Wills tells us that "passage after passage in the gospel takes on new intensity when looked at through the lens [he] has provided." But for others less spectacularly endowed, this provision may not let them see even as "through a glass darkly"—but only strabismically. The result, as all of the above critique evinces, is a blurred vision of history and a fudging mode of its narration.

We now turn from soteriology to mariology, and to the broader theme of flawed scholarship regarding the papacy. In his chapter titled "Marian Politics" on "the use of Mary for papal purposes" by various lying pontiffs, and the conferring on her of titles like "the Immaculate Conception" so "that she may preside over papal structures of deceit," Wills describes touring various Florentine galleries in pursuit of "semideified" (his term; elsewhere she becomes "the idol-goddess") depictions of the Virgin by such painters as Botticelli, Orcagna, and Sogliani. Among the artists who go unvisited on this censorious jaunt are Vincenzo Frediani, recognized by modern scholars as "Il Maestro dell'Immacolata Concezione" and, more significantly in this context of Wills' fuzzy digests of history, Giovanni Francesco Barbieri, whose "Madonna in Glory" is also unmentioned. The omission of the latter artist is a shame since Wills has genuine visionary affinities with this particular painter who was known to his contemporaries as Guercino, "the Squinter."

But what specific "structures of deceit" does Mary support¿ As always, they are manifold. *First*, the proclamation of dogmas relating to her are manifestations of Roman hegemonic discourse—as current jargon would have it—on the part of two of the three pontiffs who are Wills' prime exemplars of "papal sin." "The only two formal exercises of papal infallibility in modern times have been definitions of Marian dogmas" by Pius IX and Pius XII.[10] The *second* is brought out in the opening sentence of the chapter: "One support of the celibate system has not been considered yet [in the chapters on the pope's eunuchs, clerical pedophiles, and gay priests]—the Virgin Mary"; this leads into a discussion of "mother dominance" which leads to (*third*), "The Virgin is repeatedly used to prevent the ordination of women" and thus in general to subordinate them to men—a topic on which Mary Gordon is then cited: "In my day [echoing another female subordinate, Eleanor Roosevelt], Mary was a stick to beat *smart girls* with. . . . For women *like me*, it was necessary to reject that image of Mary in order to hold onto the fragile hope of intellectual achievement, independence of identity, sexual fulfillment." Though not exactly a model of all-encompassing democratic feminism, anyone would immediately embrace this goal, along with the two others implicit in Wills' indictment.

Apart from the fact that every doctrine or devotion Wills can mock, thereby becomes part of a hierarchical conspiracy, the real issue, again, is whether Wills' analysis is accurate enough and rigorous enough to sustain his conclusions. As always with Wills, the reader is in danger of ignoring faulty argumentation simply to support noble goals—all in fulfillment of that dictum of Lord Acton cited as epigraph to the previous chapter: "It became a rule of policy to praise the spirit when you could not defend the deed." Four-fifths of "Marian Politics" is given over to another derivative disquisition only obliquely, at best, related to those three commendable causes. The question remains whether diversion by a whole school of red herring—that is, in this instance by a treatment of the titles "Immaculate Conception" and "Mediatrix of Grace"—is the way to sink the bark of Peter (which, in another

---

[10] This ignores the theological truism that every canonization "in modern times" is marked by the charism of infallibility when exercised by any pontiff, including the "patron" of saint-making, John Paul II.

sense, is worse than its bite) and so end patriarchy, pederasty, etc..
Are not such marian doctrines too slight a vessel to bear so heavy
a burden of causality, even if they were presented accurately—
which they are not?[11]

Before getting to that presentation, I want to examine
briefly—though in this context of the Immaculate Conception—
the Willsian strategy I mentioned earlier, but did not analyze because it was unrelated to the issue of antisemitism: that is the
deliberate mistranslation of texts. Speaking of the "maximalist
principle of Marian dignities," Wills says of the position of Duns
Scotus, the *doctor marianus*: "What was possible with her was
plausible; and if it was plausible it was performed. *Potuit, decuit,
fecit.*" This conventional dictum here is derived from Jaroslav Pelikan's *The Christian Tradition*; the warped translation is Wills' own.
(What it doesn't serve Wills' purpose to appropriate from Pelikan
is his observation that "the doctrine had become the generally accepted one in Western Christendom," centuries before Pius IX.)

---

[11] One brief instance of Wills' scattershot approach. Waxing learned, he writes
that "a kind of competitive chivalry, as in courtly love, made men [women apparently had no such devotion—news to Hildegard, and several Mechtilds and
Gertrudes] pay escalating compliments. She was not only the highest of humans,
according to Peter Damian, she was greater than the angels—taking her even
further out of reach as a model for other women"[like Mary Gordon]. Yet how
explain that St. Peter Damian, this marian maximalist (and like the equally criticized Anselm, a Doctor of the Church) attacked in *The Gomorrah Book* precisely
the kind of clerical vices Wills enumerates above and, moreover, on theological
grounds opposed the "escalation" from "Queen of the Angels" (in the words of
the litany of Loreto) to "Immaculate Conception"? Wills can't explain it because
Jaroslav Pelikan, the scholar from whom Wills here derives his data, doesn't tell
him. Such "courtly love" effusions are part of the prodigal eloquence of the marian tradition, as in, *Ad Matrem Virginum:* "O rose in your spring; O branch in
your flower; O fleece in your dew; O ark in your law; O throne in your king; O
moon in your light; O star in your rays; O mother in your child," and so on for
several verses. This type of ardent enthusiasm is not only misunderstood by
Wills, who ought to know better, but is exploited for post-whateverist ends (one
is tempted to invoke,"Mother of Good Counsel, *ora pro nobis*") by authors like
Julia Saville in *A Queer Chivalry: The Homoerotic Asceticism of Gerard Manley Hopkins* (Charlottesville, 2000). Hopkins is the author of *Ad Matrem Virginum,* another member of the "sacerdotal caste" corrupted by medieval practices. For a
somewhat different reading of Hopkins, cf. Justus George Lawler, *Hopkins Re-
constructed: Art, Poetry, and the Tradition* (New York, 1998).

Regardless of the fact that Scotus was employing a text going back to the amanuensis/biographer of St. Anselm—that latter Doctor of the Church being, as we have seen, the *bête noir* out of the blue who fabricated what was traditionally misconceived as a kind of pawnshop soteriology—and regardless of the fact that Wills' wording of the text serves his own agenda, what is *astounding* (Wills' recurrent temper) is this professor of classics' decidedly unclassical translation.

The axiom, now in the word order Scotus would have preferred, was *Decuit, potuit, [ergo] fecit;* loosely but accurately, "It was fitting" [that the mother of the Savior be pre-emptively sinless]; [God] "was able to bring that about"; "therefore it was done." To translate *decuit* ("seemly," "proper," "fitting") as "plausible" makes a mockery out of the Scotist doctrine—which of course is what Wills intends. And it makes a joke, as every snickering schoolboy would attest, of the legendary last words of the emperor Vespasian: *"Decet imperatorem stantem mori."* With his dying breath Vespasian is made to proclaim in Wills' skewed translatorese: "It is *plausible* that the emperor die standing." Or one might take Horace's *"dulce et decorum est pro patria mori,"* familiar after World War I from Wilfrid Owen's poem treating it as "the old lie," and after World War II from Britten's setting of Owen in the "War Requiem." The traditional translation of *dulce et decorum* which preserves the alliteration is "sweet and seemly": compare that with "sweet and plausible." (I will not labor the point of the Italian wordplay on "translator" as "traitor.") Lastly, how about considering, "a *plausible* respect for the opinions of mankind."

Now, to the two final "Marian" *squintings,* relating to Pius IX and to John Paul II—both connected by the same methodology of textual truncation and mutilation. Before providing his interpretation of the definition of the doctrine of the Immaculate Conception by Pius IX, Wills observes that the vainglorious and power-hungry Pope "was awed by the fealty he was paying to Mary; and by the power he was using to do it. Mary was being exalted. *But so was the papacy.*"[12] After omitting the proem to the definition, Wills continues immediately with his version of the text: "To the honor of the Holy and Undivided Trinity, and to the grace and dignity of the Virgin Mother of God, to the exaltation of the Catholic faith and the advance of the Christian religion, by the authority of our Lord Jesus Christ and of the blessed apostles Peter and Paul, and *by our own authority* [Wills' italics]*,* we declare, pronounce, and define. . . . " Directly following that text, Wills quotes Owen Chadwick: "No previous Pope in eighteen centuries had made a definition of doctrine quite like this."

But neither had Pius IX. What preceded Wills' excerpt, what indeed he has *skipped*, puts the paragraph preparing for the actual definition in a broader personal and theological setting. The original version doesn't contain Wills' *tendentiously inserted* and clearly redundant repetition ("by our own authority")—the arbitrary phrase Wills italicizes in order to underline more emphatically Pius's allegedly omniverous egocentricity. Lastly, the original text has a climactic pause before the definition itself to emphasize both its solemnity and its dependence on "the Church," "the power of the Holy Spirit," and other invocatory formulae. By contrast, Wills has the passage flow directly into the text of the definition so that the emphasis ends up being on *the Pope's* "authority" to declare, pronounce, and define. The complete paragraph follows:

---

[12] Wills' conspiracy theory that marian devotion masks papal sin and deceit is simply annihilated by a passage near the end of the *Apologia* treating of the Immaculate Conception. "So far from the definition in 1854 being a tyrannical infliction on the Catholic world, it was received every where on its promulgation with the greatest enthusiasm. It was in consequence of the unanimous petition, presented from all parts of the Church to the Holy See, in behalf of an *ex cathedra* declaration that the doctrine was Apostolic, that it was declared so to be. I never heard of one Catholic having difficulties in receiving the doctrine, whose faith on other grounds was not already suspicious." This passage leads into Newman's treatment of what is now called free speech in the church—much of which Wills cites, though without indicating that his citations relate to Pius's definition of the Immaculate Conception. Acton who—in a not atypical overstatement—viewed Newman as "ultramontane and fanatic" would subscribe to the notion that Immaculate Conception was a tactic to prepare the way for Infallibility sixteen years later. If so, Pio Nono was almost supernaturally prescient. Newman, understandably embittered in the aftermath of Vatican I, recollected old rumors

Wherefore, in humility and fasting, we unceasingly offered our private prayers as well as the public prayers of the Church to God the Father through his Son, that he would deign to direct and strengthen our mind by the power of the Holy Spirit. In like manner did we implore the help of the entire heavenly host as we ardently invoked the Paraclete. Accordingly, by the inspiration of the Holy Spirit, for the honor of the Holy and Undivided Trinity, for the glory and adornment of the Virgin Mother of God, for the exaltation of the Catholic Faith, and for the furtherance of the Catholic religion, by *the authority of Jesus Christ* our Lord, of the Blessed Apostles Peter and Paul, and by *our own*:

> *We declare, pronounce, and define that the doctrine which holds that the most Blessed Virgin, in the first instance of her conception, by a singular grace and privilege . . ."* etc.

The real life situation, the *Sitz im Leben* (which our biblist and translator calls "Sitz *am* Leben") must be recognized if we are to put this text in its genuine nineteenth-century framework.[13] A twenty-first century framework might substitute "in the first instance of her full human being" for "in the first instance of her conception."

And that latter substitution would not even be necessary had it not been for the misuse of the Immaculate Conception in opposition to abortion—an opposition which few would not support, but with clearly differing arguments, applications, and motives. Before briefly considering the arguments and applications, the motives must also be closely examined. This is particularly true and particularly important now that abortion is no longer just a personal matter between mother and medical practitioner; or no

---

about such a tactic, but there is not even the faintest suggestion in the *Apologia* of giving them credence in 1864 some ten years after the marian definition.

[13] The language though florid is utterly traditional. Thus Paul III's *Sublimis Dei* of 1537 on the rights of indigenous peoples in the New World: "We who though unworthy exercise on earth the power of our Lord, and seek with all our might to bring those sheep of His flock who are outside into the fold committed to Our charge. . . . define and declare by these Our letters. . . ." Similarly, Gregory XVI's *In Supremo Apostolatus* of 1839 on the abolition of the slave trade: "Placed at the summit of the Apostolic power and, though lacking in merits, holding the place of Jesus Christ the Son of God . . . We have judged that it belonged to Our Pastoral solicitude to exert Ourselves. . . ."

longer just a social-religious issue between two antagonist groups; or no longer even just a political issue based to a greater or lesser degree on partisan, regional, and even cultural influences. For some Roman Catholics led by vociferous clerics of a fundamentalist orientation (who in an earlier era invoked "mortal" sin for a host of trivial offenses and spoke of "the culture of contraception"), it has become what can only be called an ecclesiological issue.

Opposition to abortion is now the external *sphragis*, the seal stamping one as truly Catholic; but not in the sense of a singular practice denoting affiliation, as periodic abstinence from meat once was—as much a public trait of Catholics ("mackerel snappers") as "Kosher" was of Jews. Then because such opposition is based on a communal taboo, it assumes a kind of sacramental power that functions entirely apart from its origins in maternal and fetal relations. And by the same totemic symbolism, it takes on a sacred character binding together the chosen which—again parodying the sacrament—liberates them from the *law* and its constraints.[14] Only such an explanation clarifies the obsessive equation of the Holocaust with abortion, and the clerical denunciations of the latter in the most unexpected, indeed most incongruous situations—for one common example, the feast of the nativity of Jesus. There is in ascending order a collective righteousness, a sacral purism, a Catholic tribalism abroad in the church, and it predictably can lead only to further exclusivism climaxing in doomsday fanaticism.

Keats began "The Fall of Hyperion" with the words: "Fanatics have their dreams, wherewith they weave / A paradise for a *sect*."

---

[14] Thus the mere word "abortion" itself—ironically like the seventeenth-century coinage "hocus pocus," allegedly derived from the words of consecration at mass—conjures up a necromantic power to which even our most sophisticated technology is subject. On many computers the code "ab" originally was defined as meaning "abort"—to end a process; it is *now* defined as meaning "abandon." Perhaps, even in what popular culture views as the most recondite knowledge, "rocket science," the once not uncommon exclamation, "abort mission," has become "abandon project." Thus is avoided double trouble among linguistic exorcists. "Abandon" replaces "abort," while "project" replaces "mission"—the latter switch, lest that wizard word evoke emission.

If there is anything predictable about this tinsel triumphalism it is that, unless checked, it will reduce the Church Catholic to the status of a fundamentalist cult, with an inevitable reduction of influence in the real world, and a greater and greater incapacity to read clearly the signs of the times. This is going to prove neither distinctive nor attractive, particularly to the next generation for whom the already withered ties of ethnicity will mean less and less in terms of religious commitment. That great admirer of Newman, Muriel Spark, is alleged to have said that if you're going to join a religion, you might as well join the real one. That realness is becoming less evident to those looking over the barricades being erected by the new purists who, as Newman himself said, "move in a groove, and will not tolerate anyone who does not move in the same."

So much for motives. As to arguments and applications, it is not necessarily to embrace some three-stage development of the "soul"—vegetative, sensitive, rational—to point out that a fertilized egg is not a human person. But even the three-stage notion clearly implies some temporal gap before the infusion of the fully human soul into the developing fetus, as does also the acknowledgment of bodily conception (*conceptio seminis carnis* in the old language) by Mary's parents. "Joachim" and "Anne" generated her naturally; she is Jewish in her flesh and blood. Her *actual* human soul and hence her unique "Maryness" were simultaneously created *and* sanctified (conceived immaculately) when infused into the potential human being in her mother's womb.[15]

---

[15] The time of such infusion is a matter for possibly future scientific determination. But what is to be determined by common sense is the defectiveness of arguments that imply the absolute sacredness of embryonic life or that oppose such things as blastocyte research or even therapeutic cloning because it *might* lead to everything from "euthanasia" to experiments on mentally or physically impaired human beings. The "slippery slope" argument here, like the "camel's nose" argument in church-state issues, like the "domino" theory in geopolitics— all lead to disastrous conclusions. It is not even ethically debatable that when a purely speculative, indeed imaginary, hypothetical collides with a verifiably real and certain good, the latter takes precedent. If governmental advocates of "faith based" social programs (certainly a "thin edge of the wedge"—to cite another

This was the relatively unambiguous tradition—apart from ancillary pious or legal opinings—of theologians even after Pius IX, and of canonists up to the new Code of 1917. For this to be abandoned now under the influence of a congeries of indirectly related issues—all under the blanket, "sacredness of life"—is to abandon a basic hermeneutical principle, "interpretation is in the tradition," for a loosely invoked and vaguely defined slogan.[16] It is also to contradict the larger theological principle, which Newman defined in *Anglican Difficulties*, when writing of the Holy Spirit's guardianship of the church: "He lodged the security of His truth in the very fact of its Catholicity." If there is one thing that can be said

---

argumentative cliché) affirm they can prevent those abuses that would violate the Separation Clause, why can't they prevent abuses in embryonic research that might lead to, e.g., experiments on human beings? It is more than disconcerting to read under the letterhead of the US Conference of Catholic Bishops that "Modern *debates* on abortion and euthanasia are a symptom and *leading edge* [our fourth talismanic maxim] of something more profound and insidious," i.e., "the Culture of Death."

Moreover, though the tradition of forbidding baptism of the fetus is well known, another and perhaps more significant tradition—since it relates to holy orders—seems to be less well known. For over seven hundred years from Innocent III to Benedict XV, that is from roughly the thirteenth to the second decade of the twentieth century, penitential practice was based on the tradition of what was varyingly called the "ensoulment," "animation," "quickening" of the fetus *as subsequent* to embryonic life. A candidate for the priesthood who *concurred in* an abortion could still be ordained if his involvement took place before "ensoulment," the latter defined by some canonists as one hundred and sixteen days after bodily conception (again, *conceptio seminis carnis*), by others forty days for a male and sixty for a female—already so slow-witted *she* could never be ordained anyway. This was law and practice until 1917, and even a possible interpretation until the revision of canon law under John Paul II.

[16] There was an alternative tradition—adopted mainly by civil law—based on primitive science, on customs of clan or tribe (abortion among the Visigoths led to death for the mother) which gave way to atrocious sanctions, as in sixteenth century Spain (the guilty woman was buried alive); on superstitions about childbirth (requiring ritual "purification") and midwifery (often equated with witchcraft). In short, a tradition founded on male fears of woman in general and of her control of life in particular. This tradition was mainly reinforced up to the nineteenth century not by the clergy, but by the other two "learned professions," medicine and law. Subsequently, the clergy moved in to the vanguard, resulting in a causal connection between back woods preachers and back alley abortionists.

of various interpretations of the "Culture of Death," it is that they utterly lack Catholicity, whether in the tradition of the past, or in the body of the faithful of the present.

This is all lost on James Carroll who also, as we have seen, finds in *Mary* Gordon a kind of co-redemptress—presumably of his autobiographical enormities. Carroll true to his vision of universal reality seen exclusively in the light of Jewish-Christian "relations" has a more byzantine interpretation than Wills: Marian dogmas are simply another Catholic anti-Jewish plot. Explaining his theology to assorted religious and a-religious readers, he maintains that, "In the nineteenth century, Jesus was *commonly* [no references supplied] believed to be free of the taint of *Jewish blood* first because the Virgin Birth protected him from Joseph's Jewishness. [Such freedom from that "taint" may—from the equally byzantine perspective of Arab-Israeli politics—also "providentially" explain why the Virgin Birth was sanctioned by the Qur'an.] Then the doctrine of Immaculate Conception, which declared that Mary was conceived without sin, *inoculated* him against the *Jewish blood* of his maternal grandparents."[17]

"Astonishing," as Wills would say—and who would not?—of this "in-ocular" prophylaxis. ("In-ocular," not surprisingly, also carries the meaning of "squinting.") Was not Mary a Jew, born of Jewish parents—Anne and Joachim according to the apocryphal gospel of James—and with Jewish blood. Surely it is not the lesson of Carroll's seminar mentors that it was the "blood" of the Holy Ghost flowing through Mary's veins, or that Anne was also a virgin mother, and her mother as well, and so on, back into the shadows of pre-history. As to the somewhat ambiguously named

---

[17] The word "commonly" is the waffling term in this paragraph. Does it mean "widely," "generally," among Catholics whether educated or uneducated? Presumably it includes the educated ones and, therefore, the theologians since this is a complex and even subtle argument. Why therefore in a book freighted with lengthy footnotes is there no reference to who were these people who "commonly" believed all this? If "commonly" means among "the common people" there is the similar problem of where they derived these widespread notions from. Until further clarification from a source which is not anti-marian is provided, it is reasonable to assume this is another authorial fabrication; in short, a hoax.

dogma of the Virgin Birth, in the light of salvation history it is intended to signify a new aeon, while mysteriously reconciling the Davidic lineage of Joseph "of whom was born Jesus who is called Christ," with that other text from Matthew about Mary being "found with child of the Holy Spirit." But in any case, Virgin Birth says nothing about "Jewish blood," and everything about the role of women in child conceiving and bearing—which Carroll (professed and professional feminist) with neo-Aristotelian punctilio wondrously, if not neatly, finesses.

Lastly, and also related to the "use of Mary for papal purposes," is Wills' baffling exegesis of the encyclical of John Paul II, *Redemptoris Mater,* which represents the pope's effort to "claim that Mary is the mediatrix of *all* graces." Elsewhere the pope is "eager to foist his view of the mediatrix" on the scriptural texts relating to the miracle at Cana. (In Wills' thesaurus of papaphobia John Paul II "foists his view," whereas Pius IX "flexes his authority.") The following text about the miracle at Cana is the only passage from this very lengthy encyclical that Wills cites:

> There is thus a mediation. Mary places herself between her Son and mankind in the reality of their wants, needs, and sufferings. She puts herself 'in the middle'—that is to say, she acts as a mediatrix, not as an outsider but in her position as mother. She knows that as such she can point out to her Son the needs of mankind, and in fact she 'has the right' to do so Her mediation is thus in the nature of intercession: Mary "intercedes" for mankind. [Last clause omitted by Wills.]

Wills' argument is that here in section 21 of the encyclical, the pope is sanctioning the usurpation of divine agency by Mary, and so diminishing the role of the Son and Holy Spirit in the economy of redemption. But before he introduces Augustine's view of the miracle at Cana, Wills simply bypasses the meaning of the repeated term "intercession," and precedes the quotation above with the observation: "She can actually *bend* the will of the Father, who has set the hour of her son." (One might note the Pio

Nono-Mary parallel: to "bend" is to "flex.") This would presumably be the ultimate usurpation of trinitarian power by a mere creature. But "intercession" is *not* a word that implies "bending the will." St. Paul wrote to Timothy: "I desire therefore that supplications, prayers, intercessions, and thanksgivings be made for all."

And before I introduce Wills' introducing of Augustine, I will re-introduce John Paul's detailed observations in the next numbered section, 22, which explicate the quotation above—not in his own words but in the words of scripture and of an ecumenical council; in this instance, of Vatican II.

> It is important to note how the Council illustrates Mary's maternal role as it relates to the mediation of Christ. Thus we read: "Mary's maternal function towards mankind *in no way* obscures or diminishes the *unique mediation* of Christ but rather shows its efficacy," because 'there is one mediator between God and men, the man Christ Jesus' [Paul to Timothy, again]. This maternal role of Mary flows, according to *God's good pleasure* [no *bending* the will here], "from the superabundance of the merits of Christ; it is founded on his mediation, *absolutely* depends on it and draws *all* its efficacy from it."

The text could have represented, and certainly did reflect, the viewpoint at the Council of Cardinal Congar who rightly criticized—in a citation Wills supplies—the use of exaggerated devotional language by a marian enthusiast, St. Bernardine, in an encyclical of Leo XIII.

As to the introduction of Augustine's views, other than riding a hobby, it adds nothing to the substantive issues involved—though it does begin with an interesting statement, presumably translated by Wills: "Because she was not the mother of his divinity [it would be helpful to know just how exact this translation is], and the miracle she was asking for had to be worked through his divinity, he answered her in this way: 'What claim have you on me?'. . . ." I leave to historians and theologians the determination of what this does to the doctrine of an earlier council on Mary as Theotokos, as well as to the wonderful theological adaptation of metaphor, also sanctioned down through the centuries, in the teaching of what is known as *communicatio idiomatum*—which even Luther embraced, and which has been central to the "suffering God," or "crucified God" theologies of Bonhoeffer and Moltmann.[18]

My final illustration of "bending texts to the will," and as hapless as Wills' [19] earlier overlooking of Guercino, is his selection of the oft-cited last lines of Hopkins' "God's Grandeur" to round out his animadversions on "Marian Politics": ". . . the Holy Ghost over the bent / World broods with warm breast. . . ." Again, the process is one of picking and choosing whatever can be commandeered into the service of the overarching thesis of papal duplicitousness; in this case the alleged substitution of the Virgin for Sophia as the feminine face of deity. (Apparently dependent on the degree to which he wants to enhance his feminist credentials, Wills himself oscillates between the Holy Spirit as an "It" and a "She.") How this substitution occurred under the aegis of papal sin and deceit is not explained—nor can it be, since scholars like Quentin Quesnel have shown that it was the intensity of popular devotion before the first millennium that assimilated the Eastern Church's "St. Sophia" to Mary, the mother of Jesus (Cf. "The Search for Sophia," *Continuum,* II, 3, 1993).

But also expediently ignored in this treatment of Mary and the teaching on her Immaculate Conception is a much more relevant Hopkins poem which speaks to and from the devotional tradition, his sonnet on Duns Scotus:

> Of realty the rarest-veined unraveller; a not
> Rivalled insight, be rival Italy or Greece;
> Who fired France for Mary without spot.

---

[18] Conversely the Lutheran doctrine of "imputation" is founded on the rhetorical trope, simile. (Cf. Justus George Lawler, *Celestial Pantomime: Poetic Structures of Transcendence,* 2nd ed., 1994, pp. 92–99.)

[19] As a marian maximalist, and admirer of Maximus the Confessor, I am here being rigidly anti-monothelitist regarding both the will and the Wills.

4

THE POPE AND
THE SHOAH

Proclamation v. Reprisal

> "But where are the Christians? They are
> unable to bring their influence to bear on
> world events by carrying out the eternal
> principles of our Lord because—they are
> not unified."
>
> *Father Metzger*

I now come to the most disputed issue relating to popes and
politics, as well as to possible antisemitism: the activities of
the Holy See and pre-eminently of Pius XII during the Nazi
period. We have already seen in chapter two the extremes to
which his "denigrators" and "consecrators" can be driven by their
respective ideologies. No one questions that this remains the most
tangled and the most controversial issue between Jews and Christians (as well as *among* Christians and *among* Jews) since the brutal
devastation of the Shoah began to be tentatively acknowledged in
the period before and during the second World War. From that
time of its occurrence to the present when its full impact has only
gradually dawned on the conscience of the world, no issue has so
riven the sensibilities of people of every and of no religion. But
since the enormous literature this dispute has elicited is not my
present focus, I will say briefly what I have sought to clarify elsewhere (*The Range of Commitment,* 1970; innumerable times in the
original series of *Continuum;* and in at least twenty titles published
under the Herder and Herder imprint)[1] that the failure of the pope

---

[1] To mention only two: Alan T. Davies, *Anti-Semitism and the Christian Mind:
The Crisis of Conscience after Auschwitz* (1969), and Carl Amery, *Capitulation: The
Lesson of German Catholicism* (1967). For the latter the descriptive text read:

to fulfill his threefold office as prophet, priest, and *servus servorum* is *arguably* the great tragedy of modern Catholicism. Whether in fact it will remain clearly such in the future is a judgment of history. In either case, one simply cannot justify faulty scholarship, or biased and distorted interpretations, much less arbitrary accusations in condemnation of an enigmatic figure who seems by any balanced judgment to have embodied and suffered the tension of *mystique* and *politique,* a tension that von Hügel would have viewed as the "frictional" factor intrinsic to the very nature of religion as a this-world/other-world phenomenon.

—I—

A shadow hovers over virtually all discussions of Pius, particularly since his treatment in *Der Stellvertreter* by Rolf Hochhuth. (Possibly not since *Uncle Tom's Cabin* has a third-rate literary effort had such a widespread and controversial impact.) But that shadow is not his condemnation of the pope—largely on his part a propaganda effort, easily dismissed—but his defining the terms of all subsequent discussion, so that what is asked of Pius is not a deed, an *actio,* which would achieve the cessation of the Jewish slaughter, but merely a statement, a proclamation, a *word.* As a consequence, the immense literature which grew up around the figure of the pope persistently employs Hochhuth's (Protestant) language, as though Pius's preached word would have some kind of automatic, intrinsic, even sacramental efficacy. Hence, too, all those dreary tracts focusing on "speaking out," "public condemnation," "never saying a word," "les silences," "das Schweigen,"

". . . the institutional Church cravenly subjected itself to the powers of this world"; the text then went on to consider its relevance to American Catholicism in the late sixties: " . . . in danger of abdicating its principles. . . . The witness of its bishops has been blurred by chauvinistic utterances, by the failure to speak out against such indiscriminate weapons as napalm, by indifference to the struggle for civil rights, by active opposition to the legitimate organizing efforts of underprivileged farm workers, and by a massive identification of institutional religious health with the grossest material achievements."

etc. The entire dramatic tenor of Hochhuth's play, and of the real-life situation, should have focused on the pope's seeking a word made flesh, an accomplishment which would not merely pay futile homage—however loudly, dramatically, vigorously—to some ideal order of justice, but a *deed* which would fuse the ideal with the real, which would like the sacrament of which he was the high priest, *work* what he *said*. The friction lay in that the fulfillment of his prophetic office abraded his office as priest and as servant of the servants of God. (Cf. "The Deputy," *Continuum*, Summer, 1963; *Blackfriars* [U.K.], October, 1963) Moreover, such abrasion as all the records attest, was intensified by his own uncertainty as to the consequence of deeds fraught with the possibility of reprisals more violent than those he would be seeking to prevent.

It is difficult to see how further research in *any* library or archive could aid in confirming such uncertainty. Even if it were documented that—to take the worst possible "hypothetical"—Pius had forbidden explicitly the hierarchies of every country remotely connected to the mass killings to do anything to prevent them, his intention would remain unknown and unknowable—short of discovering a detailed personal diary or written examen of conscience composed during the war years in which he had weighed the issue of reprisals vis-a-vis proclamation. Precisely this question of intention was raised by the International Catholic-Jewish Historical Commission, of which fortunately John Morley was a member: did Pius indicate either in personal papers or in communications to anyone doubts about the correctness of his "silence"? But even this begs the question. To have had no doubts would render him precisely the monster his critics have painted him as. Furthermore, his stated concern over reprisals indicates that he was indeed weighing that basic factor; indicates by definition, *dubiety* as a state of mind.

And after over five decades it would seem unlikely that any record of such obviously private doubts could exist. Moreover, there are contemporaneous attestations of his sincerity in believing he had spoken plainly and understandably in condemnation of the exterminations. If, on the other hand (perhaps the best possible

hypothetical), Pius realized that to avoid reprisals he must communicate *by spoken word only,* and in utter secrecy and through
trustworthy messengers with assuredly reliable ecclesiastics that
these latter, under guarantee of total concealment, should take
every step possible to aid the victims—what evidence, by the very
definition of the situation, could there be available in archives or
libraries, or anywhere? It might be argued that the *results* would
constitute the evidence. But the results, after fifty years of scrutiny, show only that much was done by local church officials to
frustrate the Nazi apparatus—though certainly not as much as
ideally should have been done.[2] And this raises the question of the
paradigm shift discussed in chapter two. If the ruling principle of
Holocaust history is to attain some undefined and possibly undefinable judgmental ideal, where will interpretations ever find a ter-
minal point?

The Commission's questions posed to Vatican officials do not
seem to contemplate the possibility of such a "non-ideal" resolution of what has become a cause of resentment and conflict—
largely because of a scapegoating of Pius rather than a critiquing
of the role of the whole church. A clear and simple solution with
a single guilty party might bring what is optimistically called closure, but possibly at the price of truth. Questions having to do
with specific details of specific instances of evil by Catholics acting
as Catholics must of course be answered. And it goes without saying that archives should be opened, that there should be "full dis-
closure," and that transparency should reign. But maybe it ought

---

[2] There is almost an infinite calculus of factors. Religious groups like the
French Protestants were more sympathetic to the plight of Jews than were Catholics, since the former two shared a common minority status. Bretons though a
minority were less sympathetic because they hoped the Germans would support
their nationalistic aspirations. No single definite element explains why French
Jewish survivors far outnumbered survivors from most other western European
nations. There was an active resistance movement, porous borders, and the relatively lenient Italian occupation in the south originally beyond the purview of
Paris or Vichy. So too with other countries: Holland with a population equally
divided between Catholics and Protestants lost almost 75% of its Jews, while
Belgium predominantly Catholic lost only about 30%. Why Denmark suffered
relatively few losses and Norway so many may be due mainly to discrepancies
in official zealousness. This is simply to underline the obvious fact that not just

at least to be considered whether this pursuit of a single man is becoming obsessional, and whether there might be a kind of jubilee remission, or at least a meditative pause in this four-decade prosecutorial process, while other "understanding" rather than "judgmental" avenues are followed?[3]

Certainly on the part of the Catholic writers whom I shall be criticizing there is a kind of cynicism to this incessant exploitation of Pius XII and the Holocaust for purposes that often seem remote from any quest for historical accuracy. A decade ago the Israeli philosopher of science, Yehuda Elkana, in the context of the political exploitation of the Shoah, made a celebrated plea to his fellow citizens that while other nations should abide by the injunction to "remember," Israel should "forget."[4] It is time for Catholics, while fostering genuine research—if they have the skills and freedom from parti pris, as clearly some do not—to cease using the Holocaust as a weapon for assaulting their own religious opponents; in short, to cease using it for their own purposes as some kind of ecclesiastical football. This does more to dishonor the need

---

religious elements must be weighed, but also geographic, temporal, cultural, administrative, etc.

[3] A hiatus of a couple of decades would at least mean the entry of a new generation of researchers, a cooling of understandable but perhaps narrowly focused ardor, and an opportunity for archival examination free of the urgency of deadlines, as well as of Q and A insistencies.

[4] The immediate context was the intifida, but the larger setting was a revaluation by a new generation of Israelis of the Zionist foundations of the state, of the role of victimization, of the Ashkenazi political and cultural dominance—all important issues, but for purposes of this analysis, issues of intermural Jewish concern. But for James Carroll who makes the basic relation of Judaism and Christianity the antisemitism culminating in the Holocaust, the words of Elkana may be worth reflecting upon: "For Israel to base its understanding of human existence on the Holocaust is disastrous. . . . Without overlooking the historical importance of collective memory, it is more important to take a stand on the side of life, to build a future. . . ." A Christian voice has no place in this debate, except to strengthen whatever remedies it can offer. But no one should make the essential link between two religious visions—whose goal is to see human life *sub specie aeternitatis*—the Christian evils perpetrated during what is in the light of eternity a relatively brief segment of human intercourse. Catholics *must* remember, but not to the point where the past simply negates the future, particularly the future of relations with the faith of their elder sibling.

to "remember" than do all the patently vacuous invocations of "honesty" to devalue that virtue.[5]

— II —

In any event, neither understanding nor judgment—save of condemnation—seems contemplated by the critics of Pius. While one should pity the pope in his plight, one need not praise him. But neither can one bury him under the steaming compost-heap of invective—"Hitler's pawn," "ideal pope for Hitler's unspeakable plan"—that John Cornwell piles up around Pius's memory, that Carroll naively adds his husks of spoilage to, and that Wills burrows into with ill-concealed relish. Of Pius's statement that he had "condemned on various occasions in the past the persecution that a fanatical anti-Semitism inflicted on the Hebrew people," Wills again plays fast and *louche* (the word is "squinting") with historical fact: *"That* is a deliberate falsehood. He never publicly mentioned the Holocaust." Of course, *that* word was not in currency during Pius's time—but let it pass.

In proof of "deliberate falsehood" Wills refers to "the Pope's Christmas message of December 4, 1942 [meaning December 24], the one speech that is cited to prove that he did speak out against the Holocaust." (A strange circumlocution here: "the one speech that is cited"—as though the straw-man of indeterminate "citers" exhausted the matter, and the words of the pontiff himself were not worthy of examination by historian Wills.) Never mentioned are these people who have cited only *one* speech; the reason being

---

[5] It is enlightening to read the balanced account of the popes and the Reich by the premier "Vaticanologist" and one of the papacy's severest critics of our era, Peter Hebblethwaite in *Paul VI: The First Modern Pope.* In spite of the journalistic title, this is a remarkably objective and thoroughly researched account. There are no gratuitous editorializing or slanted interpretations, nor is there any sniffing out of conspiracies and deceptions. It is a major history of the papacy covering seven decades as reflected in the life or as seen through the eyes of Paul VI. No where in the treatment of Pius XII do Wills or Carroll refer to Hebblethwaite's work.

that Cornwell doesn't provide Wills with the names. Though there is some indication that Cornwell on whom Wills is totally dependent did glance at parts of the entire message with his now celebrated assiduity and freedom from bias: "no discrimination, no insight," "lengthy and dry sermonizing," "denial and trivialization," etc., Wills himself appears to be aware of the two sentences only. Ignored by both writers, as well as most other commentators (John Morley excepted) is the context of this "one speech": the passages preceding the sentences which are "cited to prove that he did speak out against the Holocaust," and the passages that follow immediately; all of which of course must be read as a unified statement. The first passage relates to the complicity of Christians in the moral disintegration before and during the war; the second to the plight of the Jews (here italicized); and the third to the destruction of civilian centers—a recurrent theme in all the major addresses of this pope, as demonstrated in the discussion of Phayer's *The Catholic Church and the Holocaust* in chapter two.

1- A great part of mankind, and let Us not shrink from saying it, not a few who call themselves Christians, have to some extent their share in the collective responsibility for the growth of error and for the harm and the lack of moral fibre in the society of today. . . . That which in peacetime lay coiled up, broke loose at the outbreak of war in a sad succession of acts at variance with the human and Christian sense. . . . 2- *Mankind owes that vow* [to bring back society to its center of gravity in God's law] *to those numberless exiles whom the hurricane of war has torn away from their native soil and dispersed in a foreign land. . . . Mankind owes that vow to those hundreds of thousands who, without any fault of their own, sometimes only by reason of their nationality or race, are marked down for death or gradual extinction.* 3- Mankind owes that vow to the many thousands of noncombatants, women, children, sick and aged, from whom aerial warfare—whose horrors We have from the beginning frequently denounced—has, without discrimination or through inadequate precautions, taken life, goods, health, home, charitable refuge, or house of prayer.

It is obscene to call this a "paltry statement" as Cornwell does—on a page Wills must have missed when rifling through Cornwell's swollen satchel for facts, opinions, and quotations. Whether the statement represents a *"deliberate* falsehood," is contradicted by the testimony of the British and American representatives at the Vatican both of whom affirmed Pius's sincerity in believing he had spoken clearly enough, and in a manner "plain to everyone." As to Wills' and other carpers' much quoted response as to "why he did not name the Nazis. . . . [because] he would have had to name the Communists too," what is truncated or intentionally omitted here is Pius's belief that, in the words of the American representative to the Vatican: "this ["naming the Communists too"] might not be wholly pleasing to the Allies." Several critics of the statement also detect a clue to the alleged insignificance of this passage in Pius's rhetorical scheme—and therefore also in his mind—because it occurs near the end of a lengthy address. One doesn't know what has happened to the notion of *peroratio*, the summation and climactic finale to a speech; but then who these days grows up with—as did Pius—"grave Quintilian's copious work," the *Institutio Oratoria*? (The quotation is from a different Pope, Alexander.)

Wills justifies his "deliberate falsehood" and "false claim" accusations in the name of that virtue he has trumpeted as his own paramount attribute: "But the issue of honesty arises when arguments are made defending Pius with false readings of history." This is a statement with which one must agree, certainly if they are "readings" such as Wills assembled with regard to Rahner, Benoit, Glock and Stark, "the hidden encyclical," and *Nostra Aetate*. Wills then recites, in an exercise of his own *patent* dishonesty, that "it is out of these two sentences [italicized above] that he [Pius] would later construct a claim to have attacked anti-Semitism, specifically, on various occasions." But Pius claimed no such thing, and to assert otherwise is indeed a "deliberate falsehood." What he claimed was by Wills' *own* wording: "We condemned on various occasions in the past *the persecution* that a fanatical anti-Semitism inflicted. . . ." This is not a caviling distinction and certainly not one that should be lost on Wills who, when it suits his purposes, scrutinizes every jot and tittle and parses every phrase and clause in papal utterances to ferret out "dishonesties." Again, Wills' wording and interpretation suggest his seduction by Abecedarianism and his addiction to papaphobia.

As to the all-important broader issue of the Holocaust, as early as his Christmas address of 1940, Pius declared: "It is a comfort to Us that through the moral and spiritual assistance of Our representatives and through Our financial resources, we have been able to give support to a great number of refugees, homeless, and emigrants, including non-Aryans." In the paragraph preceding this quotation—and proleptic of John Paul II's introduction to the document "We Remember"—Pius had also declared: "The laws and morality of international warfare have been so callously ignored that future generations will look back on the present war as one of the darkest periods in history. Our thoughts anticipate with anxiety the moment when the complete chronicle of those who have been killed, maimed, injured, captured, those who have lost their homes and their relatives, will be known in all its details. What We know already, however, is enough to rend Our heart." Now this is certainly not the statement of someone who, according to current and past critics, was intent on clouding the historical record out of fear of future obloquy. Nor could it have referred to any other warring nation than *Germany* which had invaded in the months before the address Poland, Belgium, Holland, Luxemburg, France, Denmark, and Norway.

As I have emphasized, the three numbered sections above constitute an interlocking whole. It should also be emphasized that this message was delivered at a time when the first rumors of what is now called the Holocaust were just beginning to be independently confirmed. It is also when the aerial attacks violating the "morality of international warfare"—which the pope had first condemned two weeks after the outbreak of hostilities, and several times thereafter—were launched by the Axis powers against such cities as Warsaw in 1939, Rotterdam, Coventry, and London in 1940–41. Again, it seems obvious, without "mentioning names" whom the pope is accusing. In the context of living through "one of the darkest periods in history," Pius spoke of embracing not just Christians but Jews as well: ". . . those who are children of the Church of Christ, and those who, because of their faith in the Divine Saviour, *or at least in Our Father Who is in Heaven*—all who are very dear to us."

In June, 1941, speaking of "sin as being exalted, excused, and the master of human life," he gave this illustration: ". . . individuals and families are *deported, transported, separated, torn from their homes*, wandering in misery without support." Six months after the Christmas address of 1942, in an Allocution to the College of Cardinals which was published in *l'Osservatore Romano* (June 3, 1943) and in *La Civiltà Cattolica*, Pius mentioned specifically his concern for "those who have turned an anxious and imploring eye to Us, those who are tormented because of their nationality or race by major miseries and by more acute and grievous suffering, and who are sometimes even fated, without guilt on their part, to extermination." If these are not condemnations of "the persecution" inspired by antisemitism, then we need to revise our dictionaries. But we have to revise out thinking as well: why do students of the era persist in following almost blindly in the footsteps of Hochhuth, and displaying this obsession with "silence" and with the need for public statements, declarations, even excommunications—the latter demanded by a number of captious critics—rather than with deeds and actions? (Of the axiom, *facta non verba*, more shortly.)

Nevertheless, Wills persists: "Pius never explained his *silence* on the Holocaust." Yet he did proffer publicly and privately the reason for his circumspection: "Every word directed by Us to the competent authorities and every public reference have to be seriously pondered and measured by Us in the interest of those who suffer, in order not to make—even unintentionally— their situation more grave and insupportable." Two months before the Allocution, the Vatican Secretariat of State, after noting that "in order to avert (*evitare*) the massive deportation of Jews" it had involved its representatives in Italy, Slovakia, and Croatia. However, it added, "an open sign of this would not seem advisable lest Germany, knowing of this declaration of the Holy See, should intensify its anti-Jewish measures." But then from the wings six decades later comes the voice of sensationalizing *pasticheurs,* suddenly front and center in this carnival of recrimination—the voice of tardy "discoverers-of-the-truth-about-Catholicism"—all masters (and mistresses) of high dudgeon and low blows, bravely asserting *urbi et orbi* their own untested but, of course, heroically outspoken condemnation of such "silence."

Wills and his cicerone, Cornwell, believe the 1942 Christmas address to have been evasive and trivializing. Wills condemns it as "an address that refused to name Jews or Nazis or Germans specifically." Less than six months earlier in a broadcast to the British people, Churchill had said, "Since the Mongol invasion . . . there has never been methodical merciless butchering on such a scale," but never named the Jews, so that it was not clear whether he was referring to the war in general, to the conflict in the Pacific theater with "Oriental" peoples, or even to the bombing raids on England. Pius was clearly much more specific, and much more clearly understood. One might note also that Pius in messages—commiserating at the invasion of their countries—to the Queen of the Netherlands, to the King of the Belgians, and to the Grand Duchess of Luxembourg never named "Nazis or Germans specifically." The exercise of a modest historical sensibility, much less any semblance of empathy whether retroactive or not, would suggest that in those terrible times during the early stages of the most destructive war in history—six decades removed from life in the precincts of somnolent libraries at claustral universities with their snug professorial digs—the watchword would have simply been: *ça va sans dire.* As it would also, no doubt, have been in the face of complaints that the Declaration of Independence "refused to name" George III, or that the Emancipation Proclamation "refused to name" Jefferson Davis or the Confederacy.[6]

---

[6] Diplomatic protocol as well perhaps as political prudence dictated—at least before the Allied powers' declaration of a policy of unconditional surrender—a lack of specificity that might allow the pontiff to mediate between both warring parties. Relatively rare in the early years of the war was his mention of "the blood-stained soil of Poland and Finland" (though without naming Germany or Russia) in his Christmas message of 1939, and of his "paternal love for all our sons and daughters, whether of the Germanic peoples . . . or of the Allied states" on June 2, 1940. Nor is there any doubt that Pius was aware of the experience of

To illustrate the "triviality" of the Christmas address, Cornwell cites an anecdote from that gleeful bomber of Ethiopian peasant villages ("like blossoming flowers"), the sycophantic Galeazzo Ciano, Mussolini's son in law, who described the dictator as "scoffing" at the address: "platitudes by a parish priest in a backwater native village" was the gist of the "contemptuous dismissal of it." If that tale is credible, perhaps Mussolini was still smarting from the oblique but manifest mockery aimed at his grandiose imperial ambitions in the valediction of Pius's Christmas address of the preceding year which was delivered: "From this Rome, center, rock, and teacher of Christianity, from this city called Eternal by reason of its relations with the living Christ rather than by reason of its associations with the passing glory of the Caesars."

But in fact the 1942 message was not as cryptic and incomprehensible as latter-day critics would suggest. Officials in the Reich Main Security Bureau (RSHA) of the assassinated Reinhard Heydrich—architect of the Wansee extermination program of January, 1942, and heir presumptive to Himmler—clearly understood to whom this address was directed and to what it referred: ". . . the pope has repudiated the Nazi New Order . . . , clerical falsification of the Nazi world view. . . . The Pope does not refer to the National Socialists by name . . . , but [*pace* Cornwell and Wills] he is clearly speaking on behalf of the Jews . . . , he makes himself the mouthpiece of the Jewish war criminals." Owen Chadwick in *Britain and the Vatican* attributes these responses to the German Foreign Office. This is certainly a less anecdotally driven datum than that of the opportunist, Count Ciano, to which Cornwell gives credence.

Moreover, Bishop von Preysing of Berlin in March of 1943, three months later, also clearly understood what and to whom the Pope's address referred. In one of the letters in *Actes et Documents . . . ,* he wrote to Pius, a long-time personal friend, about

---

another pontiff when, in the words of a passionate opponent of fascism, "Benedict XV was reproached during the last war for not having denounced the arrogance of German nationalism"—reproached by French nationalists. Cf. Julien Benda, *The Treason of the Intellectuals* (New York, 1928).

the deportation of "thousands and thousands of Jews whose probable fate is that which Your Holiness has indicated in the Christmas message. . . . Would it not be possible that Your Holiness attempt *once again* to intervene in support of these unfortunate innocents?" Pius's "full response" is rarely reproduced since it would not reinforce the post-Hochhuth image in *Der Stellvertreter* embraced more by Catholic than by Jewish critics—and in fact, the acknowledged motivation of Cornwell's *Hitler's Pope.* After noting that he had referred to the fate of the Jews in that message, Pius observed that his statement "was brief, but it has been well understood." He went on to say that his love and concern were extended to all who were in anguish, but that he could do nothing effective for them except to pray. However, that "full response" to which I referred above as being rarely cited, is Pius's declaration to von Preysing: "But We are decided, as circumstances advise or permit, to speak out once again in their favor"—about which Phayer observes dryly: "Whatever the circumstances the pope had in mind evidently never came to pass," whereas a more pertinent observation would have to do with the proven fatuity of mere "speaking out," when action was called for. Nevertheless, one assumes the "circumstances" were those surrounding his allocution to the College of Cardinals six months after the Christmas address.

But I want to draw a parallel regarding "outspokenness" with the leader of another church, the world-wide communion of Anglicans. Almost exactly between the time of Pius's Christmas message and his address to the cardinals, the Archbishop of Canterbury—a socially committed prelate in the mould of Cardinal Manning—also formally broke his "silence." Speaking to the upper house of parliament on March 23, 1943, William Temple asserted "that in view of the massacres and starvation of Jews *and others* in enemy and enemy-occupied countries, [we] should take measures on the largest and most generous scale for providing help and temporary asylum to persons in danger of massacre." (Would that Pius, obsessed with diplomatic niceties, had emulated his forthright British counterpart.) As to the latter's message, one will have to imagine how accepting, how universally welcome would have been the response from Anglicans everywhere—from Sydney to Toronto, from Bombay to Nairobi—at hearkening to this brave clarion; and certainly no where more enthusiastically (at the least, *two* cheers for Anglicanism) than in the United States where Episcopalians had prided themselves since colonial times on being the quasi-official church of the republic—and well known for their openness to Jewish immigration.

Unfortunately this well-intentioned and sensible statement had to be retracted when were pointed out the constraints of immigration law and the even more humiliating possibility, as the Foreign Office so diplomatically put it, "that the Germans or their satellites may change over from the policy of extermination to one of extrusion, and aim as they did before the war at *embarrassing* other countries by flooding them with alien immigrants." How very understandable in the country about which T. S. Eliot would opine—without remonstration—that "reasons of race and religion combine to make a large number of free-thinking Jews undesirable." ("Free-thinking" has to do with religion; the "reasons of race" were never supplied.)[7] For the Foreign Office—as for the laureate—extermination was clearly preferable to *embarrassment*. All of this led to the archbishop lamely admitting that he hadn't envisaged a "flow of vast numbers of refugees"; his view being that "it would be at best a trickle." This, from a prelate of acknowledged virtue, and speaking not in Vatican City—that tiny island of fragile security in an ocean of Nazi troops who in a few months would take over Rome itself—but in the very House of Lords of the "mother of parliaments" in the heart of imperial Britain.

But the British Foreign Office, not being able to ignore the Primate's plea and the American State Department, responding to a mass rally of Jews in New York around the same time, both decided—with the furtive chicanery a Zuccotti or a Phayer could attribute only to "Rome"—on an "exploratory" conference in Bermuda (chosen because it was off-limits to the press), to which

---

[7] On February 18, 2000 (in the Roman calendar, feast of St. Simeon, cousin of Jesus and successor to James the Less as bishop of Jerusalem and crucified in 107) the reigning Archbishop of Canterbury delivered a sermon around various texts of the Nobel prize awardee, referred to "as one of *our* greatest poets."

no Jewish organizations were invited and which, at the State Department's insistence could not discuss relaxing immigration laws, and at the Foreign Office's insistence could not discuss changing immigration policy in Palestine. "And so it came to happen" that the surrogate representatives to what has gone down in history as "the Bermuda [not Laputa] Conference," spent their days in the sun talking about possible asylum for alien (and embarrassing) Jewish immigrants in places like Libya and Honduras.[8]

The ironies are too farcical to labor. But if this charade had played out under the aegis of the Vatican, we would still be hearing about it, with insistent demands for detailed explanations filling the daily papers and book reviews more than half a century later. As to Archbishop Temple, a noble-minded prelate (as some might even dare to say about Pius), he died two years later, and thus was spared the recrimination that longevity brings in its wake. And his defenders could always say—citing the dictum of Acton preferred in chapter two—that, anyway, there is really no parallel here at all, since the Anglican communion is both much smaller and more episcopally democratic than the Catholic church.

But even given that latter factor, national bishops conferences did have considerable freedom of action under Pius XII, as he himself emphasized during the war. So if there is a fault it may have been less with the pope than with the German bishops, and more particularly with Cardinal Adolf Bertram president of the Conference who had a history of antisemitism as well as of disagreements with the outspoken von Preysing. It is certainly arguable that agitation by the bishops, acting individually as local church leaders among their own diocesans, would have been more effective than public declarations by the Vatican—or rather by the pope, since Vatican radio made many such declarations. Much is

---

[8] There is an unfortunate replication of the Wannsee Conference of a year before, also held in a resort area, where as a passing sop to any latent flicker of remorse among the conferees the notion was floated of Madagascar as a possible destination for soon to be dispossessed Jews— though it was a foregone conclusion by the organizers and by Heydrich, the Chairman, that the "Final Solution," could only mean extermination.

made of the oft-alleged monolithic and pyramidal structure of the Church, and of the prepotent influence of the figure at the peak; but it was a figure in 1942 with moral authority only, unlike the even more egregiously waffling Roosevelt or Churchill, both of whom ignored pleas by Jewish representatives in England, America, and Palestine for relaxing immigration laws and for the bombing of the death camps. Moreover, concerning the myth of the monolith, several non-Italian prelates *had* criticized Pius XI for his failure to oppose Mussolini's Ethiopian adventure, including Hinsley of England whom Pius later named a cardinal; there is also the well-publicized personal attack—albeit in the early 30's—on Hitler himself by the American Cardinal Mundelein which was never retracted; and finally the joint statement—the first on a major socio-religious issue—by American Protestant leaders and Catholic bishops condemning the ravages of Kristallnacht.

When Cardinal Bertram acted as head of the Conference in opposition to the Nazi program for the dissolution of marriages between Jews and non-Jews, the program was aborted. When in the summer of 1943, the bishops agreed to consider a proposal sponsored by von Preysing that would have squelched "rumors regarding the mass deaths of deported non-Aryans," it was Cardinal Bertram who successfully led the opposition. (Cf. Michael Phayer, "Nazism and Some German Bishops," *Continuum,* Autumn, 1990.) Pius's notion of subsidiarity was carefully communicated to von Preysing: "We leave it to senior clergy to determine if and to what degree the danger of reprisals and oppression . . . may make restraint advisable to avoid greater evils, notwithstanding the reasons for intervention." Pius's reliance on national episcopates was effective throughout the English-speaking world (both the British and the American bishops condemned racism), as well as—given war-time conditions—in his own country, Italy, Southern France, Belgium, and Holland;[9] less well-served were Catholics in Hungary, Romania, and Slovakia. Nevertheless, it cannot be denied

---

[9] Morley provides the original text with translation (Appendix H) of a communique— from the Berlin Nunciature to the Vatican two weeks before Pius's Christmas message—which observed that "churchmen and laity have noted with amazement that until now the German episcopate has not made any collective manifestation on the question of the grave mistreatment inflicted on the

that such reliance would have been more understandable had the pope himself secretly but vigorously insisted on action by his sub-ordinates—as indeed he may have.

But can anyone say there was "deliberate falsehood" on the part of Pius in any of this tragic history? Certainly not if the unbi-ased reader—as the rubric "honesty" would dictate—take into ac-count not only the texts cited above but also the repeated references in a multitude of addresses and allocutions to "the per-nicious errors widespread today" that ignore the "indissoluble unity of the human race," "the common origin of all peoples," and that "elevate the state to the supreme criterion of the moral and juridical order," that foster "acts irreconcilable with the law of na-ture and the elementary sentiments of humanity," that frustrate "the just demands of nations and populations and racial minori-ties," or that "hinder or restrict their economic resources, for the limitation or abolition of their natural fertility." It is certainly not inconceivable that these and scores of public statements on the violations of the law of nature, on the indissoluble unity of the human race, and on the atrocities of the wartime period were be-lieved by Pius and were, in fact, condemnations of the persecution of all who died in the Holocaust. The question is not whether such condemnations were emphatic and clear enough—they obvi-ously were. The question is whether more muted and ambiguous public statements *combined* with straightforward but clandestine directives through nunciatures would have had any real alleviat-ing effect, or would also have simply exacerbated the slaughter of the Jews.[10]

Jews, while the French episcopate immediately took a position against racial legislation . . . ; also voices of protest were raised in other nations."

[10] It is simplistic and uninformed for Carroll to say: "If Pius XII had done what his critics, in hindsight, wish him to have done—excommunication of Hit-ler, revocation of the concordat, 'a flaming protest against the massacre of the Jews,' in Lewy's phrase—it would have been *only a version* of what Pius IX did in 1875 against Bismarck, and in 1871 against Garibaldi when he excommunicated all Italians who cooperated with the new Italian state." *Constantine's Sword,* (p. 534). First, in neither instance were the *lives* of millions hanging in the balance; second, neither nineteenth-century figure had anything in common with Hitler apart from being a leader of a political group; third, there were no consequences

— III —

Moreover, through all the messages delivered after the outbreak of hostilities was the refrain condemning weapons of mass destruction (a clarion taken up by Vatican II and by Paul VI at his address to the United Nations) along with the repeated denunciation of wanton violators of the principle of noncombatant immunity. This raises an issue, to be considered shortly, bearing on the Holocaust as well as on the differing burden of guilt borne by both of the warring parties. As I have already noted, many of these condemnations of the destruction of urban centers were made before the aerial attacks on such cities as Warsaw, Rotterdam, and London by the Luftwaffe; but even more significantly in *this* present context, they were also before the RAF "thousand plane" bombardments of Cologne, Essen, and Bremen. The most lethal of these early attacks was in the summer of 1943 when 50,000 civilians died in Hamburg. The *US Strategic Bombing Survey,* published a month after the grand dénouement at Hiroshima, reported that a fifth of all dwellings in Germany had been destroyed "rendering homeless seven and a half million German civilians." Among those engaged in the survey were such unquestionably upright officers, and later widely admired figures, as George W. Ball, John Kenneth Galbraith, and Paul Nitze.

One has to ask this question as a matter of historical honesty—it is indeed the single ineluctable issue for both admirers and denigrators of Pius. Why did not that exemplary model of probity—again, one must ask in all sincerity—that general who publicly and unembarrassedly invoked Christian values and whose war memoir was called a "crusade," why did he not heed the plain

---

whatever to the alleged nineteenth-century excommunications. Five times in his book Carroll complains that Hitler was not excommunicated, as though this were a notion to be memorized, but not to be questioned and then analyzed—anymore than we are expected to analyze what appears from the above to be the excommunication of Bismarck (which never happened—he was a Lutheran by birth). The disconnect in the above quotation is incomprehensible. Pius IX—hitherto in all these accounts a fool and a villain—here becomes a model and a hero to be emulated by his successor; and this, because Pio Nono engaged in some papal gestures—then and now recognizably otiose.

and clear statements of the "Vicar of Christ" denouncing what would subsequently be called in more calloused times, "city busting," and later, "carpet bombing"—and more importantly, what may be the lessons for later generations of that heedlessness? If the Pope's well-publicized statements were so utterly ignored by military leaders who honestly believed they were engaged in necessary retaliatory measures, who were motivated not by ideological ethnic hatred of the "enemy," and who were convinced their tactics were a moral imperative; if such statements were so utterly ignored by such leaders, what would have been the response to similar statements, raised in condemnation of their Nazi counterparts who were inspired and led by a pathologically depraved racist, a ruthless megalomaniac, supported by literally millions of entranced followers including Roman Catholics who had been indoctrinated over the years into mass acceptance of their own systematic dehumanization? At the very, very least those statements would have been ignored.

But, if not at *the most* or at the *very most,* it is certainly not impossible, it may even be probable, that they would have been more than just ignored; that they would have been met by demented rage as an affront to the very person of "the Führer," and followed immediately by intensified acts of persecution and extermination. There is here a history of the acceleration both of motivation and of subsequent violence. Kristallnacht was virtually unprovoked, so much so that its fabricated motive still remains highly tenuous if not absurd. The assassination of Heydrich as an indirect attack on Hitler himself was certainly provocative, and it brought about not merely punishment or retribution, but the *total annihilation* of anything whatsoever connected to the little town of Lidice in a *literally* diabolic effort to erase its very existence. What would have been the next stage of violence if the provocation were a direct insult to his office, to his rule, and to his self image? It has been suggested that there was little imaginable that could be much worse than what Hitler had already planned and achieved—as though to a madman evil were a finite entity. And he could certainly have accelerated the extermination process, particularly in countries like France and Italy where bureaucratic procedures were encumbering it.

An equally not inconceivable scenario, indeed one implicit in Hitler's Ostpolitik and explicit in the Wannsee Protocol, would be to strike at that nation of Slavs where almost all the death camps were already located and functioning (across the border, lest refined Aryan sensibilities be offended); to strike at that nation Pius—in his first encyclical six week after the war began—referred to as witnessing "the blood of so many cruelly slaughtered, even though civilians, [which] cries to heaven . . . , our beloved Poland." Five million Poles died during the war; it is impossible to say how many more it would have been if their methodic extermination could have been assured through the utilization of the most sophisticated German technology. A nightmare fantasy? More likely to a rabid fanatic, a dream fulfilled: at once a blow to that haughty aristocrat in the Vatican, that "diplomate de l'ancien régime," as well as the elimination of a negligible, incommodious, and—at least temporarily—brazenly disruptive "subhuman" people. And finally the fulfillment of the Reich's historic destiny, *Lebensraum*.

By the beginning of 1943, Hitler was enraged that only a million Poles had been driven from their homes and replaced by Aryan settlers. It was the "gradualism" of the elimination of the Jews that led to the Wannsee Conference in January of 1942. What pretext or demented motive would it have taken for Hitler, a year later, to hit upon a "final solution" to his Polish problem? Particularly given his growing instability as the war progressed, it is not preposterous to assume that the kind of public papal condemnation insistently demanded by Hochhuth and his successors would have triggered some such reaction. The utter irrationality of Hitler's declaration of war against the United States had already indicated the emergence of a clearly discernible streak of increasing fanaticism and lunacy.

This was precisely the issue in the Historikerstreit, with the "functionalists"—the very language tends to distance and reify the horror—arguing that the mass murder of Jews was not the result of a systematic plan developed by Hitler, but rather an *ad hoc* improvisation resulting from disorganization in the regime, from unanticipated military and political setbacks, etc.[11] One certainly need not embrace the thesis of William D. Rubenstein's *The Myth of Rescue* (1997) that virtually *nothing* by outside parties would have made a difference regarding the Holocaust, "difference" here meaning anything more "than the most minor and insignificant numbers." But his emphasis on the *absolute* centrality of Hitler in the decision-making process is far from a wild assumption. That Rubenstein implicitly exonerates Allied indifference to the plight of the victims in the camps is but another illustration of the kind of selective innocence and guilt that surrounds the Holocaust, since he also argues that, "In all likelihood—a likelihood probably amounting to near certainty—Hitler would have paid no heed whatever to any pronouncement on the Jews made by the Vatican."

One indication of Hitler's state of derangement as the war progressed was his absolute refusal, against the advice of all his advisors, to abandon any conquered territory regardless of its political or military insignificance, and regardless of the number of casualties suffered—all that, to satisfy what was clearly an egomaniac whim. That refusal continued until the surrender of Stalingrad in February, 1943. Given this deranged condition compounded by his habitual arrogance and vanity, "any pronouncement on the Jews made by the Vatican" would certainly have resulted in some act

---

[11] The Israeli historian, Yehuda Bauer, while sharply differing with one functionalist historian, Goetz Aly, who argues in *Endlösung* (Frankfurt, 1955) that not racist ideology motivated Holocaust perpetrators, but primarily the geopolitical ambition to transfer all ethnic Germans from the Baltic states, the Balkans, and ultimately the Soviet Union to "the Eastern marches of Germany," that is, to conquered Poland. This would mean the "displacement of non-German populations—mainly Polish, *but also* Jewish and Roma." Bauer of course rejects the argument that the Holocaust was merely a "but also" item in plans for Germandom, but he recognizes the fact "that there was nowhere to push these hundreds of thousands of Poles, Jews, and Roma." We know what happened to the Jews and Roma. What provocation, added to such Lebensraum concerns would it have taken to seek the Endlösung to the Polish problem? (Cf. Yehuda Bauer, *Rethinking the Holocaust,* New Haven, 2001.)

of vengeance, if not aimed directly at the person of the pope,[12] then quite likely at more innocent victims—who were conveniently located in the very lands needed for more German living space. Philippe Burrin in *Hitler and the Jews* (1989) suggested that it was in late summer of 1941—when Russian armies in the area of Stalingrad encircled and then captured 250,000 German troops and when the impact of American aid was beginning to be felt—that Hitler being personally insulted *definitively* made the long-contemplated extermination decision which would be implemented by the Wannsee Protocol. (Christopher Browning suggests on much more complicated and more plausible grounds, a decision date of shortly before July 31.) From Burrin's point of view, the specific decision at that particular time was conceived as expiation for German deaths and as an act of revenge against those aiding the Allied powers. Certainly it is possible that a similar act of expiatory revenge would follow on a public papal affront, "a flaming protest," to the German chancellor.

When asked during the war why he wasn't speaking out more forthrightly, Pius replied that indeed he had, and that he had been ignored. The parallel is with Hochhuth's *other* play, *Die Soldaten*, now either intentionally or out of ignorance overlooked by Catholics-come-of-age. The subtitle to the play is, loosely translated, "Death Notice on the Geneva Conventions." The central plot relates to opposition to the aerial destruction of civilian centers by Bishop George Bell of Chichester—also an outspoken advocate of nuclear disarmament in the post-war period. In *The Soldiers* he pleads in vain with Churchill to discontinue a tactic known as "saturation bombing" that would further erode the principle of noncombatant immunity and—more specifically in this drama—result in the incineration of Dresden. That city, well known to the Allies as a refuge for the aged and infirm, for children and women, and of absolutely no strategic importance, was engulfed in an enormous fire storm only three months before the end of the war.

---

[12] Some authors seem to envisage with complaisant acceptability a *Murder-in-the-Cathedral* (or rather -*Basilica*) scenario, as indicated by their frequent references to the apparently regrettable fact that "only one Catholic bishop died in the war"—actually there were three, but only the ghoulish would be counting.

(For the carping critics of the pope's "silence," the message here is: *De te fabula.*)

It should go without saying that of course there is no equation whatsoever of even the *aggregate* of these bombings with the monstrosity of the extermination camps. The latter has nothing to do with comparative numerical totals, as Judge Benjamin Halevi patiently but insistently pointed out when deflating at the Eichmann trial the latter's attempt to treat the two as morally equivalent. (But Allied bombing had posed a problem among those planning for the Nuremberg Trials, since it was seen as possibly giving an opening to countercharges—as a consequence, the issue was suppressed.) But there is a "proportionality" argument—and certainly one not lost on as politically and ethically sensitive a figure as Pius XII— relating to a publicly proclaimed condemnation. If his invocation of the traditional doctrine of noncombatant immunity from the very beginning and throughout the war was utterly ignored, even by the party of justice, it is surely uncertain that there would have been any different response to his condemnation of the initially almost inconceivable and historically unprecedented evil of the death camps. Concerning precisely this latter point, the historian Gerhard Weinberg in *Germany, Hitler, and World War II* (1995) suggests one, possibly anodyne, reason why the Allied powers did so little to aid the Jews: "The governments of Britain and the United States expressed repeated concern in public but would take few or no practical steps to help. This was due in part to a continuing inability to believe that what they knew was happening was indeed taking place." This argument, as noted earlier, Susan Zuccotti also employed to exculpate innumerable European leaders—except the pope.

In the final analysis, what does all this say of Pius XII? At the least it says that he like his predecessors and his successors was a man *in* history and *with* a history. Does it exonerate him? Certainly not, as I said at the beginning of this discussion, if one think of his office as threefold: prophet, priest, and *servus servorum*. As prophet, one may believe he should have vigorously and publicly proclaimed the truth, regardless of the consequences of such proclamation. One might even invoke Newman: "A silent saint is the object of faith rather than of affection. If he speaks, then we have the original before us." But as priest and servant Pius would have had other missions to fulfill. Though precisely as priest and servant, one of those missions was not *proclamation* but certainly *action*, no matter how silently carried out—indeed, to avoid retribution, intentionally carried out *silently*. Only those gifted in searching the reins and the heart can judge definitively whether he believed he had acted truly as Christ's vicar. But even the ungifted can decry the strident and facile affirmations that would make this Pope guilty of "deliberate falsehood." So, at the most, one can affirm with Kenneth Woodward—whom Wills cites when it suits his purpose—that "the Pope became the first figure of international stature to condemn what was turning into the holocaust."

But having acknowledged that fact, is there something else that must be affirmed? Certainly in the light of the perils attached to any strident condemnations or excommunications, one can even insist that precisely what Pius shouldn't have done was as prophet to "speak out" more clearly and vigorously. However, it certainly may be urged that that would hardly exhaust the demands of his office as priest and *servus servorum*, the foremost of which would have been—once the enormity of the Nazi extermination program became clear to him (a date that can now only with difficulty be regarded as historically uncertain)—to secretly but effectively employ the worldwide network of ecclesiastical officials from episcopal conferences and nunciatures down to parishes, religious orders, and their auxiliaries in an immense effort to frustrate in every possible way the criminals that brought to pass what history knows as the Holocaust. What he should have *done* is what he *apparently* was in fact somewhat half-heartedly doing. But even that observation needs to be nuanced since there is no way to know what the response to such a secret effort would have been on the part of his own subordinates.

The same critics who are convinced that a wholesale and wholehearted condemnation of the exterminations would have at the least partially frustrated them, because the power of the pope is presumably absolute and unquestioned, are those who doubt the possibility that insistence on secrecy by Pius—regarding his direct command to frustrate the Nazis in every possible way—would have been so totally obeyed as to remain utterly unknown over the last six decades. This issue is clearly hypothetical and I introduce it again mainly to point up the selectivity of judgment at play in the controversy. Anyone who would say, "I have no need for this hypothesis," must explain, why if the first assumption of obedience to the demands of the pontiff regarding a public condemnation of the Holocaust is valid—why is it not equally valid to assume an even greater degree of obedience regarding his command to maintain secrecy, particularly since the latter would relate only to a small select group of trusted subordinates?

— IV —

As is not unexpected, this treatment of Pius XII and the Holocaust ends in a question. But this is not the "Q and A" kind of "question" I referred to earlier in which one side insists on answers to highly imaginative and often purely speculative questions posed out of a desperate though admittedly understandable need for anything that might hold even the slightest possibility of that elusive thing called "closure." Rather, this is the kind of question that leaves one asking for surcease—for the hiatus I also mentioned earlier—in the hope of re-examining the issues with a fresher eye after the ill-concealed though well-understood acrimony of the post-Hochhuth era has further subsided. We owe it to Pius's successors that the suspicions and recriminations of that past are gradually being replaced by mutually assuring gestures, and in the case of John Paul II, by mutually assuring deeds.

Of course there will always be some professional historians, of varying degrees of accuracy and of motivation—as this and the preceding chapter well illustrate—who should continue their investigations, and there will undoubtedly be more and more revelations of antisemitic acts in the past, just as there will be more and more revelations of vicious acts of cruelty toward chattel slaves on this continent and in Africa. These will remain disturbing and distressing to all people of conscience who in the first instance have been struggling against antisemitism all of their adult lives, and in the second instance who have supported the cause of reparations from the very beginning. So long as this research is not exploited for personal ends whether by the historians or their auditors, and so long as the intent is not to scapegoat the sincerely remorseful present-day heirs—whether biologically or morally—of the original perpetrators of those evil acts, such scholarly efforts can only be applauded.

Concerning the pursuit of "personal ends," I proffer another parallel; again, I trust, not in violation of Acton's admonishments to Mary Gladstone that I alluded to earlier. The parallel is with Eugenio Pacelli and another major twentieth-century leader who was also acclaimed during his lifetime, though admittedly within his own community he was also a controversial but beloved figure. However, after his death, and particularly in the final two decades of the last century, he became (and continues to be) the object of attack and even vilification. All this is common enough for any powerful figure, though the parallel becomes more telling since this particular leader has also been denounced for indifference to the most frightful phenomenon of the modern era, the Holocaust—and I do not have reference to either Roosevelt or Churchill: both likely candidates, but posthumously almost apotheosized. Among charges brought against the leader I have reference to were that he had goals and interests that converged with those of Hitler—though without any complicity between the two; that he did little to counter Hitler's "final solution" as he was by his religious views and by his position absolutely required to do; that he and his followers were deceptive about precisely when they knew of the existence of the death camps; finally, and most unforgivably, that he and his followers gave precedence to their personal political concerns rather than to the rescue of Europe's Jews. There are other minor parallels having to do with temperament and administrative style: a certain air of haughtiness, of relishing the exercise of authority, of overriding opposing views, etc.—but those are obviously of little import.

The various charges I mention above have in varying form been brought against David Ben-Gurion and others associated with him in the foundational days of the state of Israel. One specific book representative of a "school" of revisionist Israeli students known as the New Historians is *Seventh Million: The Israelis and the Holocaust* (Tel Aviv, 1991; E.T., New York, 1993) by an American trained scholar, Tom Segev. Many of those charges as well as others dealing with the Palestinian question had been anticipated, and for many observers effectively refuted by Dana Porat in *The Blue and Yellow Star of David* (Tel Aviv, 1986; E.T., Cambridge, 1990). The charges have been directly addressed more recently by Shabtai Teveth in *Ben-Gurion and the Holocaust* (New York, 1996).

But at this point I want to move from the figures at center stage to their critics, some would say, their detractors. Since we are not talking about identical but about *"parallel* lives"—a genre with an ancient and honorable lineage—there is necessarily some imprecision involved, but the broader outline remains accurate. Just as the attack on Pius is putatively motivated by the need for "honesty" in the church and the larger good of Catholicism (as defined by some Catholic authors), so the attack on Ben-Gurion is motivated by "justice" for Palestinians and the larger good of the state of Israel (as defined by some Israeli authors). Denigrating Pius becomes a way of advancing an agenda of church "reform," just as denigrating Ben-Gurion becomes a way of advancing an agenda of political "reform"—and I have no doubt that there are scrupulous scholars of unquestioned integrity who can make a case against either or both men, a case that will be resolved only in the court of history. (Though it is obvious I haven't found that case being made with integrity or scrupulosity by the authors I have been criticizing.) It should go without saying that I hold no brief for Ben-Gurion or for partisans on any issue relating to Israeli politicians or politics. But just as I cited earlier Yehuda Elkana on the misfortunes attendant on the exploitation of the Shoah for Israeli political and cultural ends, I would here raise objections to its much more grievous—because extramural and arbitrary —exploitation by Catholics for ecclesiastical ends.

I present a final illustration of the latter. In a review of David L. Kertzer's *The Popes against the Jews: The Vatican's Role in the Rise of Modern Anti-Semitism* in *The New York Times* (September 23, 2001), Garry Wills writes of the author's "sickening task" covering "a stretch of two centuries" while not "giving way to the indignation most readers must feel," and resulting in a "staggeringly thorough job." To all of which anyone would probably say "amen," since the church's role in the horrors of antisemitism is a theme on which too much repetition or too many variations—of which Kertzer's book is clearly another—can never be enough. Equally enthusiastic was James Carroll in a front page story in the weekend "Arts & Ideas" section of *The New York Times* three weeks before Wills' review, where this author "of a critical history of the church's treatment of Jews" (i.e., Carroll) is quoted as saying: "The Vatican is obviously trying to backpedal as fast as it can from the dark history of the Catholic church. Kertzer is telling the truth."

As to "dark history" Kertzer acknowledges that he used the Vatican archives, and as to "trying to backpedal," it is difficult to see what makes it so obvious, since the last four decades have witnessed a vigorous program of dialogue and of public repentance moving forward at a pace unimaginable even during (much less, after) the conciliar years. Short of deliberate distortion it is almost inexplicable how Wills and Carroll could keep ignoring such progress, [13] and insist on living in the past, as if nothing had occurred in the forty years since Vatican II regarding Catholic-Jewish relations—particularly when most observers would say there has been a quantum leap towards increasingly amicable reconciliation. One is tempted to say: get a life *now*—stop all this gloating. Don't keep telling the gullible press, "I told you so!" at every putative exposé of the failures of historic Catholicism.

---

[13] One explanation may be found in the following bit of anonymous pseudo-Victorian doggerel:

> Wills the journalistic sleuth
> Discovers popes don't tell the truth.
> In *Constantine* Carroll cries
> Theology's a pack of lies.

> Such statements how can we combine?
> This perhaps explains the mystery:
> Wills thinks Carroll a divine,
> And Carroll looks to Wills for history.

No Catholic feels any sense of vindication when reading that an Israeli "New Historian" has found a possible source of Christian blood libels in the alleged killing of their own children by Jews fearful of attacks by crusaders. (The thesis seems tenuous at best, and useless in exonerating Christians for perpetuating the myth.) Similarly, with another "New Historian's" contention that for centuries on the feast of Purim Jews would mock Christians by burning images of the crucifix. Why would anyone be surprised or embarrassed that people persecuted from time immemorial would seek some retaliatory measure, whether symbolic or not? Yet these disclosures have roiled not just Israeli scholarship but the population at large.[14]

The ardor of both Wills and Carroll regarding Kertzer's book is not due to the latter's belief that "the debate over what Pius XII might have done during the Holocaust is a distraction from a more important question—what did the Catholic church do to help bring on the Holocaust in the first place?" ("Much too much" is the obvious answer of history—an answer which has been reaffirmed again and again by the second Vatican Council and by two popes.) But the ardor exhibited by our two critics does indicate that a different target than Kertzer's concern with antisemitism is in view. All those superlatives, "staggering," "thorough," "formidable achievement," come to their fine point in Wills' concluding comment on Pius IX: "Owen Chadwick said there was only one pope who would have canonized Pedro Arbués—Pius IX."[15]

---

[14] The two illustrations are described in *Hadassah* magazine (February, 1998); the historians' conflict has been widely discussed in the United States, in *Commentary, Tikkun,* and even *Lingua Franca.*

[15] During the reign of Ferdinand and Isabella, the Augustinian canon regular, Pedro Arbués—who had been appointed chief inquisitor of Aragon by Torquemada, the grand inquisitor of Castile—was murdered a year after his appointment while at prayer in the cathedral of Saragossa. His supporters believed he was martyred by what were variously called marranos, conversos, new Christians, i.e., Jews, who over two centuries in order to save themselves from extermination by mobs had accepted baptism. In folk memory, Arbués is recalled as a master of excruciating torture, but that memory is verifiably uncertain. All of these events were prelude to the final solution of their Catholic Majesties' Jewish problem when after the conquest of Granada, all Jews were expelled, and the inquisition continued to persecute the marranos/conversos, throughout the Spanish and Brazilian colonies.

The next sentence, and the last statement in the review: "I am afraid, *in the same way*, that there was only one pope who would have beatified Pius IX—*John Paul II.*"

How difficult was it to predict that this was where we would end up? The route is not merely circuitous, it is tortuously convoluted: from a nineteenth-century pope to a murdered fifteenth-century Dominican inquisitor, who was beatified in the next century by Innocent X who opposed the "Chinese rites," and then canonized three centuries later by that same nineteenth-century pope, Pius IX, who was in turn beatified in the twenty-first century by the suddenly emergent and climactically invoked—John Paul. (Through this daedalean maze of history, what thread was followed, with Mary Gordon perhaps as Ariadne, to bring the monster slayers out of that labyrinth?) So, now these doughty warriors have the real target in their sights and are once again ready to fire away. But there is a kind of perverse, self-destructive obsessiveness at work here that leads one to think that strabismus is symptomatic of myopia. *John Paul II* can certainly be criticized, as I have in these pages, for being increasingly centralist in his administration, for insisting on curial micromanagement of episcopal activities, for supporting the condemnation of wayward theologians, for trying to control traditionally independent agencies such as Catholic universities. The one thing he cannot be accused of is engaging in acts even remotely antisemitic—though he has certainly done things that offend individual Jews or Jewish groups, even as he has offended individual Catholics—Wills and Carroll for two—or Catholic groups. I excerpt from a statement of the Central Conference of American Rabbis and the Rabbinical Assembly in the year when it had been long known that Piux IX would be beatified (March 14, 2000):

> The Pope has affirmed the irrevocable nature of God's covenant with the Jewish people. He has condemned anti-Semitism as a "sin against God." He has forged diplomatic relations with Israel, recognizing the Jewish State's right to exist within secure borders. He has called upon Christendom to engage in *teshuva* for the atrocities of the Holocaust. He has apologized for the excesses of the Crusades and the Inquisition.

John Paul II has so little in common with Pio Nono—except occasionally, a white soutane—that to link them ideologically is to
be blinded to the obvious. Nor was Pius himself the creature of
total evil Wills habitually depicts—though he certainly was no
saint: nor is he now. But he did assure Rosmini of a fair, though
lengthy, investigation by the Roman censors, and he also canonized that gentle exponent of *l'humanisme dévot*, Francis de Sales.
But the depiction is not even apparently motivated by the claims
of historical honesty. It is motivated simply by a compulsion, once
again, to magnify the enduring monstrosity of John Paul. (And to
arbitrarily introduce his name into a book review of yet another
dismal tale of Christian antisemitism is as astonishing and unexpected as it was a few years back for a dramaturge-theologue to
suddenly bring up John Paul's name as that of a "homicidal liar
and endorser of murder.") However, if indeed Paris was worth a
mass, then who would question that the politic beatification of
the sad figure of poor obsidian Pius—a bone for rightists to gnaw
on—was worth getting down to the more serious business of, say,
empaneling historians to investigate the inquisition, or cementing
relations with Israel, or opening the door to church reunion, or
denouncing the evils of capital punishment, even in the very capital of that mode of punishment, the United States—and all this
at the cost of aggravating the pope's physically infirm condition.

One more parallel. In the year 2000 Lerone Bennett published
Forced into Glory: Abraham Lincoln's White Dream, one of several recent critical books, which also included *The Confederate War* by
Gary Gallagher, and *The Glittering Illusion* by Sheldon Vanauken.
It was the Bennett book, however, that received the most widespread attention in the majority of "mainstream" reviews (e.g.,
The New York Times, under the heading, "Lincoln the Devil"), accusing the author of not only bad scholarship but of failing to understand the genius of Lincoln, his political astuteness, and his
recasting of the constitution to give primacy to the union over the
states—though these criticisms did little to answer Bennett's fundamental contention that Lincoln was a white supremacist at

heart, and that the Emancipation Proclamation, however strategically beneficial in winning the war, was in effect a hoax because it had no effect on slavery in the Confederacy, and explicitly did not apply to slaves in regions controlled by the Union. The state of Lincoln's "heart," is of relative unimportance; the second contention, however, is a crucial issue relating to an ethic of universal humanity.

That contention would be that Lincoln was responsible for crimes committed against slaves in the exempt regions from the period of the Proclamation to the passage of the thirteenth amendment—even though he had been assassinated a few months before the latter was passed. So for a span of approximately three years, people who could have been given their *human* (not "citizen") *rights* were treated as chattel, and this in the regions where the Union government was in control. Unpunished were such crimes—indeed, such acts were not even recognized as criminal—as the continuing dissolution of slave families, the selling of slave children, the rape of slave women, and on and on. (It says something about the callousness of the modern conscience that such acts are, even today, justified in the name of political expediency—after all, it was *only* three years, and for the "long-term greater good.")

I introduce first a hypothesis, and second a familiar trope, concerning a laudatory review of Bennett's indeed quite worthy book—and certainly in terms of scholarship at least as commendable as those books that have been the primary focus of all my criticisms. Let us suppose that a hypothetical reviewer, after commending the author's detailed descriptions of slavery's evils, praised him for "not giving way to indignation," in "undertaking his sickening task," and in the end for producing a "formidable achievement." The reviewer then contrasted the book with the "orthodox" treatments of Lincoln, singling out a particular work that had glorified the president as a noble figure, a paragon of democratic vision. The reviewer went on to maintain that it would take a monster to praise a president who had been responsible for so many crimes against so many innocent and helpless people. The reviewer added that even if Lincoln's encomiast *professed* to ignorance about all those crimes of a century and a half ago, *he simply must have known* the truth.

Now I introduce my trope, *parvis componere magna* ("to compare great things to small"), our hypothetical reviewer concludes, dramatically and possibly rather exaggeratedly: "I know of only one writer who would have so exalted Abraham Lincoln—Garry Wills in *Lincoln at Gettysburg.*" Compare this with the conclusion to the review of Kertzer's *The Popes against the Jews* above: "I know of only one pope who would have beatified Pius IX—John Paul II." Both are seemingly arbitrary assaults; but in the case of Bennett's Lincoln book there is at least a historic figure arguably guilty of the evils alleged of him.

Who is to say how much John Paul knows about the crimes attributed to Pedro Arbués or the evils attributed to Pius IX—or even how much Pius IX knew about events four centuries after they allegedly took place? We do know that John Paul in his address of October 31, 1998, to the Study Conference on the Inquisition which he had established said: "The problem of the Inquisition belongs to a troubled period of the Church's history, which I have invited Christians to revisit with an open mind." He then declared as he had earlier, "Another painful chapter of history to which the sons and daughters of the Church must return with a spirit of repentance is that of the acquiescence given, especially in certain centuries, to intolerance and even the use of violence in the service of truth." (Again, to compare great things to small: that is more than we have heard the orthodox Lincoln scholar say about the Emancipation Proclamation.)

Anyone having a passing familiarity with Henry Kamen's *Spanish Inquisition: A Historical Revision* (New York, 1998) or Edward M. Peters' *Inquisition* (New York, 1989) knows how fluid and unstable are old convictions based on folklore, prejudice, and superstition relating to the inquisition. Kamen's book is not just a revised version of the original *Spanish Inquisition* of thirty years ago; it is a new book, hence the unusual subtitle. Peters devotes much of his account to the popular and anti-Romanist "myths" (his word) that grew up around *this* peculiar institution. To briefly illustrate the fluctuations surrounding the inquisition in general and specifically the murder of Arbués, Henry Charles Lea, the canonical nineteenth-century historian (after whom Edward Peters' professorial chair is named), believed the murder was an act of revenge by "conversos" or "new Christians," pejoratively known as "marranos." In this he had been followed by almost all scholars until *The Origins of the Inquisition in Fifteenth Century Spain* (New York, 1995) by B. Netanyahu—certainly the new standard bearer in the field—who believes Arbués was killed by the inquisition itself acting at the behest of King Ferdinand. "Revised" Kamen doubts this possibility for want of documentary evidence.

No one can defend even a single auto-da fé, but the point is that if for four hundred years the assassination was shrouded in fictions, fabrications, folktales, and even today is clouded by controversial versions, how would the truth be known to Pius IX, much less to the villainous John Paul? But among Lincoln students, save for Lerone Bennett and sympathetic followers, no one in authority and place has called for the establishment of a kind of truth and reconciliation commission or even a truth and justice commission to assess a possible historic evil on the part of a beloved president. There *is* such a commission for the inquisition, and it is looking at the relation of that body to several beloved popes.[16]

There are two lessons—which intermingle—to be drawn from this final illustration, first, on the relatively narrow ecclesial level, and second on the larger societal level. First, for the Catholics whom I have been discussing, the papal icon can be gleefully smashed while the political icon is to be carefully burnished; the "Holy Father" is to be demeaned while the "Founding Fathers"

---

[16] For the same reason that a majority of ecclesiastics would not be regarded favorably in an investigation of popes and the inquisition, few would look favorably upon the presence of conventional scholars from the Lincoln history guild on such a truth and justice commission which would be concerned with first, findings of fact, and second, compensatory redress if called for. Moreover, since there have been so many congressional hearings resulting in legislation relating to such things as civil rights, equal opportunity, even quotas, and since there are partisan and regional issues involved, such a commission would ideally be made up predominantly of social philosophers formed in the tradition of John Rawls' *A Theory of Justice*.

are to be exalted; many evils of modern life, both communal and individual, are less the fault of the national ethos and heritage than of historic Catholicism and the papacy; lastly, in both the practical and the speculative order, patriotism trumps piety (precisely one of the fears alleged by a few of the defenders of Pius XII's "silence") as Catholics settle comfortably into the "non-lasting city" rather than seek "the one which is to come."

Second, on the larger societal level, if antipapalism is the real antisemitism of all intellectuals, spiritual and physical racial animus is the antisemitism of the mass of white America, regardless of class. And this may be indicated in part by the reception given to Bennett's book ("Lincoln the Devil") by those who have no problem with the demonization of popes—while whitewashing America's two and a half centuries of slavery. The palliation takes the form of such bromides as that, while admittedly it was a problem, it was traditional, it was customary, it was a social convention, it was sanctioned over time, etc., and as far as the North was concerned it was on the way to being solved, according to Lincoln, "as fast as circumstances permit"—all made abundantly clear by books such as *Lincoln at Gettysburg*.

To return the discussion to *this* book's primary focus, it should be noted that Pius XII's relation to the actual Holocaust during the war years—even if given the worst possible interpretation—is provably slight. This stands in sharp contrast to the glorification of Lincoln whose relation to the slave holocaust is provably causal during the last of the war years and before passage of the thirteenth amendment. Whether Lincoln from the period of his election onward intended to free the slaves is *sub judice* (perhaps to be resolved by the optative commission envisioned above), and remains unknown notwithstanding the verbal contortions and textual fundamentalism entailed in proving that Lincoln's "new birth of freedom" refers to fulfilling the promise of the first birth at the Declaration of Independence with its reference to "all men are created equal."

5

CONTEXTUALIZING PAPAL SINS

A Cautionary Tract on Reform

> "You write with haste and without consideration; you write on subjects which you have not studied, and do not understand, and which are out of your province."
>
> *Provost Hawkins*

Having just concluded this treatment of the arbitrary certitudes brought to bear on Holocaust judgments with all their related implications, and after previously discussing what I have referred to as the methodology of mendacity in chapters two and three, it now remains to begin the promised reconstructive phase of this book. I continue to take Garry Wills' *Papal Sin* as "exemplary" (though I will glance occasionally at James Carroll's ancillary venture) since its prosecutorial indictment is the widest ranging and most intensely pursued of all the books I listed at the beginning of the second chapter. Though I shall be pointing out errors of fact rather than of interpretation, the major contribution of this chapter will be to put such errors in a historical setting that will help illuminate how the forces of renewal and reaction have played off one another in the past and in our own time.[1] Thus while Wills' many errors are the point of departure, it

---

[1] The motif here is from Bernard Häring—in what is his spiritual testament to the church—writing of experiences at Vatican II: "When there was absolutely no progress being made, no movement at all, I held on. I had a natural instinct, and a grace too, no doubt: I always saw, first and foremost, the encouraging signs of the time. . . . Anyone who experiences a historical epoch, where the dynamic of thesis and antithesis clearly manifests itself, can dare to hope, after close in-

is their historic contextualization which begins the process of "bridge building" that I referred to in chapter one. This process will be concluded in chapters six and seven where I treat of what might be called after Cardinal Congar, "true and false reformers."

— I —

The corpus of Wills' work is large, and often marked by a polemic style which, particularly in his religious books, can be characterized—among other traits—as crotchety. *Bare Ruined Choirs, Politics and Catholic Freedom,* and now *Papal Sin* are explicitly about religion, *Confessions of a Conservative* implicitly so. Had one not read the analysis in the two previous chapters, one might assume this merely bespeaks the significance of the religious and the theological in Wills' scheme of things. But it now should be evident—and will be increasingly so as we progress—that this represents what is traditionally known as *odium theologicum*: in David Hume's well known definition, "that degree of rancor which is most furious and most implacable." Such would seem to be, at least in part, what motivates the methodological excesses considered earlier and the factual blunders to be considered now—both of which undermine his program for restructuring Catholicism and stand in sharp contrast to the reformative efforts of his historically more effective antecedents. The "cautionary" element in the chapter title above, is merely to indicate that Wills' *Papal Sin* may be regarded as being in many ways, a how-*not*-to-do-it book.

The very title itself is arresting, and certainly calculated to shock great numbers of Roman Catholics, while also pandering to the exploitation of scandal among the general public and of prejudice among the adherents of traditionally anti-Romanist groups. It is not merely the juxtaposition of the pope with sinning, which will suggest to almost everyone at best some kind of dubious paradox; even more, it is the use of the singular noun. Papal *sins* would

---

spection of the whole picture, for a new synthesis. And that is the case *right now*" (*My Hope for the Church,* 1999).

indicate merely the failings or aberrations all mortals are heir to—as self-righteous journalists have over the past few years casually referred to presidential sins. Their very multiplicity diminishes their gravity. "O Luther, thou hast ninety-five theses; how terrible! But in a deeper sense, the more theses the less terrible," wrote Kierkegaard in his *Attack upon Christendom*. But "papal *sin*" sounds generic, sounds as though it were a type of evil which defined the papacy and a term to be entered into the lexicon of students of the "discipline" (a discipline which Wills denominates with a nineteenth-century coinage "papolatry") who will cooly, scientifically, and of course bravely, employ such argot where historical rectitude demands.

The subtitle of the book, *Structures of Deceit,* as is not unusual, amends the title. Relative to "misreadings, misinterpretations, and misrepresentations" regarding "the church's behavior" over the centuries, Wills affirms that "there is nothing here as clear-cut and direct as simple lying. That is why I speak of the 'structures of deceit' that recruit people almost insensibly to quiet cosmetic labors buttressing the church by 'improving' its substructure." But in moving from papal sin to structures of deceit, we have also moved from the very concrete person of the pope to the very abstract notion of the church. Is it that the former sins, while the second merely ("nothing clear-cut and direct") deceives? The danger in the use of such hypostatized abstractions is that they lead to the victory of historicism over history. I cite an exemplary sentence from Wills' earlier critique of Catholicism, *Bare Ruined Choirs*: "In the wake of Vietnam, America which has been very skilled in certitude throughout its history, has become a new Rome capable of self-doubt." Now, it is true as Toynbee said in *A Study of History* that, "It is hardly possible to write two consecutive lines of historical narrative without introducing such fictitious personifications as 'England,' 'France,' 'the Conservative Party,' 'The Church'. . . ." But it is also true that when this leads to the attribution of interiority and self-direction to abstractions or artificial constructs, one is more likely to be chronicling the fictional than the factual. It is as we have all seen the favorite device of propagandists whether of the left or the right: "Russia is still intent on world conquest"; "the Democrat party solves problems by throwing more money at them"; "the Republican party favors people over government," etc.

Wills never defines "the church" though he speaks of "the great truths of faith—the Trinity, the Incarnation, the Mystical Body of Christ," the latter traditionally being defined as church. (Curiously, among these great truths there is no mention of resurrection.[2]) I proffer two efforts at definition from two quite different sources, both of which may help advance the issue of where precisely to locate this alleged sin and deceit:

> The Church is something of a monarchy since its unique head is Christ, and since the first of its human pastors was the bishop of Rome. It is something of an oligarchy if one considers the small number of those who exercise power in it. It is also something of a democracy by the royal priesthood of the faithful and the apostolic mission which is confided to all its members. But strictly speaking it is nothing of each of these in particular and it is something of all of these at once.

That is taken from Patriarch Maximos IV *(L'Eglise grecque melkite au Concile,* 1967), one of those Patriarchs concerned about *Nostra Aetate*, not out of antisemitism but out of fear of political repression—all part of the price of being in a world-wide church. The second definition is from an earlier era and a different continent: "Let there be individual action [in the Church]. Laymen need not wait for priest, nor priest for bishop, nor bishop for pope. The timid move in crowds, the brave in single file." That is taken from Archbishop John Ireland *(The Church and Modern Society,* 1896).

---

[2] What resurrection is for Wills is not brought forth—except that it is apparently dispensable. For James Carroll the resurrection is not a dogma but a consolatory myth recorded for a primitive community by a scribe dispensing comfortable palliatives about togetherness. "Immediately after Jesus' death, the circle of his friends began to gather. Their love for him, instead of fading in his absence, quickened, opening into a potent love they felt for one another . . . and a repeated *intuition* that there was 'one more member' than could be counted. That intuition is what we call the Resurrection. . . . To *imagine* Jesus as risen was to expect that soon all would be. . . . His love survived his death—which is what Resurrection means" *(Constantine's Sword,* pp. 124–25).

Both definitions give us a notion of the church far different from that set forth in Wills' book. Indeed, most of the issues chosen to illustrate *papal* sin and structures of deceit have proved to be balking points for other religious bodies, including many that are identified with "liberal"postures. Are they too trapped in Romanist structures? As I pointed out in the two preceding chapters, issues such as the holocaust and antisemitism, contraception and abortion, clerical abuse and "hierarchology" (the term is Cardinal Congar's), as well as prejudice based on race, gender, or sexual preference—all have spawned intense controversy and hateful practice in virtually every institution in Western society from major universities to major religious groups to major corporations to major governmental agencies.[3]

Why then the dredging up here of these and other institutional

---

[3] At the end of this chapter I shall discuss in detail the nature of these putative "structures" that engender sin and deceit Here it is merely necessary to observe that the sociological nomenclature is itself deceptive since, as so often with technical jargon, it obfuscates more than it clarifies: one may think of those who would describe the Holocaust as a "functionalist" phenomenon. Possibly, the most magnificent passages in the *Apologia* occurs in the climactic final chapter—a peroration to the tedious historical reckonings that precede it— which can only be described as a personal statement and a defense of Catholicity almost overwhelming in its grandeur, and its truth. I will cite only its conclusion which gets to the core of what culture theorists want to call structures of deceit: "And so I argue about the world;—*if* there be a God, *since* there is a God, the human race is implicated in some terrible aboriginal calamity. It is out of joint with the purposes of its Creator. This is a fact, a fact as true as the fact of its existence; and thus the doctrine of what is theologically called original sin becomes to me almost as certain as that the world exists, and as the existence of God." Sin or evil does not become a structure or "structured" by repetition whether over the centuries or over numerical increases, however dramatic, in the human race. Did brutally punishing or lynching black people become evil only in 1865 after the passage of the thirteenth amendment?

What Peter Damian condemned at the dawn of the medieval period in *The Gomorrah Book,* what was condemned a century before the Reformation in *De squaloribus Romanae Curiae,* what was condemned in the nineteenth century by Antonio Rosmini in *The Five Wounds of Holy Church,* what Protestant Kingsley condemned in his statement that "truth, for its own sake has never been a virtue with the Roman clergy," what protesting Wills condemns in *Papal Sin*—none of these is due to some new cultural insight resulting in a sociological categorization that blurs the nature of perennially recurring vices and of attendant individual responsibility.

vices as though they were unique to Catholicism? There is, as I also mentioned in chapter three, an allegedly reformist agenda here; but that doesn't explain the noisome details, the incessant accusations, the exaggerations and distortions. By way of answer to the question, Richard Hofstadter's "paranoid style" comes first to mind; then there are all those motives referred to in the previous chapter, psychological, political, *and* journalistic—the latter being particularly salient since we live in media-dominated age, that is, an age of overstatement in tone and overreaching in scope. But one still has to raise the question of "why" this concentration on Catholicism *only* when treating of evils diffused throughout the whole of western society. That answer cannot be, as I said in chapter one, an innocent declaration to the effect that "because I'm Catholic that's what I know best." Nor regarding the immediate point of Wills' book, can the answer to that question be that one should expect more of "the church" on the ground that it embodies the one true religion ("outside the church, no salvation," as the old maxim had it). Such expectation is foreclosed because in the final paragraph of his book, one may read: "I do not think that my church has a monopoly on the [Holy] Spirit, which breathes where She will, in every Christian sect and denomination . . . , among Jews and Buddhists and Muslims and others."

Of course, it may merely be that from his position these evils appear darker and more heinous, just as the moon being closer to the observer looks larger than the sun. If the last half a millennium of Christianity is seen through the narrow lens of the dark night of the spirit that has engulfed many Catholics during the past three decades, then one may indeed be tempted to chronicle only sin and deceit. But the spectacle of vision through such a narrow lens may also reflect its source in a narrow mind. Nor is "chronicle" the precise term. What we have here is the result of "investigative reporting," as contemporary euphemists would term it. In less pretentious times it was simply called "muckraking," and its product appeared on the "front page" celebrated in drama and cinema, and known as a "scoop"—though not now in the sense of Evelyn Waugh, but rather—to call a spade a spade—in the sense of implement for scavenging. In any event, I shall not concentrate on Wills' detailed and somewhat breathless exposé of those personal and social moral issues implicit in the larger culture and exhaustively and exhaustingly treated in the religious, the general, *and* the tabloid press.

— II —

My focus here is on Wills' slant on the politics of authoritative ecclesiastical decisions (and of course on the context of those decisions), because that politics is the theological and historical foundation on which are allegedly built the "structures of deceit" relating to all the evils mentioned above. But given the fact that those latter have indeed been so broadly treated in the secular and religious media and all their lesser adjuncts, the companion question emerges as for whom precisely the present book has been written. Every educated Catholic is not only utterly familiar with the nature of these evils, but is also, according to her position, her conviction, and her lights engaged in the struggle against the social and intellectual defects which Wills reprises. Many of these Catholics for over four decades have been citing at length and in detail the same intellectual warriors—according to Wills his "own heroes include . . . Lord Acton and John XXIII"—in the same battles described in his book.

Moreover, much of this took place during the time when he was snidely denigrating Pope John's efforts: *mater sì, magistra no,* was it not? And although in support of his thesis on deceitful structures he now introduces Acton's oft-cited judgment on papal abuse of power, he had in an earlier day at the height of the controversies listed above, and in the cavalier style of Lytton Strachey for whom Acton was "a hysterical reviler of priestcraft," dismissed the import of this "unfortunate dictum": "What 'absolute power' and 'absolute corruption' are supposed to mean in the mouth of an historian, no one can say"—except, fortuitously, one liberal *converso* and practitioner of the Higher Journalism, and one autobiographical exhibitionist who discovered the papal allusion nowhere but in *Papal Sin*—and this, apparently only after the process of composing a two millennia, 700 page "history" *cum* memoir of Catholicism and antisemitism.

Even when employing a moderate hermeneutic of suspicion in this assessment of the politics of authoritative decisions, this is not the appropriate place for a detailed consideration of Wills' familiarity with the history of his own church—a "history" summarily sketched in the beginning of chapter three where I pointed out more than a dozen egregious errors of fact, and then went into a series of distortions relating to some of the most revered figures in contemporary Catholicism relating to the Holocaust and the period of the second World War. My concern now is with what might generously be called voodoo history, but with an emphasis on the significance of serious errors that go beyond the mere failure of Wills to have done his homework—errors that suggest that in his reading of contemporary and past history he clearly appears to be practicing the very deceit he so freely denounces in ecclesiastical officials: as did another "hero," Fra Paolo Sarpi.

As for "deceit," we read that "in 1937 . . . Pius XI signed the Lateran treaty . . . , at a time when Mussolini *wanted church approval for his actions*." However, as every Catholic "schoolboy and even every Bachelor of Arts" (cf. "The Golden Trashery of Ogden Nashery") used to know, the treaty was signed by Cardinal Gasparri *in 1929*. In this shift from the actual date to this fabrication, we encounter—at least in this chapter— the first instance of Wills' exercising the same deception he elsewhere vigorously censures. In 1929 Mussolini had had control of the government for only six years, and there was little widespread criticism—"made the trains run on time" was the complacent outsiders' view—and thus no need for "church approval." But by 1937 Mussolini was reviled in most of Western Europe, in Africa, and in North America. His war in Abyssinia had been condemned by the League of Nations and sanctions were imposed on Italy; the deposed emperor, Haile Selassie, was a universally pitied but revered figure, though less in his own country than on the world stage; and Mussolini had forged an alliance with Hitler that among other evils in that very year led Italy to join Germany in the infamous bombing of Guernica. Surely 1937 was an opportune time for seeking "church approval." To drive home this particular "papal sin" Wills adds in a footnote that, "Mussolini so wanted church approval in the middle of the 1930s that he moved *almost* to the right of the Pope on some issues."

In passing, it may be noted that the year 1937 for the Lateran treaty is assuming canonical status. Karen Armstrong, invariably credentialized by her publishers as "a former nun," intercalates it in a *New York Times* Op-Ed piece illustrated by a four-column drawing (July 16, 2000), where it is combined with other chronological errors to support her pro-PLO position regarding Jerusalem in the peace negotiations. From her point of view Jerusalem is to all of East Jerusalem as Rome is to the Vatican City, regardless of the Lilliputian topography of the latter. We have perhaps a new school of Catholic revisionist historians aborning, and one dismissive in the name of a grander vision of the claims of chronology. [4] This latter phenomenon is worth briefly pursuing, as Ms. Armstrong observes: "The city *only* became central to Judaism after its destruction by Nebuchadnezzar in 586 B.C," whereas it "has been sacred to Muslims *ever since* the Prophet Muhammad began to preach in 610 A.D." As the preceding three chapters illustrate, for these media-driven historicists facts don't necessarily relate to theories.

First, biblical scholars are unanimous in dating the Davidic kingdom at ca. 1000 B.C.E. (so Ms. Armstrong errs by "only" four

---

[4] There seems to be something about Pius IX in particular that discombobulates Wills. A scholarly detective of the sort I have defined in chapter two might find here a useful clue or, what less inquisitorial scholars would call, "a heuristic device"; since mention of *that* Pius is always linked to inexcusable gaffes of interpretation and of dating. As to the latter, on Pius's watch, Wills' own chronology goes awry: concerning Pio Nono's *Syllabus of Errors* delivered in 1854, Wills discusses "the first draft of January 1869." Again, Wills describes how Pius "could almost be said to have wept himself into power," so that "to criticize him became a way of joining his persecutors, who drove him from Rome in 1858." I don't want to keep introducing Macaulay's mythic schoolboy, but the fact is Pius fled from the Italian nationalists ten years earlier. Finally, he adds ten years on to Pius's reign. All this may hint at some deeply rooted animosity which might be helpful in explaining the kinds of distortions we saw regarding the dogma of the Immaculate Conception, and which we will see again regarding the *Syllabus* and papal infallibility.

centuries); second, the Prophet neither preached in Jerusalem nor about Jerusalem (save to admonish the praying faithful to bow *not* to Jerusalem but to Mecca); and, third, its sacrality is based not on the Qur'an but on its pious glossators who—after the fashion of devout commentators, whether Christian or Muslim—asserted that Jerusalem was the locus of the Prophet's oneiric ascent into the heavens. If Ms. Armstrong buys into that etiolated etiology there's a house in the town of Loreto in which she might want to invest some intellectual capital; or she might want to look at this assumption of an Assumption in Tom Robbins' "The Sixth Veil" (*Skinny Legs and All*, 1990).

But such facts (and fictions) don't get in the way of allegedly noble goals, whether Wills's unmasking of deception or Armstrong's promotion of peace. Nor can one be sure what is worse, their arrogance or their ignorance—probably the latter, in confirmation of the rustic adage that you can lead the worse to *hauteur* but you can't make 'em think. (An interesting footnote: the *Times* after being informed of the error regarding the Lateran treaty acknowledged the "misstatement" without mentioning author, title, or informant. Thus do "journals of record" keep the record straight.)

Wills next tells the reader that one Don Luigi Bosco was a leader of a Catholic party "undercut" in *the aftermath* of the allegedly pro-Mussolini Lateran treaty. This is intended primarily to illustrate the baneful consequences of papal acts, even on patriotic Catholic priests. Ignored, or unknown, by Wills is the fact that Alcide de Gasperi, another party leader and later post-war premier who was a close personal friend of the deceit-ridden Pius XI as well as of "Don Luigi," affirmed that even the latter would have approved of the treaty. The latter is of course Don Luigi Sturzo, founder of the Partito Popolare who went into exile in 1924, *five years before* the actual signing of the treaty. (Maybe our author had in mind the Hollywood flick, "Donnie Brasco," and again distraction resulted as the plot hit the fan.) What *is* odd here, however, is not so much the presence of more impossible chronology, but the conflation of a nineteenth-century founder of a religious order, Don John Bosco, with the founder of a twentieth-century political party. Our mythic Luigi Bosco was possibly exiled to the equally mythic Boscobel, W. Zembla of Nabokov's *Pale Fire.*

I cited Sturzo's monumental treatise, *Church and State,* in a *Commonweal* essay on Congar's *Vraie et fausse Réforme dan l'Eglise* which bears on the present discussion—though it doesn't get into "papal sins." The date of the article, ironically, was August 15, feast of *the Assumption*—if the "Prophet" why not the "Blessed Virgin"? The latter, as we saw in the conclusion to chapter three, another of Wills' haunting bogeys•whom he describes as having had doctrinal, ferial, and titular honorifics "heaped on her" to reinforce papal deceptions. His daimonic heebie-jeebies were unsuccessfully exorcized in that tour described earlier to various Florentine galleries sniffing out apotheoses of Mary—and presumably ending his peregrinations at the itty-bitty-Pitti Palace. In any event, Don Sturzo wrote: "Clement XIV is the last of the Popes whose acts have been subjected even by Catholic historians to open criticism [largely for his suppression of the Jesuits]. It is fortunate that we find this precedent in respect of a recent pope, so that no irreverence can be imputed to anyone using the same historical method towards some of his successors"—but historical method, not historical retribution. To this day, I believe it is uncertain whether pontiff or incipient dictator was behind Sturzo's exile, though Sturzo himself told Cardinal Bourne that it was Pius XI, acting through his Secretary of State. But the exile did have the unexpected boon of bringing Sturzo for a couple of decades to England and the United. States, where he was a frequent and vigorous participant in public debates on the dangers of fascism as well as a contributor to the major liberal journals. (Unquiet goes the Don.)

— III —

I don't know if this confusion over Don Luigi *whoever* betrays some latent stereotype; but such would certainly seem lurking behind the description of Paul VI "with his sad sunken eyes in their smudgy Italian sockets." (Those familiar with Willsian journalese may recognize the spin on "smudgy Italian sockets" as indicative of a "dim bulb.")[5] Pope Paul of course is *mise en scène* (sin¢) as the pontiff responsible for appointing the commission whose views were ignored in the composition of the encyclical *Humanae Vitae*. The context is the euphoria "over new freedoms . . . that characterized the 1960s." But the record demands noting again that Wills only very tardily responded to these "new freedoms"—witness his comments on John XXIII. One is put in mind of A.J.P. Taylor's observation on the revolutions of 1848 when Germany reached a turning point—only Germany refused to turn. Nevertheless, he does explain the issues, discusses the major players, and weaves the various historical threads into an adequate chronological depiction—the latter perhaps a bit redundantly, as when detailing the *quondam* condom leap in the mid-nineteenth century of vulcanization engineered by Charles Goodyear—at this point the

---

[5] Wills often writes like a latter-day physiognomist gifted with the uncanny power of interpreting facial features. There is the memorably nasty instance of his comparing a mere youth courting his bride at the White House—who grew up to become a major military historian, David Eisenhower—to the puppet character, Howdy Doody. Less vicious, since it relates to a nineteenth-century figure, whom Wills professes to admire, is what can only be described as eighteenth-century psychology applied to Cardinal Newman. Our Lavatery analyst describes him as a man "whose *personality* seemed to elude men behind his great hawk beak of a nose, his effeminate manner, his softly seducing voice." In this case, Wills eclipses Geoffrey Faber's fabricated Freudian assay, *Oxford Apostles* (who were implicitly being compared to the even more gay Cambridge ones), proving Wills to be indeed *il miglior fabbro*. Moreover, most portraits before Newman's later years show no such deformity which, to the degree it may exist outside of Wills' imagination is attributable to the onset of old age, perhaps like Wills' own unanalyzed *menton triplé*. Or perhaps he is merely again confused among these *personae dramatis;* here identifying Newman with W.G. Ward who boasted: "I have the mind of an archangel in the body of a rhinoceros." From Newman we have a more modest, and profound, estimation: "I am an old man; my hair white, my eyes sunk in, but when I shut my eyes and merely think, I can't believe I am more than 25 years old, and smile to think how differently strangers must think of me from my own internal feelings." This was written two years before the *Apologia* where there is an undeniable playfulness (evident particularly in the retorts to Kingsley) and an energy in writing that any twenty-five year old would envy. The portrait that it is generally agreed best represents Newman in his old age is Lady Coleridge's done sixteen years before his death.

saga goes flat and the reader is tempted to retire from the discussion.

But though the yarn ends, the spinning does not; particularly as it relates to the moralist John C. Ford who, notwithstanding his unenlightened views on contraception, had vigorously *during* World War II, and following the lead of John K. Ryan, condemned obliteration bombing as immoral (one may recall from the last chapter, Hamburg and Dresden), and courageously maintained the same position *in the sixties* with regard to a national policy of nuclear "deterrence"—this when an assortment of cold warriors were embracing the doctrine of massive retaliation, and people like Wills were so obsessed with individual morality as to appear oblivious to social morality. Not all consistency in ethical issues is reprehensible as—one might add in this context—is illustrated by the dantesquely demonized Cardinal Ottaviani who in 1947 and again at Vatican II called for the condemnation of the instruments of total warfare, and was supported by such of his myriad opponents as Archbishop Roberts and Patriarch Maximos.

What Wills inadequately conveys regarding *Humanae Vitae* is the reaction in its aftermath which was calm, consistent, and both universal and unceasing among educated Catholics in opposition to the curial view. This opposition was articulated in books, magazines, and public forums that were focused not only on contraception as such but also on the relevance of natural-law principles, on infallibility, on the authority of encyclicals, on the social and political implications of the condemnation in a pluralist society, and above all on the right to active dissent from ecclesiastically sanctioned teaching. Nevertheless, as to whether even the members of the papal commission were complicit in wrongdoing, Wills does not waver: "A cultivated submission to the papacy had been, for them, a structure of deceit, keeping them from honesty with themselves, letting them live within a lie."

And so overwhelming, he alleges, was such a structure that even this highly educated body of people was "surprised" at the notion that the church can and must change. But such a "surprise" is simply unbelievable to anyone living through the period and aware of what I have referred to as the universal opposition to the curial view. The articles, the debates, the books (among many, one by Canon Drinkwater, and another edited by Archbishop Roberts with an interesting title suggested by the German-Canadian theologian, Gregory Baum, *Contraception and Holiness*)—all affirmed that on this issue change was a ubiquitous reality. If Wills in his conservative days as a contributor and supporter of *The National Review* could explicate in print the notion that the encyclical *Mater et Magistra* was an "exercise in triviality," why would it be surprising that a majority of Catholics could acknowledge change in the nature of their sexual relations, and view the encyclical *Humanae Vitae* as a relatively trivial intrusion into their personal lives?

The judgment that a structure of deceit, kept the members of the papal commission or *a fortiori* the members of the Roman curia "from honesty with themselves, letting them live within a lie"—this judgment exposes the fatal sociological flaw of the book. I have noted from the beginning of this chapter that it is not just Catholicism with its "cultivated submission to the papacy" that has succumbed to the scandalous prejudices and practices enumerated earlier; it has been virtually every religious, educational, political, and cultural body in Western society. Yet we know many of these bodies to be composed to a greater or lesser degree of individuals of unquestioned rectitude. Herein lies a quandary that has perplexed, or rather bedeviled, political moralists from at least Aristotle to Burke and Niebuhr: the tendency of every social organization, every institution, every consortium to enlist its membership in the pursuit of controversial goals, however alien to the individual member's personal inclination. Of course, it is *not* a question of collusion in evil, or of extremist groups. I am talking about "mainline" organizations of ordinary well-meaning citizens: chambers of commerce, unions, professional associations, fraternal (and sororal) organizations, support-groups and auxiliaries of every religious persuasion.

I will not go into the social-psychological explanation; there is certainly a reciprocal "trade-off" here, a voluntary subordination of the individual to the *esprit de corps*, a subordination of personal

view to the supportive, collective, and cohesive ideology. Instances abound: ethical political party members decline to oppose
a children-endangering embargo against a harmless nation, while
advocating trade with another nation previously responsible for
the deaths of thousands of its own and other nations' children. A
government official of utter probity follows his legislative or exec-
utive overseers in advocating a celestial Maginot Line in the form
of an endangering and technologically unfeasible missile "shield."
(I intentionally draw examples from non-ecclesiastical issues and
from both sides of the partisan division.) This is the nature not of
"structures of deceit," but of social instruments as such; and in a
fallen world, instruments that do enmesh the holy and the sinful,
enmesh Mann's "holy sinner," Rolfe's "Hadrian VII," and Duffy's
"Saints and Sinners"—to return this to matters papal.

One additional social-psychological datum may be adduced
here. Wills' book has had well over a score of reviews which were
followed by an almost uncountable number of letters expressing
for the most part enthusiastic support for his opinions, and vehement indignation at any criticism of them. Such unanimity regarding a professedly controversial book is inexplicable in terms of
its exposure of abuses which are, as noted earlier, prevalent
throughout American society. Whence, then, the almost universal
sense of outrage this book provoked among its defenders at their
alleged victimization by those practitioners of papal sin who authored *Humanae Vitae*? The question is even more baffling since
ecclesiastical condemnations of obliteration bombing or of the nuclear deterrent or of capital punishment or of economic greed have
apparently not sufficed to validate religious authority and wipe
away the putative stain of its endemic structural deceptions.
There was but one major issue, amidst all the societal evils afflict-
ing this entire culture, which was relatively unique to Catholicism, and which is pivotal to this book: contraception.

But the phenomenon of its centrality raises an additional problem. While *Humanae Vitae* engendered consternation and dismay
in other "first world" Catholic countries; while it brought forth
theological debates and clarifications from episcopal conferences
in France, Holland, Germany, Spain, and England, it never was *the*

test of adherence to Catholicism that it became over the next decade in the United States—only to be supplanted by the abortion issue in the latter part of the century. The reasons are twofold, and for reasons of brevity must be somewhat over-simplified here. There is, first, the gradual enervation of the American episcopate—to be discussed in detail in the last chapter— in the aftermath of the Americanist crisis with its attendant shift from public and social to personal and individual morality. One might contrast the interventions in support of labor unions by Cardinal Gibbons, of strikes (a much more controverted matter) by Archbishop Riordan, of racial justice by Archbishop Ireland ("obliterate absolutely all color line"), and of opposition to the war with Spain by Archbishop John Lancaster Spalding, not on the ground that Spain was Catholic, but on the ground of anti-imperialism: one might contrast all of that with what seems the dominant concern of the present hierarchy, sexual ethics regardless of how broadly defined.[6] Second, and more important, is the significance of devotion to the papacy with concomitantly the exaltation of the magisterium in a society shaped by the cumulative experience of successive waves of immigrants who found in such devotion the mark

---

[6] It is true that during the period of debate over contraception some broader "social" issues were discussed. There is most notably the intervention of Cardinal Spellman and Archbishop Hannan a few days before the close of the final session of Vatican II which asserted that the conciliar text on the avoidance of war contained "errors," and that unless they were corrected the entire schema should receive a non-placet vote. The two prelates asserted: "We deny that 'recent popes' have condemned total war as categorically as it is condemned in this section . . . ," of what would be article 80 of *Gaudium et Spes*. Bishop Schroeffer and Archbishop Garrone, on behalf of the redactors of the schema, charitably suggested that the Americans had simply failed to read carefully the text in question, and went on to cite Pius XII, concluding with the observation: "As to indiscriminate destruction, as here understood, no Catholic theologian admits or is able to admit that it is morally licit." A year later this same Archbishop of New York affirmed that his nation in Vietnam was fighting "a war for civilization." Emboldened perhaps by this Weltgeschichtlich *aperçu* from the East Coast, Archbishop Thomas Connolly of Seattle in June of 1969 publicly advocated that Hanoi and Haiphong be bombed and mined, citing in support of this position the precedents of Dresden, Hiroshima, and Nagasaki—all in illustration that not the entire episcopate was preoccupied merely with issues of personal morality.

and seal that distinguished them in the face of a militantly antagonistic Protestant culture.

Similarly, it was the contemporary heirs of such immigrants
who exulted in the election of John Kennedy, and found in that
election the legitimation of their Americanism.[7] But here too personal morality trumped social morality. For ignored in that exulta-
tion were the facts that his election pivoted on a non-existent
"missile gap," that his administration's first foreign-policy venture was an amoral invasion of Cuba, and that its most highly
touted triumph, in violation of every just-war principle, was a nu-
clear-weapons gamble entailing a threat of piracy in international
waters which were treated by this "Catholic" administration the
way Mussolini treated the Adriatic, as *mare nostrum*.[8] All that was
of little moment to Catholics growing accustomed to ignore social
evils and to concentrate mainly on the personal. As a consequence
the aura and image of John Kennedy—a man whom a priest *sociol-
ogist* had publicly promoted as worthy of canonization—was only
muted and disfigured by the subsequent exposure of his private
sexual activities. And so the sinning papacy and the deceitful
curia, with their repeated condemnations of total war went un-
heeded and unheralded, while failure to sanction condoms or dia-
phragms provided—as attested by the salient sections of Wills'

---

[7] James Carroll, Klieg lights in focus, writes with habitual hiererotic verve:
"When I described myself early on as a child of Vatican II, I thought that the
greatest significance of the reforming council was its concern with various aspects of Church renewal, but after *this* exploration [pp. 1–546 of the memoir] of
connections between theology and politics, I see its significance for an entire society beyond the Church. Even among non-Catholics, for example, the figure of
Pope John XXIII is linked in memory with that of John Kennedy, and for good
reason. Pope John's *aggiornamento*. . . . " So self-absorbing is the auto-manipulat-
ing that the "good reason" is never supplied and John Kennedy is never mentioned again. Wills, *on the other hand*, hits the parallel bars, equally without any
sense of irony: "Catholics had the Pope, their own John, to balance against 'secular John' in the White House. But for a while they [Catholics] had no Jackie." But
providentially out of the cosmic matrix of history emerges one Sister Jacqueline
Grennan, nun (such) president of a college near St. Louis as "our own" Jackie—
though never memorialized quite as fulsomely as either of the Johns.

[8] Cf. Justus George Lawler, *Nuclear War: The Ethic, the Rhetoric, the Reality*

book as well as by its public reception—an occasion to vent widespread and inordinate rage at the betrayal of (residually immigrant) Catholic loyalties, a "betrayal" which Wills here shamelessly exploits.

Indeed, when discussing *Humanae Vitae* the tone reaches an almost hysterical pitch: the encyclical "dealt the most crippling, puzzling blow to organized Catholicism in our time"; "the most disastrous papal document of this century"; "the equivalent, for sheer wreckage achieved, of the nineteenth century's most disastrous papal document, Pius IX's *Syllabus of Errors.*" But as I shall note shortly, the hullabaloo attached to the latter was a *hallucination publicitaire* of nineteenth-century "No Popery" crusaders, as was made clear from the widespread indifference by the faithful to its flagrant anachronisms, even in the very next decade as well as later in the century. Only six year afterwards, Newman was in agreement with an Irish bishop at Vatican I concerning the supporters of the Syllabus, "They have not come into contact with the intellectual mind of the times," and two decades later Archbishop Ireland would observe that the "propositions reported in the Syllabus as *at one time or another* 'censured' by Pius IX, represent the excesses, the extravagances of the movements of the age, and not the movements themselves." Moreover, how Wills could *so* describe *Humanae Vitae* is incomprehensible in light of the concordat with the Third Reich. And one wonders if he has ever read what was arguably "the most disastrous" theological document of this century, Pius X's own *Syllabus of Errors, Lamentabili,* with its companion document *Pascendi Dominici Gregis,* an encyclical which for decades hindered Catholic theological speculation (nearly forty years later in a prison camp, Congar would learn of Père Chenu's *Une Ecole de théologie* being placed on the index),[9] and

---

(Westminster, Md., 1965); "the Reality" in the title refers to the Cuban missile crisis.

[9] In *Chrétiens en dialogue,* he wrote: "The starved messenger who came to us in Silesia gave us no details on the extent, the exact nature, nor above all, on the motives of the blow. And even today [1964] after questioning, searching, and studying closely these details, I am so stunned by the contradictions and the incomprehensible nature of it all that I can see it only as an error or a malicious act."

was the forerunner of the revanchist *Humani Generis* with its dire consequences not only in the speculative order—where were silenced the future Cardinals Daniélou, de Lubac, and Congar—but also in the practical; being the rehearsal to the suppression of the Mission de France in 1953 with its ill-fated but proleptic steps towards a theology of liberation.

As to the specific contention that members of the group convened to resolve the contraception issue were living "within a lie," it must be emphasized that all thinking Catholics past their nonage know that popes, bishops, and even pontifical commissions are prone to errors and misjudgments—all of which in the rational order of things are subject to correction by individual conscience. Moreover, if these errors, misjudgments, etc., are crystallized in sins and lies, how explain such changes in official teaching as John T. Noonan discerned in his massive work on contraception? "Use of the sterile period, once attacked by Augustine when used to avoid all procreation, approved in 1880 for cautious suggestion to onanists, guardedly popularized between 1930 and 1951, was now fully sanctioned [by Pius XII]. The substantial split between sexual intercourse and procreation, already achieved by the rejection of Augustinian theory, was confirmed in practice." (*Contraception: A History of Its Treatment by Catholic Theologians and Canonists,* 1966). What was not further developed *doctrinally* by Paul VI's encyclical was developed *practically* by the laity. Was this too reflective of sins and deceit?

— IV —

I think not. After all, as Cardinal Newman, affirmed councils come and go, and what one pope has done another can undo—and frequently does, as noted in the first chapter.[10] Is this not what is

---

[10] In the background of Newman's observation is the Council of Constance, now remembered more for its dissolute ambience and unfortunate condemnation of Hus—a condemnation regretted by the original John XXIII, a legitimate pontiff but deposed after opening the Council—than for its distinctly reformist agenda. But its historical significance—as Gallicanists of every national origin recog-

meant by living in history? As to remedies for those struggling through any attendant painful period, perhaps a touch of realism would be mitigative. This, from the archeologist Msgr. Duchesne during the early period of the Modernist crisis, which had to do with Catholic dogma not morals, and when he was more suspect than the leading biblical revisionist, Alfred Loisy: "I am not a theologian, that is why I can praise God with joy." Or in a similar vein: "Religious authority rests on tradition and on its adherents who are most devout—and also most unintelligent." Or less whimsically, "Every year is for me a lamentable spectacle of an episcopate composed of imbeciles. Our present archbishop is a mitred sacristan"—a comment reminiscent of Newman's reference to such zealous partisans of infallibility as W.G. Ward, and Cardinals Manning and Vaughan, as "the three tailors of Tooley Street."

Perhaps even a touch of curial pragmatism would not be a bad disposition to cultivate, as exemplified by Archbishop Robert Seton, for a while America's most decorative prelate in Rome: "Theologians make difficulties and canonists get around them." It was also in Rome that the leader of the British Modernists, Baron von Hügel, was advised, "Never ask for an *imprimatur*, it is the first step to the *Index*." And when Archbishop Errington was dismissed to the Isle of Man (much like Archbishop Charbonneau of Montreal under Pius XII being sent to a convent chaplaincy in Vancouver), he sardonically noted that "it is not the Holy Ghost that

---

nized—was its convocation by what would be defined today as laity (regardless of titles or place in society), and its endorsement of conciliar over papal authority, an endorsement condemned four decades later by Aeneas Silvius Piccolomini, who became Pius II not out of devotion to his predecessor but to the poet of two centuries earlier who wrote "sum *pius* Aeneas." Never was there a period in which Newman's "do/undo" dictum was more exercised. The future Pius had for years supported the cause of antipopes, but on becoming reconciled with Eugene IV, he was ordained, consecrated, and ultimately elected. Following the lead of the Council of Constance, he appointed a commission to reform the curia, canonized Catherine of Siena, sought to restore monastic regularity, and like Nicholas of Cusa (whom he had presciently referred to as a "Hercules"), reversed his earlier conciliarist stance; he also—now like Augustine—authored a palinode repudiating his youthful writings and personal indiscretions ("forget Aeneas, remember Pius"), and died en route to a crusade against the Sultan whom he had earlier sought to convert. In sum, a life of remarkable reversals that illustrate historically and personally the principle of homeostatic equilibrium discussed in chapter one.

governs the Church, but Msgr. Talbot"— the latter an adviser to Pius IX, an antagonist of Newman, and an unfortunate who was subsequently confined to an asylum. More pertinently one might think of the contemporaneous *mot* about that long-awaited contraception decision having been delayed until Msgr. Marcinkus could get some pharmaceutical stocks into the Vatican portfolio.

Perhaps Newman is the best guide. "Now the Church is a Church Militant, and, as the commander of an army is despotic, so must the visible head of the Church be; and therefore *in its idea* the Pope's jurisdiction can hardly be limited." But of course in its execution it will invariably be limited, and not by some imaginary "structures of deceit," but by the pressure of what Karl Rahner, called, "free speech in the church." Part of the exercise of that free speech is the kind of conscientious resistance which translates into a *consensus fidelium*—as when the great mass of faithful Catholics simply ignored Vatican views on contraception.

Newman wrote about why the laity took upon itself the right to ignore "official" views: "There was true private judgment in the primitive and medieval schools,—there are no schools now, no private judgment (in the religious sense of the phrase), no freedom, that is, of opinion. That is, no exercise of the intellect. No, the system goes on by the tradition of the intellect of former times." But Newman, in "internal exile" ("shelved" was his word) at Birmingham and under a cloud far denser than any hovering over the church of the third millennium, added: "this is a way of things which, in God's own time, will work its own cure, of necessity; nor need we fret under a state of things, much as we may feel it, which is incomparably less painful than the state of the Church before Hildebrand, and again in the fifteenth century." So to a sense of history we must add a sense of providence, a sense that "truth defends itself, and falsehood refutes itself," as Newman concluded.

If von Hügel regarded the reign of Leo XIII as an interregnum, then the reign of John Paul II is a benign despotism with occasional but significant glimmers of enlightenment. Some of the latter are certainly his moving and effective overtures to Jews and Judaism, his rehabilitation of past Catholic thinkers like Rosmini and Newman as well as of the more recent victims of the hoopla over Nouvelle Théologie—the latter being the prelude to Vatican II and the final flare of the Modernist comet. Also to be noted are the present Pontiff's frequent denunciations of weapons of mass destruction, and his impassioned condemnations of capital punishment—this latter as much ignored among conservatives as the condemnation of contraception is among liberals. But both the Pope's consistency on the latter issue and the pew-Catholic's indifference to it illustrate once again the inconsequentiality of Papal sin and structures of deceit as the locomotive either of religious corruption or of religious reform.

No one could be more transparent and lacking in guile than this pontiff—unless it be Dostoevsky's Grand Inquisitor. But who is to judge, and why would anyone want to? Though it is true Newman defined the authentic hypocrite as someone who genuinely believes in his own sincerity, it is also true that he once ironically observed about religious debate that one's own doxy is orthodoxy, one's opponent's is heterodoxy. John Paul II is neither the prisoner of the Vatican nor the prisoner of deceitful structures, any more than are his gnostic critics, ensconced in their own imagined structures of blissful integrity. He like them is a being *in* history and *with* a history. To say otherwise is reductionistic, simplistic, sophistic; and as far as the analysis of theological/sociological complexities goes, it is utterly useless.

The fecklessness of employing the reductivism of Wills' titles was brought out in his treatment of Pius IX and of the dogma of the Immaculate Conception discussed in chapter three. Now, in Wills' account of the *Syllabus* and of papal infallibility simplistic historical theory goes hand in hand with simplistic practice of the journalist's art. So many curial villains, so many papal sins, so much toadyism by papal lackeys, so many Vatican conspirators crowd the stage that one loses sight of the actual events in the salvoes of derogatory expletives and epithets that Wills fires. Nor can one overlook the factual errors that mar the narrative and suggest that the omnicompetent tone and sweeping anathemas may be tactics to obscure flawed research and *ad hoc* conjectures.

Again, I draw from Newman and his description of another journalist, Richard Simpson, editor of the *Rambler,* a Catholic publication that Newman tried to salvage: "He will always be flicking his whip at Bishops, cutting them in tender places, throwing stones at Sacred Congregations, and, as he rides along the high road, discharging peashooters at Cardinals who happen by bad luck to look out of the window." Part of Newman's salvage effort took the form of assuming the editorship and publishing his celebrated essay "On Consulting the Faithful in Matters of Doctrine,"[11] an essay which affirmed what his great German counterpart, Matthias Scheeben, would say a few years later: "It follows that the public profession of doctrine by the body of the faithful, being a witnessing of the Holy Spirit relatively independent, ought logically and briefly to precede the precise declaration of the teaching body, and in such circumstances influence, as a means of orientation, its future judgment" (*Dogmatik,* Freiburg, 1873).

Because few curialists could read German, Scheeben went unscathed; but because Pius IX had Msgr. Talbot at his elbow, Newman was criticized and in the end turned over the editorship of the *Rambler* to Lord Acton who subsequently changed its name to *The Home and Foreign Review* and a few years later, also after criticism from Rome, abandoned the project altogether. Matthew Arnold publicly lamented the loss, and contrasted the independence of Acton with the servility of *The Dublin Review* under the editorship of the ultramontanist, W.G. Ward—now remembered only for his boast that at his daily breakfast he would like to read a

---

[11] Relative to Newman's "consulting" and to the apparent indifference of the American episcopate to issues of social morality discussed in footnote 6, an exception should be noted, again regarding the Vietnam war. In July, 1965, ten diocesan ordinaries signed a declaration which had been proposed by *Continuum* in response to warnings by the State Department. The bishops affirmed that "the possibility that either side may bomb any purely civilian center would entail a clear and direct violation of Christian ethics and must be denounced as an immoral action." The background and history of the declaration appeared in the Summer, 1965, issue under the heading: "On Consulting the Episcopate in Matters of Practice." Cf. *U.S. Catholic Historian* (Spring, 1984), "The *Continuum* Generation."

papal decree along with *The Times.* The interrelationships bear examination. Ward had been a devoted disciple of Matthew Arnold's father, Thomas Arnold, before joining Newman's Tractarians whom the elder Arnold referred to as "thugs" in a celebrated *Edinburgh Review* article titled "The Oxford Malignants." As editor of *The Dublin Review,* W.G. Ward's zeal in defense of the papacy led him to attack Dr. Döllinger, Acton's former teacher, mentor and ally in the anti-papal party. Interestingly, in another chronological jumble Wills makes no mention of Simpson, and has Acton turning over the *Rambler* to Newman, not vice versa; this unfortunately leaves no opening for the significance of *The Home and Foreign Review,* nor for examination of the fascinating web of personalities involved in a controversy that seems in Wills' view strictly ideological, a conflict of the party of sin and deceit with the party of virtue and candor.

In any event, the conflict intensified with the appearance of Pius IX's *Syllabus* of modern errors, the tone of which is evident from its famously execrable eightieth and last condemnation of those who believed that the Pope should reconcile himself with progress, liberalism, and modern civilization. Other propositions condemned advocates of freedom of religion and of the press, of separation of church and state, and all those who differed from the Pope on what was then called in the chancelleries of Europe "the Roman Question" on the fate of the Papal States. As a result of the *Syllabus* the non-Catholic and anti-Catholic world had a short-lived lark exploiting the church's incompatibility with nineteenth-century life and thought; the ultramontanists were confirmed in their adulation of the papacy; and what came to be called cisalpinists[12]—all liberal Catholics north of Umbria—

---

[12] The original "cisalpinists" were a group of Catholic laymen who in 1789 rejected the "deposing power" of the British monarch first invoked by St. Pius V, abandoned the dreams of a restoration of the Catholic Stuarts, and rejected the detailed regulations and religious practices they believed had been dictated by the Roman curia. Newman as a Protestant and as a Catholic would have joined them. Four decades after their founding, he wrote in *Lectures on the Prophetical Office of the Church*: "When religion is reduced in all its parts to a system, there is hazard of something earthly being made the chief object of our contemplation instead of our Maker. Now Rome classifies our duties and their reward, the things to believe, the things to do, the modes of pleasing God, the penalties and

engaged in various strategies to deprecate the document. In England where there had been a Liberal Party since the 1830s, a distinction was made between the dangers of liberalism's extremist *advocates* and the benefits of liberal *institutions*. In Italy the *Syllabus* was put in the context of the Roman Question, and was viewed less as an attack on the modern world than as an impetuous response (politically) to the advocates of Italian unification, and (theologically) to the Munich Congress of the previous year which had asserted the independence of scholars from ecclesiastical supervision. In France the most ingenious antidote to the temporary embarrassment took the form of a proposal that, although in the hypothetical order the propositions in the *Syllabus* were tenable, in the real order they were not necessarily applicable. This hypothesis/thesis explanation was the creation of Bishop Dupanloup of Orleans, several times in this book and in *Bare Ruined Choirs* referred to as "Cardinal"—though it is never explained why Pius IX would have elevated a prelate who had eviscerated the *Syllabus* and vigorously opposed the decree on Infallibility.

The preceding thumbnail sketch is a fairly straightforward though abridged account of the *Syllabus* affair—and "affair" is the *mot juste* since as noted above it was a transitory epiphenomenon of no lasting historical significance. How it can be construed as "papal sin" requires on the part of Wills a good deal of verbal legerdemain, as well as a discriminating use of sympathetic sources. His first fudging is to blur the document's origins in a suggestion of Cardinal Pecci who is unmentioned because he later becomes the open-minded successor of Pius IX, much like John XXIII after the later years of Pius XII. If one is going to prove the ubiquity of papal sin, one has to be highly selective in one's choice of villains *or* willing to portray the innocent as the villain. So the spin commences: all in accord with the axiom of Msgr. Knox, "any stigma will do to beat a dogma." The origin of Pius's propositions, the reader is told, was a "list drawn up by *an opportunistic ex-liberal,*

---

the remedies of sin, with such exactness that an individual knows (so to speak) just where he is upon his journey heavenward, how far he has got, how much he has to pass; and his duties become a matter of calculation."

Philippe Gerbet, who had *scrambled to the right* after the Pope's condemnation of his earlier hero, Felicité de Lammenais [*sic*]. Gerbet, a bishop *who was not respected* by other members of the French hierarchy, *liked to address grandiose* pastoral letters to his diocese." *This* villainous opportunist was in fact a prelate who was known as a second Fénelon, whose writings were praised by Sainte-Beuve, and who was the closest collaborator of de Lamennais at La Chênaie, "one of the factors, and perhaps the most effective at this time, of a renewal in theological speculation"—so says Edgar Hocédez in *Histoire de la Théologie au XIXe Siècle* (1948, I).

Indeed, de Lamennais was not only a theological innovator but a social reformer whose pleas went unheard in Rome for six decades, until the successor of Pius—the innominable Leo XIII—addressed issues relating to the working poor. As for ex-liberals or ex-conservatives scrambling to the right or to the left, one may be reminded of a *mot* relevant to Wills' own scramblings. When the poet Lamartine was elected to the French parliament in 1833, the question was raised as to whether his chair would be on the left or on the right. The prosaic response was, "M. Lamartine's chair will be on the ceiling," i.e., not above the debates but irrelevant to them. It should also be noted that when de Lamennais was elected to the assembly in 1848—after the revolutionary furor that drove the younger Pius IX from Rome—there was no question as to where his chair would be.

Wills' bias becomes even more transparent when—as is the case with his use of almost all secondary sources—he cites only a single distinguished scholar on a particular issue. Giacomo Martina, author of the three-volume definitive life of Pius IX, is quoted (apparently from the Italian though an English translation of the single-volume abridgment appeared in 1990) on the development of the *Syllabus:* "Finally, the contributions of mature theologians like Abbot Guéranger, Monsignor Pie, and Monsignor de Ram, had little effect, while the basic initiatives came from an obscure French bishop, Monsignor Gerbet of Perpignano [*sic*] . . ." —this last for "Perpignan" serves to let the reader know that Wills *qua* polyglot is looking at the authentic Italian text. But if Martina wrote "obscure," he shouldn't have.

Moreover, there is no way Guéranger or Pie could be described as "mature theologians" save in terms of age. Regarding Guéranger alone, it must be noted that he too "scrambled to the right after the Pope's condemnation of his earlier hero, Felicité de Lammenais" [*iterum sic*]. Anyone who has read Guéranger's massive assemblage, *l'Année liturgique,* will know that here we have to do not with a theologian but a collator. As for Pie, there is nothing but (eponymously) unctuous pieties. If he were living today, as a theologian he would be in a class with Rev. Jerry (no priestly caste here) Falwell—and not too different from the latter politically. The only prelates who could be described as "mature theologians" were the Germans influenced by such scholars as J.A. Möhler, Scheeben, and Dr. Döllinger, editor of Möhler's essays, and also a friend of de Lamennais. As we have seen, German theology was ignored or contemned in Rome, and hence the eminence of French mediocrities like Guéranger and Pie. But, again, who here is now caught in structures of deceit in attempting to prove how tainted are the sources of the *Syllabus*? The latter document is bad enough, it doesn't need this tissue of tendentious embroidery.

— V —

Now—with a Copland fanfare for the common Catholic—come the ultimate exposé of papal sin and its, so to speak, cardinal instance: the Constitution *Pastor Aeternus* containing the decree on infallibility. Again, deceit (accompanied by historical error) abounds. At the debates on this issue during the first Vatican Council one meets some of the same players. Monsignor Pie notwithstanding his theocratic notion of "the Pope-King" is among the "moderates." While Bishop Dupanloup, who continues to wear the red hat Wills had conferred on him in *Bare Ruined Choirs,* is among the leaders of the opposition. Allied with Dupanloup was Georges Darboy, Archbishop of "Parigi" (as Martina/Wills would have it). Darboy was a martyr in the etymological sense of being a "witness" to the authentic tradition, and in the general sense of dying for his faith during the communard rule of Paris a year after the Council. One of the most vociferous opponents of the decree, Wills tells us, was "Cardinal Strossmayer the Bavarian leader of bishops against infallibility." Unfortunately, Strossmayer was neither a Cardinal nor a Bavarian. He was a Croatian, a recognized leader in the Panslavic movement, and intent on bringing about a reunion of Orthodox and Catholics—which, as subsequently with Anglicans and Lutherans, the infallibility decree would render almost impossible. (Witness the failed efforts of John Paul II to receive an invitation to Moscow from the Russian Orthodox Patriarch.)

In the end, after months of debate and following the departure from Rome of most of the opposition, including Darboy, the reader is informed correctly that "only three negative votes were cast at the last session." (In passing, one notes a nice touch missing. One of the three was a bishop from Arkansas; and so the headlines bannered that Little Rock had opposed Big Rock.) But Wills ceases neither to toil nor to spin, as the perpetration of another "papal sin" is ferreted out: "Even if all the bishops who first assembled for the Council had remained for the final vote, they would not have been representative of the entire church, since the Pope had named many more bishops from Italy and Spain than from the more distant and less docile lands." Thus is illustrated once again the obsessively regnant structural deceit, and in support are mustered detailed statistics gleaned from Gertrude Himmelfarb's dissertation on Lord Acton. (Mrs. Irving Kristol at least is not among those heinous ex-liberals who have "scrambled" to the right. She was there from the beginning.) But overlooked in this assumption of a duplicitous conspiracy to weigh the scales in favor of his loyal countrymen is the fact that Pius IX appointed more non-Italian cardinals than any of his predecessors in modern history. As for the statistical evidence, the eminent theologian and historian, Roger Aubert, assesses the numerical accounts quite differently. "By dint of their [the Italian delegates] numbers they lent decisive support to the informal compromise faction. This group, conciliatory from the outset, finally succeeded in having a more flexible formula accepted, which occupied a middle ground between the neo-ultramontane and the anti-Curial extremists, and which allowed for adjustments in the future" (Hubert Jedin, editor, *History of the Church,* 1993, III).

Wills continues: "The Council would be broken off when war against Austria made France withdraw its troops, so that an independent Italy's warriors came flooding up to the very gates of the Vatican City." One can overlook the hypostatizing of Italy, and the metaphoric mélange of flooding warriors—maybe through the cloaca maxima of the Vatican. But one can't overlook another curious conflation: the Franco-Austrian war of 1859 is identified with the Franco-Prussian war of 1870. This latter, "as every schoolboy used to know" brought the end of the Council and the end of the Papal States. The quotation is adapted from Macauley, one of those historians Wills had earlier commended for affirming "that history was no longer the province of institutions impervious to outside scrutiny or committed to official versions of the past." It should be added, "and no longer committed to *unofficial* versions either."

But perhaps as with Shakespeare and the Hundred Years War or the War of the Roses, one can get a more vivid sense of the political events surrounding the Council from the poet Paul Claudel in the third play of his *Oresteia,* "Le Père humilié."[13] The "Father" of

---

[13] Two aspects here are relevant. The play was published in 1916 when Benedict XV, whose reign began at the time of the first World War, was consistently rebuffed in his peace efforts by both the Central and the Allied powers—to a degree that could be called a public humiliation. Second, Claudel though briefly maligned as a Vichyite, was the first major writer—among many others who remained silent throughout the occupation—to express in a public letter to the Grand Rabbi of France "the disgust, horror, and indignation which all good Frenchmen and especially Catholics feel at the iniquities and ill treatment inflicted"on the Jews. This was three months before the first trains left for Auschwitz (Cf. Marrus and Paxton, *Vichy France and the Jews*). People who have read Auden's metrically interesting but sermonically tedious poem on the death of Yeats should be mystified by the Hyperion/Satyr conjoining of Claudel and Kipling, and the pointless puzzle of *for* what exactly Claudel should be "pardoned." Jeffrey Hart thought the names were tossed out like a couple of poker chips, but George Steiner, polymath pre-eminent, though maybe still suffering the disaster of his Hitler novel, cites Yeats' other platitude about poetry making "nothing happen" and goes on in all sincerity about people writing poetry, performing music, and "then proceeding to bestiality the next day." ("Festival Lecture," Edinburgh, 2000) This is a rare lapse for so awe-inspiring a mind since he illustrates the condition by noting "that it was under the occupation that French drama—

the title is Pius IX, and the central character is a blind young Jewish woman (a shekinah figure like Trophaëa in Gertrud von le Fort's *Papst aus dem Ghetto*) in love with one of the Pope's nephews whom she upbraids for his indifference to a unified Italy: "You're fighting against this people which is struggling to live. . . . each of its parts is trying to weld itself to the next, like a body coming to life, you're doing all you can to stop it." The nephew replies: "I can't *stand against* my Father"—precisely the position of the minority bishops at the Council. The heroine, named Pensée, and one of the most touching figures in Claudel's enormous repertoire, responds: "Is that futile old man, to whom time and progress means nothing, forever going to stand between you and life . . . ¿"

In the aftermath of the Council, the opposition bishops who had left the city to avoid "standing against" the Holy Father eventually accepted the decree, in some cases through a kind of Fabian ecclesiology, only after annulments for their diocesans ceased being delayed by Roman officials. Lord Acton's fellow agitator against infallibility, Dr. Döllinger, was excommunicated along with several thousand German, Swiss, and Austrian "Old Catholics"—a sect which continues to this day, among a dozen or so other groups with the word "Catholic" in their name—whom he had inspired but as a matter of conscience refused to join. Wills says, "Döllinger left the Church": Wilfrid Ward said he had been driven out of it. In fact, Döllinger refused to join the "Old Catholics" and professed himself a loyal Catholic to the end, which is why his piteous cry still resonates: "Je suis isolé."

Noblesse oblige left Acton untouched, and he later went on to a Professorship at Cambridge where he initiated the Cambridge Modern History, but never saw its publication, as was equally true of his projected history of liberty, since renowned as "the

---

Claudel, Sartre, Montherlant—reached new heights": omitting Camus, and failing to note that Claudel refused to allow production of *Protée* unless the music of Darius Milhaud, a Jew, were included (Cf. Julian Jackson, *France the Dark Years* [New York, 2001]). As to Auden he was just saddled with the problem of finding a rhyme—though Sacheverell could have been made to sit well enough.

greatest book never written." Acton's former supporter, Gladstone, published an attack on the decree on infallibility—with the assistance of Richard Simpson—to which Newman replied in a subtly argued open letter addressed to the leading Catholic peer (a Cisalpinist by birth, heritage, and politics), the Duke of Norfolk: thus the future cardinal utilized an Earl Marshall in a rejoinder to a Prime Minister. It was a whim of the same Duke of Norfolk that later resulted in Newman's elevation by Leo XIII, as it had earlier been a whim of Newman in his reactionary Anglican days to oppose Catholic Emancipation which the then Duke of Norfolk supported. In Newman's long history, there is no end of Howards.

Finally, for the record, and to refute the historically warped concept of *structures* of deceit, I would note three post-conciliar transforming reversals of view. The first see-saws through several decades of the twentieth century and begins with Pius X's refusal to authorize the condemnation of the antisemitic and inchoately fascist, Action Française. The condemnation was then enforced during the reign of Pius XI, much to the consternation of monarchists and Jew haters. At the beginning of his reign the condemnation was lifted by Pius XII in a placatory gesture to Franco; this latter against the firm counsel of the advisor who would become Paul VI—again, all in verification of Newman's "do/undo" dictum. Second, and closer to Vatican I is the reversal of position by Cardinal Manning, the "majority whip" at the Council who later vigorously criticized what he called a "Catholic presbyterianism" which reduced the episcopal college to "only the pope's vicariate"—precisely the position of the minority in 1870. Third, and mentioned earlier, although the initial impetus for the justly reviled *Syllabus* came from Cardinal Pecci, his views were radically revised when as Leo XIII he—in an understandably mixed fashion, symbolized by the condemnation of "Americanism"—made peace with the Enlightenment and with post-revolutionary France, and wrote an encyclical on social reform whose very title would have made Pius IX shudder: "Concerning the New Things."

A sense of the shock that Leo's reign caused is amusingly brought out in André Gide's *Les Caves du Vatican* in which a young vagabond impersonator, a kind of clerical Felix Krull, cons elderly ladies into donating cash and jewelry to ransom the true pope and drive from the throne the false pope, Leo XIII, patently a creature of evil Jesuit plotters—no doubt caught in their own unique structures of deceit. Leo's papacy was called an "interregnum" by Baron von Hügel not as a pejorative but rather as descriptive of a period of sanity, a reprieve between the ruthless infallibilist ambition of Pius IX and the equally ruthless anti-Modernist crusade of Pius X—Loisy, whom Leo had refused to excommunicate, was excommunicated by Pius. As I have noted, Leo XIII succeeding Pius IX, like John XXIII succeeding Pius XII, illustrates the fact that there are no inalterable structures of deceit *or* of candor, though the latter as history shows ultimately triumphs. This is the meaning of the equilibrium between center and periphery that was discussed in chapter one.

In the past Catholics were wont to refer to "holy mother the church"; in the present they "botanize upon their mother's grave"—a Wordsworthian *mot*. Wills' book is not distinguished by any discernible narrative sequence or development, save for its leitmotiv of papal sin and deception. And it is as jumbled thematically as it is chronologically. To use a term favored in the nineteenth century, where much of this narrative is concentrated, the book is a kind of "miscellany." As we have seen, it begins with a caricature of John Paul II and Jewish relations, goes back to Paul VI and such still current issues as celibacy and the ordination of women, then proceeds to the events of the reign of Pius IX. It closes with two chapters on Augustine and lying, and one on soteriology based on the sacrificial-surrogate theory of René Girard.

The discussion of Augustine on lying perhaps reflects what Coleridge called our "hobby-horsical devotion to old authors" and does not help resolve some issues earlier in the book. Of the much depicted rape of Lucretia by Tarquin and her subsequent suicide, Wills notes without demurral: "Augustine says that Lucretia's crime was greater than Tarquin's: 'He took her body, she took her life. He raped, she murdered'." Again, with cool detachment: "When Christian women were tempted to suicide after being raped in the fall of Rome, he [Augustine] said that the violation of their bodies could not violate their souls if they did not intend what happened." Wills' gloss: "He is being consistent here," may remind a few of John Paul II's condemnation of abortion *and* capital punishment. But for many, this line of reasoning will strike them as entailing a dangerously casuistic literalism which, for the sake of scoring a "logical" argumentative point, ignores the concrete situation of the subject being violated. (It also evokes the moralizing fundamentalism, not to mention the implicit "tritheism" that has led some feminists to call God the Father the archetypal parental child abuser.)

Fortunately, this is not how one of Wills' "heroes," Newman, taught Christians to think. On the title page of *An Essay in Aid of a Grammar of Assent* Newman quotes one of his favorite Fathers: "Not by dialectic did it please God to save his people." (This is from St. Ambrose, a central villain in Carroll's autodidactic autopsy on the mystical body, and grand auto-da-fé of half the saints of christendom.) Three decades before in the *University Sermons*— the first testing ground of the *Grammar*—Newman had written that all people, "gifted or not gifted, commonly reason—not by rule but by an inward faculty." Or again, "Reason is a living spontaneous energy within us, not an art." And who for Newman writing *as a Protestant* is the model of such supra-rational thought? None other than Our Lady, the Blessed Virgin, dismissed, and even contemned, by Wills writing *as a Catholic* as the "idol-goddess." Again, the issue of picking and choosing only what subserves his private goals leads one to wonder how deeply Wills has actually penetrated not just the mind, but the spirit of his "heroes." Newman, critic of Rome, is embraced; Newman, devout traditionalist and consummate Christian existentialist, if known at all, is dismissed. To Wills' catalog of Marian aberrations, of which I will cite only one more: "her very flesh was a cosmic marvel, like kryptonite, unable to die"—to such a catalog, Newman would simply have observed that it was "not acceptable to every part of the Catholic world." He later added, such forms of piety "do not color our body," i.e., have no influence on the Catholicism to which he had converted. Nor do they have any influence today, except for scoring cheap polemical points.

In fact, the whole discussion about Augustine on lying seems adventitious—if not just hobby-riding pedantry—in the context of Wills' book, which might have been better served by an analysis of Newman's own treatment of "Lying and Equivocation" in an appendix (Note G) to the *Apologia*. Newman should also be invoked on the broader issue of historical veracity. When discussing the prospects of a Catholic magazine, he observed: "nothing would be better than a historical review, but who would bear it: Unless one doctored all one's facts one would be thought a bad Catholic." Now it is by doctoring facts that one proves oneself a "good Catholic."

The chronological, historical, and thematic pastiche that constitutes *Papal Sin: Structures of Deceit* concludes with a commendable autobiographical homily: "I do not think that my church has a monopoly on the Spirit, which breathes where *She* will [that pronoun should allay any concerns for poor Lucretia, though earlier in a less pro-feminist mood the Spirit is a mere "it"], in every Christian sect and denomination. In fact, She breathes through all religious life, wherever the divine call is heeded, among Jews and Buddhists and Muslims and others [surely those three are no more coequal than they are coeval]. But we Christians believe She has a special role to complete Christ's mission in us. Unworthy as we are, She calls us." The irenicism runs a little thin in that last dispensational— though admittedly humble—opining. But then the irresistible itch is scratched; and what briefly appeared to be an olive branch is launched—now, as from a catapult: "She calls us. She even calls the Vatican. All Christians need to respond to that soliciting. *Including Popes.*" So the supplication—suitably from the nineteenth century—remains: No Popery! "But wherefore could not I pronounce 'Amen'?" Because I (like so many others of "my church") had as lief be embraced by a gaggle of foreign or domestic prelates as to antiphonally "respond to that soliciting."

This book shouts to the rafters the dismal, hopeless cry of yesterday's bigots, *No Popery*! But much less portentously, much less cosmically the clarion rebounds. As in the leaden echo of Hopkins' choral ode, to the cry "despair, despair," the modest golden echo replies, "spare," "spare." Spare us these dissonant, conglomerative medleys, whether historical, thematic, or chronological: *No Pot-pourri!* The method of history like the lesson of history is single and simple. Truth calls us. She even calls the journalistic guild. All people need to respond to that soliciting. *Including Wills.*

— VI —

The fundamental flaw in the invocation of structural sin or structural deceit as the explanatory device for all aberrant acts, all failures and errors that the contemporary church has inherited, and even occasionally reinforced, is not that such invocation depends on distorted scholarship and deliberate falsification—though those as we have seen are bad enough—but that it removes the church from its historic reality as a temporal institution undeniably progressing, by fits and starts like any other institution, over two millennia of growth. The phrases *"structures* of deceit" and the more frequently heard "structures of sin," should be excised from our vocabulary, because they literally have no meaning in the modern era. If they are intended to suggest that an institution has a kind of built-in pattern of sin and deception, that pattern comes only from repeated acts of those individuals who sin or are deceptive. Moreover, if there were such a thing as a "structure" of sin, its only practical consequence would be at most to exonerate the evil or at least to blur the guilt of the responsible agent—precisely the opposite of not only what these structuralizers would wish for but of what they have repeatedly defined as endemic to antisemitic popes and power-hungry hierarchs.

I take my "text" from Acton's Inaugural Lecture for his chair at Cambridge where earlier Charles Kingsley had also been professor of modern history:[14]

The plea in extenuation of guilt and mitigation of punishment is perpetual. At every step we are met by arguments which go to excuse, to palliate, to confound right and wrong, and reduce the just

---

[14] I am quoting this from the essay; "Antisemitism and Theological Arrogance," in *The Range of Commitment* (1970). It is instructive to compare the tone and content with that of the works discussed above.

man to the level of the reprobate. They set up the principle that only a foolish Conservative judges the present with the ideals of the past; that only a foolish Liberal judges the past with the ideas of the present. The mission of that school was to make distant times, and especially the Middle Ages, then most distant of all, intelligible and acceptable to a society issuing from the eighteenth century. There were difficulties in the way; and among others this, that, in the first fervour of the Crusades, the men who took the Cross, after receiving communion, heartily devoted the day to the extermination of Jews. To judge them by a fixed standard, to call them sacrilegious fanatics or furious hypocrites, was to yield a gratuitous victory to Voltaire. It became a rule of policy to praise the spirit when you could not defend the deed. So that we have no common code; our moral notions are always fluid; and you must consider the times, the class from which men sprang, the surrounding influences, the masters in their schools, the preachers in their pulpits, the movement they obscurely obeyed, and so on, until responsibility is merged in numbers, and not a culprit is left for execution.

As we saw, among the devisals of the German historians known as "functionalists," in their effort to prove that causes other than personal adherence to an ideological fanaticism begot the Holocaust, were the attribution of it to such generalized factors as the strategic demands of the war, the pressure of bureaucrats driven to fulfill impossible goals (like clearing Poland for German settlers), the "culture" of Aryan superiority, the "tradition" of Jew-hating, etc.. The response which scholars, whom I have cited in chapter four, made to the first argument, i.e., that the Holocaust resulted from pressure by a massive and largely anonymous bureaucracy, was to ask why then was it necessary to seek the death of Jews in places as remote from the "Eastern Marches" as Japan, and why was it necessary to accelerate the executions when defeat was universally acknowledged as imminent.[15] To the use of "culture" or the "tradition" as a structural

---

[15] Among the most eloquent and persuasive chapters in Daniel Jonah Goldhagen's creative synthesis, *Hitler's Willing Executioners,* are those dedicated to the exterminationist goal of programs ostensibly created to increase worker produc-

escape clause from responsibility, the response was why then did so many, even at the peril of losing their lives, oppose everything connected with the Holocaust. Certainly it cannot be that an evil becomes a "structure" simply by being repeated by thousands of individuals (e.g., the bureaucracy), or simply by being repeated over many generations (e.g., the culture, the tradition).

Regarding the church, the reality is simpler. It is not a matter of assuming a posture of moral superiority or dressing onself up as a judge of history in order that one can dredge up every real or imagined "evil," whether trivial or crass—from smoking bishops as with Wills to smoking guns as with Cornwell. (In the latter's crude conceptualization, it looked often like a mystery tale of a shepherd and the flock or a shepherd and the Glock.) Nor is it a matter of assuming that every act resulting in something bad or something just plainly stupid is always the result of a power-hungry conspiracy. Were we not told that the Latin mass was enforced *in order to* maintain the superiority of the "priestly caste"? But this caste system allegedly *still* exists in full flower—as lubriciously detailed by our nationally inquiring reporter on clerical pederasty—more than half a century after the extinction of the tridentine liturgy begun by Pius XII's *Mediator Dei* and concluded by Vatican II. (One can imagine the evasions of responsibility and guilt: "the structure of sin made me do it." Surely this can't be what reformers want.)

Of course we are talking about advanced cultures, about cultures whose members have undergone the process of emerging from barbarism and of thus becoming individually responsible for their acts. This will vary from society to society and from age to age. But one can say that it occurs when the sense of selfness and personness as the principle of identity gradually eclipses the sense of unthinking tribal or ethnic membership as that same principle—in short, when the individual realizes his or her uniqueness regardless of place or status in any group or social organization.

---

tivity, and to the "perplexing phenomenon" of the death marches in the waning month, weeks, and days of the war when "the fidelity of the Germans to their genocidal enterprise was so great as seeming to defy comprehension. Their world was disintegrating around them, yet they persisted. . . ."

Certainly, for speculative, that is, for scientific purposes, the determination of the chronological moment of such "emergence from barbarism" is up to culture anthropologists and historians. But for practical purposes, it suffices to know that when this "awakening" occurs, so too does individual responsibility.

As for most of western Europe after the barbarian invasions, Lord Acton in his *Lectures on Modern History* traced—perhaps too linearly—this emergence from barbarism to the discovery of the stoic writings around the eleventh century as the causal element that planted the seed of self-consciousness, the seed of an awareness of the uniqueness of the individual ego and its transcendent value—which by empathetic acculturation (or spiritual contagion) led to the acknowledgment of that transcendent value in one's fellow human beings. At that point personal virtue and personal sin, personal self-determination and personal culpability are present in any given society. In medieval and modern Europe one would certainly say this meant that burnings at the stake, torture or persecution for religious, racial, or cultural reasons were sins for those persons who supported, colluded in, or enforced such acts.[16]

So, too, for modern America. When the founders accepted the notion of self-evident truths about human rights, they did not mean truths that were "obvious" or "unarguable"; they meant truths that came to conscious awareness when one considered the nature of one's own self, of its aspirations and destiny. The tragedy which still besets American society is that the founders didn't look, or didn't let themselves look, deeply enough to recognize those aspirations and that destiny in chattel slaves. Thus political expediency, resulting in the perpetuation of evil, trumped human experience. In moral terms, one would have to say that those founding fathers were guilty of a sin that can not be mitigated by subsequently viewing the peculiar institution—another distanciating bit of sociological jargon—of slavery as a mere "structural" affliction of the American body politic.

---

[16] It is worth noting that it was the evils of the Inquisition not so much as a judicial tribunal but as an instrument of the most horrendous torture that Simone Weil singled out in her communication with Father Perrin, *a Dominican,* as a major factor in her refusal to embrace Catholicism.

Concerning the "old debate" over whether many Southerners tormented themselves with guilt over their ownership of slaves, Eugene D. Genovese writes; "A good many able scholars have thought they did. In contrast, other scholars, myself included, have argued that the mass of the slaveholders—and nonslaveholders for that matter—accepted slavery as ubiquitous in history, as sanctioned by Scripture, and as a fact of life." The question naturally arises as to how then did the slaveholders live with themselves. They did what their "Papist" and "Romish" enemies had done in earlier ages: they dissipated the horrors of burning at the stake (albeit by the "secular arm") by concentrating on the evils of heresy. Genovese continues: "For if few slaveholders showed any guilt about their ownership of human beings, a great many confessed guilt over their inability to live according to their own professed standards of Christian slaveholding, and they worried about their ability to give a satisfactory account on Judgment Day of the stewardship upon which their own salvation depended" (*The Consuming Fire: The Fall of the Confederacy in the Mind of the White Christian South* [Athens and London, 1998]). (One cannot but admire the allusion to W.J. Cash's *The Mind of the South.*) But we don't call this slaveholding notion of "stewardship," invincible ignorance, much less "affected ignorance"; we call it culpable self-deception.[17]

Thus something does not become a structure of evil—and hence implicitly nobody's individual responsibility—by reason of its sheer immensity, whether in time or space, whether by its age or by its geographic extension. Throughout previous centuries of the medieval/modern era, pogroms in Europe and slaughter of indigenous peoples in the New World, the fiefdom of the European

---

[17] It would be lacking in politesse, or just exercising political incorrectness, to point out that intrinsic to slaveholding was not just the frequent breaking up of slave families, but even more the almost inevitable profiting (a bonus of capitalist stewardship) from the sale of offspring: thus a fertilized egg represented literally "seed money." This may explain the paradox of an obsession with "family values" and a total opposition to embryo research and to all abortion—even in cases of rape, incest or threatened maternal life—among the present-day legatees of this social system. No slave woman, under that "structure" of society, could *ever* suffer forced impregnation; nor do there seem to be *any* records of *any* legal redress for such rape.

Catholic monarch in the Congo, serfdom in Russia, slavery in the Americas, abuse of children and women in Victorian England, obscene treatment of the insane, of prisoners, of vivisected animals in the "developed" nations—all and many more would be euphemized away by such coinages as "systemic" or "structural" or "functionalist." All these practices and scores of others had a beginning in individual sinful acts, a middle and perpetuation in individual sinful acts, and an end (to a considerable degree) in individual virtuous acts: a Las Casas, a Wilberforce, an Engels, a Charles Kingsley ("I am a Chartist parson"), a Susan B. Anthony, a William Lloyd Garrison, an Elizabeth Cady Stanton, a John Brown—some motivated by patriotic motives, some by the influence of that amorphous movement known as the "Enlightenment" (trendily, now much maligned); others by Christian principles, and so on.

If there are any enduring social structures, their names are sin and virtue—as banal as that.

So what is needed, if not a theology of original sin—about which Newman wrote with great pathos in the entire passage from which I excerpted only a brief section—is a sociology of institutions: or both. If there must be social or institutional structures engendering corruption, they are simply structures of delusion—of evil perceived as good—based on culpable ignorance, ambition, pride, or greed. As to the church, the fact is that every modern pope has been in most respects an exemplary human being, an adequate administrator, and according to his lights a faithful servant of the servants of God. And *mutatis mutandis* this has been true of the majority of bishops. (And there seems no evidence to assume otherwise, of the majority of clergy and members of religious institutes.)

The degree of resentment evidenced in the critics' indictments seems to raise the question as to how and why do popes and bishops differ from ordinary Christians: why must they be so elevated in station, so restricted in relations with their flock, so absorbed in their own circles of power and authority? Or as Wills, another emerging memoirist, puts it: "Most bishops conduct their lives sequestered from the people. I had occasion at one time to seek a bishop's attention. It was easier to get that of my senator."[18] And the answer to that complaint is, *very* simply put, because that "sequestered" he or she is a busy person in a big organizations with big responsibilities. The "Mother Church/Ma Bell" solution to that is to break up the large units into much smaller units—which will mean, of course, a remarkable increase of the number of bishops, and the number of "sequestrations." (Here Wills is just adding another gripe to his list, since the issue is intrinsic to any complex society.) Of course these bishops are going to have to struggle against the temptation—as John XXIII did with remarkable effect—of succumbing to bureaucratic ways of living and administering: otherwise they lose what is well described as "the common touch." And of course, they are going to get caught up in the normal ambitions of preserving the organization, of expanding it, seeing it flourish—while at the same time maintaining the primacy of the individual person over against the institution. Does this mean that even if the institution is "church," they don't much differ from the heads of IBM, Harvard, General Motors, the Red Cross, Wal-Mart, etc.? At this point in the discussion, the temptation would be to answer, not really. Nor do they differ much, except perhaps by being more circumspect in their language, from journalists anxious to write a good story (and maybe win a Pulitzer) or novelists anxious to write a good memoir (and maybe get a National Book Award).

Wills supplies as a concrete instance of "papal sin"and "the structure upholding the legacy of wrong"—the issues relating to the ordination of women. After a fairly conventional and certainly

---

[18] The next sentence contains a curious slip. After the mention of "my senator," he adds immediately: "If addressing the needs of the faithful were the *real concern*, access to them [bishops] would be more readily achieved by, for instance, having women priests in whom other women could confide more easily." Unless women priests are viewed as episcopal amanuenses, it is not clear how the "real concern" with access would relate to them—regardless of how much they confide in other women. Wills, always the logic-chopping literalist, seems to be taking at face value Chesterton's masculinized whimsy at the beginnings of the feminist rebellion against domestic servitude: "Thousands of women rose up and said, 'we refuse to be dictated to,' and went out and got jobs as secretaries."

widely acknowledged recitation of historic patterns of discrimination against women, he observes that, "the ban on women priests matters. It is not so much that women are clamoring to become priests (especially as the priesthood currently exists), but the perpetuation of this ban keeps alive the *whole* ideological substructure on which it is based. It is the last fierce bastion where the great Christian lie about women has entrenched itself." The parting shot about "the great *Christian* lie" can be dismissed since as Wills himself had already shown, it is really the "human" lie with its origins in pre-history, crystallized by custom and law in various near Eastern cultures, systematized in Greek and Roman civilization, and transmitted down the centuries by various societies, Christian and non-Christian. But what cannot be so readily dismissed is the haughty suggestion that ordination is being sought primarily *as a gesture* of the rejection of male hegemony. But if ordination is really the *last* bastion where the *great lie* is entrenched, it is difficult to avoid the impression that women are patronizingly being accused of inability to discern symbolic from real issues.

Wills needs to elevate ordination, regardless of his own allegation of its incidental import, to the status of an absolutely crucial element—"last bastion," "keeps alive the whole substructure"—in order to magnify the sin and guilt of the papacy, not merely in regard to Catholic women aspiring to the priesthood, but in regard to women in general. The consequence of this tactic is to reduce women to ideological pawns in a conflict that has less to do with women's rights than with Wills' passion for papaphobia—just as the Holocaust had less significance among anti-papal ideologues as the *ultimate horror* than it had as a *useful means* to assault Pius XII and the Vatican Secretariat of State—and by extension, the papacy itself. (One might recall here the deceptive strategies of Carroll, Cornwell, Phayer, and Zuccotti.)

To illustrate, I draw upon some early twentieth-century "secular" history. If someone, perhaps feigning for noble or ignoble motives to be a devoted feminist, would have said—after several

generations of suffragists had been humiliated, pilloried, impris-
oned, and force-fed—that "the vote" was important *not* because
it would put women into congress and into state legislatures, *not*
because it would empower women to legalize control over their
own bodies and their own destinies; if that "someone" had said,
on the contrary, that "the vote" was important because it undermined "the ideological substructure of inferiority"; and furthermore, if this dedicated advocate then observed that there was "no
clamor among women to become politicians (especially as politics
currently exists)"—would not the response to all that be outrage
at such a display of patriarchal condescension?. —a condescension
(we now move forward fifty years) compared with which Paul
VI's confession of the "undeniable influence of prejudice unfavorable to women" in the church's past would make him look like a
wild-eyed (albeit "smudgy") crusader for ERA? —and speaking of
which: is that too now to be reduced to the status of empty
symbol?

Wills' real goal is not the redemption of "excluded women" (his
chapter title), but the exclusion of unredeemed popes, as the following makes clear:

> Those past injustices were not papal sins, since those who commit-
> ted them—*our* thinkers like Albert the Great, *our* saints like Aqui-
> nas—did not realize they were doing wrong. But not to realize now
> when the evidence is so overwhelming, when the opportunities for
> redress are available—to perpetuate the wrongs to women *as a way
> of maintaining that the church could not have erred in its treatment of
> women*—that is the modern sin, and it is a papal sin. The structure
> upholding the legacy of wrong is not invincible ignorance but a cul-
> tivated *innocence, ignorantia affectata.*

In his Introduction to the entire book, the phrase in latin (subsequently derided as the language separating the priestly caste from
everyone else) is not translated as "cultivated *innocence*" but as
"cultivated ignorance," the latter being, I assume, what he intends

here.[19] In this virtually unparseable sentence, what is not clear is whether the *evidence* for the modern sin of violating human and civil rights is as "overwhelming" as the evidence for the "papal sin" of enforcing an ecclesiastical ordinance. I think not, and therefore wonder why the word "sin" appears here at all, a sin which is not mitigated by being the result of *ignorantia affectata*, but is intensified. "Affected ignorance" is ignorance deliberately pursued and fostered, that is, it is the state of someone choosing deliberately to not know something in order to be free to continue in evil ways. The term originated in the ancient and medieval context of those who remained intentionally oblivious to "the true church" in order not to be obliged to convert. Its relevance to the twenty-first century is not explained by Wills, since it is difficult to imagine that even the "sequestered" hierarchy is ignorant of contemporary feminism and other liberation movements for civil and political rights. The latin phrase functions here merely to justify by one type of ignorance ("invincible") *our* thinkers and saints, and to condemn by another type ("affected") popes and bishops—whether they also are "ours" is not disclosed. Similarly, the italicized clause in the above passage serves an obfuscating function by making the apparent sin not discrimination against women, but merely that of "maintaining that the church could not have erred" in the past. So once again Wills' cause is not redress of evil, but condemnation of popes. Moreover, if the errors are *in the past,* they are exonerated by "invincible ignorance," not just among our "saints and teachers" but our popes and bishops as well. Rather than this elaborate embroidery around types of ignorance and sin, why is it not just admitted that what has happened is that—the no-doubt-passing—ban on ordination is simply

---

[19] Though it should be noted that a basic hermeneutical principle is that, first, a garbled text such as this one, and, second, confusion evidenced by a mistranslation (particularly on the part of a manifest polyglot) key the reader into anticipating confusion or obfuscation. The parallel is with the multiplicity of flaws, linguistical, historical, grammatical, surrounding the mere mention of the name "Pius IX." This latter seemed to set off the most preposterous assertions and chronological errors—all cumulatively providing clues to the possible presence of uncontrollable authorial obsessiveness or some other personal intellectual disability.

carrying to an extreme a tradition in a church that is founded on tradition¿

As to the *present,* short of outright evil, which no one has suggested is either very widespread or intentionally unpunished, similar aspirations and ambitions, similar drives for success, similar foibles and follies that animate the wisest and the worst among us will at least tempt—and sometimes successfully—these pontiffs and bishops. Short of individual psychopathology, which certainly does exist in every society, and which collectively infects the ill or the ignorant, there is in this age arguably less abuse of others' human and civic rights within Catholicism than within any other religious body of comparable influence. There are what many would see as abuses regarding religious rights—e.g., sacramental marriage for homosexuals, or even ordination of women—but *ex definitione,* their solution can come only by persuading through all the channels of public opinion the religious authorities. As for sexual abuse by clergy, by boy scout leaders, by athletic coaches, by teachers, by law officers, by parents and neighbors, everyone knows there have been coverups motivated by the desire, real or fabricated after the evil, to save the institution—the church, the youth club, the team, the school, the police force, the family—from the consequences. Such a "saving" effort occasionally takes the form of ruthless sacrifice of the victim in the name of the alleged well-being of the institution. But that effort has nothing to do with structures—as the not infrequent violation of group loyalties indicates—and everything to do with individual responsibility and guilt.

For Wills, celibacy is one of those structures of deceit. "When sexual scandal has arisen in the modern church priests have shown *more than* the ordinary institutional bias to protect their own. [The reference here is not to sexual *abuse of* others but to sexual *relations with* others.] Part of this comes from the bad faith that had them pretending, for the consumption of their superiors, to believe things they did not about celibacy, either for gays or for straight men." The sociological basis for the assertion that more than the ordinary institutional bias motivates priests in such cases is not presented; neither is it validated here by any statistical data—so that to the degree such motivation does exist, a simpler explanation than reliance on bad faith just might be institutional loyalty or gratitude, or just plain *esprit de corps*. But *mandatory* celibacy, like ordination of women, relates to issues that are already on the way to being solved by agitation from the periphery, and by the natural evolution of institutional mores.

As for structures of deceit, best exemplified according to our authors by Pius XII, I have already raised the issue of intention. What motivated his alleged silence is simply not knowable. Nor, it may be said by way of riposte, does any one know with absolute certainty if these authors' factual distortion and biased interpretation *are* intentional—even though it seems they can easily discern the intention of each pope or each bishop who is the object of their criticism. Moreover, it is even conceivable that under the umbrella of "structural deceit" they too might find justification in the journalistic "tradition," or "culture" for their exposés of flawed ecclesiastics. (Maybe at this point both structures collide and self-deconstruct.) And so, it comes to pass that in the common mind, one person's deceit is another person's spin; one person's duplicity is another person's diplomacy; one person's deception is another person's "public relations." But at least, then, we have reduced it to an *agent* who is guilty or innocent, not to an abstract category like "structure" which is by definition beyond good and evil. Moreover, we are taking a stand against that erosion of social morality which is the real ethical blight on the contemporary state, not the erosion of personal morality, much less the erosion of what are mistakenly—and for political purposes—called "family values."

I proffer another cautionary illustration. One man who ambitions mediating peace between rival powers, who speaks as Vicar of Christ, and who condemns on a number of occasions antisemitically inspired persecution, ends up in the historical record, if only by sheer volume of attacks made on him, almost universally denounced as a hypocrite. Another man ambitious for political unity, who speaks under guidance of his better angels, and who authors a proclamation which explicitly refuses to emancipate thousands of slaves, ends up in the historical record, if only by the sheer volume of laudatory accounts, almost universally admired as a courageous liberator. The first's "silence" is alleged to be the result of an obsession with diplomacy; the second's blatant discrimination is touted as brilliant "politics." Moreover, years after their deaths, when the first by a quirk of destiny is to be canonized and named a saint by the institution he led, the voice of outrage is heard throughout that body. When the second, by public acclaim is in effect canonized and named "the great emancipator" by the institution he led, there is national approval. Call it luck, chance, providence, divine superfluity; what it cannot be called is structural deceit or structural virtue. The only thing those two men, with such different historical fates, had in common was an overriding ambition to attain their goals, and that has nothing to do with institutional structures, but personal passions; sometimes ignoble, sometimes admirable—more often mixed. Slavery from the seventeenth to the nineteenth century in America, as I indicated at the end of chapter four, is the crucial test case demolishing the principle of structures of sin.

Since many of these critics come from the relatively cloistered world of the academy, one has to wonder if they imagine that some vast abyss of virtue or vice separates the scholar who seeks advancement from professor, to chair, to dean, to provost, to president of—*not* Boondocks University, but (ah!—cartoon balloon— *"gasp"*) *ultima Thule,* some ivy clad learning center.[20] —do these

---

[20] Every experienced academic has harrowing tales of administrators, allegedly suffering from budgetary restrictions—and which one is not?—pursuing with a fury tenured faculty in the hope of de-commissioning them by scheduling classes at impossible hours, by shifting offices to dreaded locations, by enforcing *ad literam* long-forgotten regulations, by canceling student assistants, etc.. Of course no record exists, nor is the institutional head visibly involved. Once the need is conveyed to deans and other fonctionnaires, the presidential hand is invisible, and the satraps go to work. One university excised eight senior professors on the (academic, naturally) grounds that, first, the student body was youthful, and, second, becoming more female. The professors it was maintained being male elders "couldn't adequately communicate with these students." A law suit followed, but an immortal institution has no concern with the passage of time, so as that time passed, the professors just abandoned the effort, went elsewhere (under a cloud of sorts)—or cultivated their gardens. The scenario evokes Nabokov's *Pnin,* Jarrell's *Pictures from an Institution,* Amis's *Lucky Jim*—an entire genre

critics imagine that a yawning moral chasm separates all that raw or cooked ambition from that of the ecclesiastic going from reverend, to very reverend, to right reverend, to most reverend, to— (ah! etc.) "your eminence"? How much difference is there between the celebrated athlete, ardently seeking a trophy that has only symbolic value, and the prelate, ruling the most grateful and appreciative and flourishing diocese, ardently seeking—a red hat? (Maybe both churchman and academic official began their careers merely ambitioning "an expensive stereo.")

From Aristotle to Durkheim and Weber, and to Berger and Bourdieu this is the nature of the people that manage the institutions that fulfill collective and individual human goals. Such people act in general harmony with others; they are often overprotective of the institution; they punish faults and reward achievements occurring in the pursuit of those goals. Throughout all this, they have to be responsive to public opinion, to various sanctioning powers of law, to the norms and standards of the "marketplace," and to other social and civic codes. In the church we call these controlling codes and sanctions, scripture and the doctrinal and prophetic tradition, both of which can be violated or respected in greater or lesser degree: *violated* by people deluded by ignorance, ambition, pride, or greed, and thus seeking their own goals rather than those of the collective body; more frequently, *respected*—as seen in the first-chapter discussion of historically validated equilibrium between the periphery and the center. And that phenomenon, born of grace and providence, is attested by the continuum of an institution that has survived by its being manifestly an exception to the rule.

---

of administrative follies well symbolized by E.M. Forster's Mr. Pembroke with his "exhortations to be patriotic, learned, and religious that flowed like a three-part fugue from his mouth." Transpose to a higher level: with Cardinal Newman being shelved, Archbishop Hunthausen being humiliated, Archbishop Charbonneau being exiled—concerning the latter two, more in the next chapter. These result not from structures of deceit but, on the part of the perpetrators, from individual ignorance or greed or ambition relative to institutional success. All of those traits in varying degree may become "customary" by repetition, but are no less evil for that.

But whatever is the result of sin and deceit depends on the individual agent, subject to the only structure history knows—original sin and the grace to transcend it—and not subject to some autonomous mythic entity independent of that agent and his relation to that sin. No one imagines as true the picture painted by these critics of some vast lumbering edifice moving like a juggernaut through history, and engaged in some enormous conspiracy to destroy its own children—all because of structures of deceit. What one can imagine is a pilgrim church composed of people *in via,* people by definition seeking a goal not yet attained. A people of God faithfully, but falteringly, going toward their promised land. The next two chapters will seek not to chart *a* path to that destination, but to set forth some indicators and signals, some resting places and short cuts (maybe a shrine or two) along the route to be followed.

Of the critics of the church in his day when the "night battle" was more dark and fearsome than it is at present, Newman wrote about that faithful and faltering journey in (as seems appropriate) a clumsily titled book, *Certain Difficulties felt by Anglicans in Catholic Teaching Considered:*

> Resentment and animosity succeed in the minds of the many when they find their worldly wisdom quite at fault. . . . They accuse the Church of craft. But, in truth, it is her very vastness, her manifold constituents, her complicated structure, which gives her this semblance, whenever she wears it, of feebleness, vacillation, subtleness, or dissimulation. She advances, retires, goes to and fro, passes to the right or left, bides her time, by a spontaneous, not a deliberate action. It is the divinely-intended method of her coping with the world's power. (London, 1850, Volume I, p. 179; Volume II is on Catholic devotion to the Blessed Virgin, and on infallibility, a revision of the letter to the Duke of Norfolk.)

6

BEYOND THE POLITICS OF RANCOR I

The Varieties of Personal Renovation

> "From the beginning of 1947 until the end of 1956, I have known only an unbroken series of denunciations, warnings, restrictions, discriminatory measures and scornful delations."
>
> *Cardinal Congar*

Two of the preceding chapters have ended with a reference to a poem by Gerard Manley Hopkins. It is more than mere symmetry that suggests that this chapter should begin with another of his poems, "Andromeda," since it was written during the year after the election of Leo XIII, and reflects Hopkins in a bleak visionary mood as well as, possibly, a mood prevalent among some European Catholics after the long reign of Pius IX. Andromeda represents the church, founded on the rock of Peter, still sacred but bearing the scars of the past: "Now Time's Andromeda on this rock rude, / With not her either beauty's equal or / Her injury's. . . . Time past she has been attempted and pursued / By many blows and banes." The poem then briefly becomes apocalyptic in its description of future "blows" that are almost catastrophic in their violence: "A wilder beast from West than all were, more / Rife in her wrongs, more lawless, and more lewd." ("Lewd" has the sense of vulgate ignorance, and the reference is probably to the ravages of "laicism"—*laïcité* cognate of "lewd"—then emerging in France, and much bemoaned as the real "heresy of heresies" both before and after the Modernist crisis.)[1]

---

[1] The identity of the "beast" is controverted because west of the British Isles would suggest America, and so the allusion is alleged to be to everything from

The poem concludes with a depiction of the Church during this in-between phase as it awaits "her Perseus," Christ: "All while her patience, morselled into pangs, / Mounts." There is no clear relationship to actual historical events save what can be gleaned from chronological coincidence; but the plain lesson is, as in "The Leaden Echo and the Golden Echo," patient perseverance in the face of personal or religious devastation. It is the lesson of Häring's "hope, after close inspection of the whole picture, for a new synthesis."

But in the nineteenth century a counsel of patience would not have satisfied either the unyielding papal party intent on enforcing the triumphalist might of ecclesiastical conformity and rigidity, or the schismatic Old Catholics embittered by the collapse of a church which they believed only their notion of conciliarism could salvage—and from whom little since has been heard.[2] The historical upshot is simply that the ultramontanists of the nineteenth century begot in the twentieth, the neo-Montanists, who in turn have spawned querulous twins—like Girardian rivals. On the right the sanctimonious "First Thingers," e.g., McInerny and Neuhaus, and on the left, the vehement "last enders," e.g., Wills and Carroll: both extremes virulently impatient with the center.[3] The process has been sketched by Bernard Lonergan in less adversarial terms:[4]

"suffragism" to the poetry of Walt Whitman—both rather unlikely candidates. Given Hopkins' penchant for obscure origins and the fact that the legendary site of Andromeda's enchainment was the coast of Ethiopia, anything west of that would qualify. Hopkins was, however, much concerned with governmental discrimination against the Catholics of France and Germany. Cf. Justus George Lawler, *Hopkins Re-Constructed* (New York, 1998), p. 69.

[2] Benjamin Jowett, that utterly worldly figure—and liberal heir to Newman's mantle as dominant personality at Oxford—said curtly when he realized the Old Catholic movement could exercise no effective power over events: "It has come to nothing." *Letters of Benjamin Jowett,* edited by Evelyn Abbott and Lewis Campbell (New York, 1899), p. 76.

[3] Nevertheless—and adding to the mix of history and fable—it must be said that a church of patient griseldas is preferable to a potemkin church of papaloters (made up of anathematizing orthodox radicals) or a kronos church of papaphobists (made up of sappers cannibalizing the ranks in the name of "honesty").

[4] *Collection* (New York, 1967), p. 267.

There is bound to be formed a solid right that is determined to live in a world that no longer exists. There is bound to be formed a scattered left, captivated by now this now that new development, exploring now this and now that new possibility. But what will count is a perhaps not numerous center, big enough to be at home in both the old and the new, painstaking enough to work out *one by one* the transitions to be made, strong enough to refuse half-measures and insist on complete solutions *even though it has to wait.*

— I —

How the center reacts is brought out in the following historical "parable." Well over a century and a half ago, Abbé de Lamennais, traveling back from Rome where his democratic views had been condemned by the highest ecclesiastical authorities stopped in Munich to meet with a then relatively unknown priest-historian, Ignaz von Döllinger, whom we have encountered in the treatment of the first Vatican Council. De Lamennais then continued on to Paris and shortly after wrote *Les Paroles d'un croyant,* a book in which he described a satanic conclave assembled to uproot "religion, science, and thought," and to destroy "Christ Who has restored liberty to the world." The allegory was transparently antipapal and anticurial, and the book was condemned by Gregory XVI as being "tiny in size but immense in perversity," and its author, who had been offered a cardinal's biretta and characterized by one of Gregory's predecessors as "the last of the Fathers," was gradually "hounded out of the Church" to use Wilfrid Ward's phrase.[5]

Around this time a young Anglican cleric in a bitter polemic

---

[5] But even here, Bernard Häring's "encouraging signs of the times" can be discerned. A few years after the condemnation of de Lamennais, Gregory XVI approved the Institute of Charity whose founder was another republican reformer, Antonio Rosmini, who would also be offered the cardinalate by Pius IX in the early "liberal" years of his reign. Cf. Charles Sylvain, *Gregoire XVI* (Paris, 1899), p. 193; *Life and Letters of John Lingard,* edited by Martin Haile and Edward Bonney (St. Louis, 1913), p. 226; Maisie Ward, *The Wilfrid Wards and the Transition* (New York, 1934), p. 317

entitled, "The Fall of M. De La Mennais," attacked the Abbé for seeming to "believe in the existence of certain indefeasible rights of man." And in an even more reactionary tone, the young Newman wrote: "Hence he is able to draw close to the democratical party of the day; in that very point in which they most resemble antichrist; and by a strange combination takes for the motto of his *L'Avenir,* 'Dieu et la Liberté'." Nearly half a century later this same cleric, who only gradually came to realize that de Lamennais had been doing "a service to religion," also planned on stopping in Munich on his way back from Rome where he had been raised to the cardinalate, and he too intended to meet with Dr. Döllinger.[6] Cardinal Newman hoped, among other things, to persuade Döllinger to accept the Vatican decrees. But Newman's intention, as we know, was never fulfilled; and like de Lamennais before him, Döllinger died an outcast from the Church. Both Döllinger and de Lamennais were men born out of due time. For if a doctrine of collegiality, such as that which Vatican II adumbrated, had been proclaimed in 1870 there would have been no "defection" by Döllinger. If the principle of freedom of conscience proclaimed at the Council had been tolerated by churchmen in the early nineteenth century, there would have been no tragedy of de Lamennais.

But there is a lesson even in de Lamennais' failure. His severest modern critic and one of the most learned religious analysts of that historical era is Alexander Dru who sees him as one of the *terribles simplificateurs:* "It should be remembered that no one reads de Lamennais unless they have to: there is no future in it. His philosophy is admittedly worthless, his theology non-existent, his spiritual writings painfully mediocre." But this strongly negative critique begins with the words: "What was wanting in the most powerful religious leader which France produced can be felt immediately at the mention of the names of Möhler, Baader, Newman, and Kierkegaard."[7] But with those representing the standard, few

---

[6] John Henry Cardinal Newman, *Essays Critical and Historical* (London, 1891), p. 157; Wilfrid Ward, *Life of John Henry Cardinal Newman* (London, 1912), I, p. 484.

[7] *Erneuerung und Reaktion: Die Restauration in Frankreich 1800–1830* (Munich, 1966), p.134.

religious leaders of the century could meet it, much less exceed it. It was of de Lamennais among others that Acton was writing when (proleptic of our time) he wrote of French speculative theorists: "If one puts their thoughts into one's own [English] language, little remains."[8] But he had in mind specifically the *Essay on Indifference*, a de Maistrean "traditionalist" work, of admitted historical and theological irrelevance even a few decades after it was written. But it should be noted that contemporary humanists, such as Waldemar Gurian and Kenneth Rexroth, are much less critical than were Acton or Dru.

Notwithstanding de Lamennais' evident failings as a speculative thinker and, notwithstanding his occasionally erratic personal conduct—though we have learned to live with tempestuous popes—there is his undeniable sincerity and steadfastness in the service of the poor, qualities which even so detached an observer as Disraeli recognized.[9] Moreover, he does offer two, seemingly opposed, lessons in his life and works. First, he provides to *present-day* European and North American Catholicism, which is currently preoccupied with various notions of "reform" both radical and gradual, a kind of negative criterion; indeed, a model of what a genuine reformer in Europe and North America cannot be.

Quite simply his vision, unlike that, say, of Newman was too tied to his own historical era and circumstances. Thus he could see nothing save in the light of church and politics, of religion—in its strictly ecclesiastical sense—and society. Any such restriction, any such simplistic dichotomy has to erode the ground of solid reform. But the implications of this crude duality are more significant for twenty-first century European and North American Catholics than they were for de Lamennais' contemporaries. If, as in our time, all the evils of militarism, of patriarchal imperialism, of individual or group neurosis, of rampant sexual abuse, of racial hatred: or if (to use Rahner's ironic terms) in our time all the evils committed in the "name of good order, national pride, the good of the country, . . . theology and philosophy, beauty and symmetry—really everything on the face of the earth" *are related to* some

---

[8] *Letters of Lord Acton to Mary Gladstone* (London, 1913), p. 164.

[9] *Lord Beaconsfield's Correspondence with His Sister* (London, 1886), p. 208.

alleged failing of the institutional church, we are victims of the same time-constricted distortions that led to the Mennasian lack of perspective; and without any of the exonerating factors that even today allow us to vindicate much of what de Lamennais stood for.[10] Geometry built Chartres. There is more to the renovation of European and North American society than any mere ecclesiastical system can proffer, and more to the degradation of that society than can be laid at the door of the churches. (But de Lamennais does have a second and affirmative lesson for twenty-first century Catholicism that I will consider shortly.)

There are many morals to be drawn from this opening historical narrative, not the least of which is that the second Vatican Council should not be praised too extravagantly for having embraced the age of reason, for endorsing views, e.g., the decree on religious liberty, which have largely been commonplaces for over two centuries among the creators and heirs of the Enlightenment—even though (I note yet once again) the latter has been much disparaged by critical theorists and postmodernists. But the more immediately relevant lesson of this historical parable has to do with the manner in which de Lamennais, Döllinger, and Newman responded to the encroachments of an abusive ecclesiastical authority.

No theme runs more constantly through Newman's Catholic years than that of the need for bringing sure truths into line with historical conditions—one of those conditions being in Newman's own time an indisposition on the part of Pio Nono and the ultramontanist party to accept even the surest of truths. Faced by the condemnation of some of his most deeply held Catholic convictions, Newman could have continued to press his claims. That he didn't was not a matter of expediency, was not a mere tactical

---

[10] It is this nineteenth-century Mennasian error that Garry Wills *appears* to succumb to in expanding the ecclesiastical ban on the ordination of women to the all-encompassing factor that "keeps the whole ideological substructure" of anti-feminism alive. I say "appears" because Wills' ideological intent is to make Christianity, the church, and the papacy part of a grand conspiracy that is responsible for virtually every ill in society. He thus has less in common with de Lamennais than with fundamentalist preachers fulminating on late-night weekend television over "the whore of Babylon."

maneuver, but was the result of a conviction that once he had borne his witness as vigorously as possible it was not for him to attempt to force circumstances, to attempt to bend the times to his own will: ". . . and that having said my say, time will decide for me, without my trouble, how far it was true, and how far not true."[11] It is generally and correctly assumed that Newman was one of the "kings of modern thought" Matthew Arnold referred to when he wrote in "Stanzas from the Grande Chartreuse":

> Silent they are, though not content,
> And wait to see the future come.
> They have the grief man had of yore,
> But they contend and cry no more.

The future would appear to have sided with Newman when he was named a cardinal a quarter of a century after Arnold wrote. But before explaining why it only *appeared* so, I want to turn briefly to the institution of the cardinalate itself. Ours is not the first epoch in the history of the church when even dedicated reformers have advocated the elimination of the office of cardinal. "We could do without cardinals altogether," says Bernard Häring in *My Hope for the Church*. But an office with a millennium of history is not lightly to be dissolved. Even though its official role has only been the election and occasional counseling of a pope, there remains a place for an institution that honors the highest order of Catholic temporal achievement—particularly if that institution were open to lay persons (as it once was) as well as clerics of both genders (as it will no doubt be in the future). If nothing more, it represents the simple sociological phenomenon of rightful ambition fulfilled that was discussed at the end of the previous chapter. But it also has an important symbolic significance both in the church and in the larger world. In the nineteenth century if de Lamennais had been made a cardinal as Leo XII originally sought, or if Rosmini had been made one as was Pius IX's early intent,

---

[11] In Henry Parry Liddon, *Life of Edward Bouverie Pusey* (London, 1897), IV, pp. 106–107.

their history, and possibly that of the church and the political order, would have been drastically different.[12] In the twentieth century it seems certain that if Newman had not been raised to the cardinalate, he would have been condemned in the anti-Modernist purge of Pius X. After Vatican II, Patriarch Maximos IV, one of the leading progressive prelates at the council, and a vocal defender of the priority of the patriarchate over the cardinalate, shocked his brother patriarchs by accepting the purple. But what looked briefly like a betrayal of ancient tradition, resulted in his having a greater influence in the universal church.[13]

More recently there has proved to be no more effective means of repairing bruised reputations or recognizing admirable services than being raised to the cardinalate, as with de Lubac (whose original rejection led to the elevation of Daniélou), Congar, von Balthasar, and Dulles—or, it should be mentioned, as an effective means for submerging eminence abused, as with the purpurate "defrocking"of Billot for persistence in supporting the Action Française. As for papal elections, they will certainly at some point in the future be opened to representatives of major Catholic bodies whether lay or clerical as well as national and international.

And herein lies a lesson about the temporal record—Newman's "future"—which relates to the "personal" and that record as it

---

[12] It is noteworthy that the year of de Lamennais' condemnation by the encyclical *Mirari Vos* (though he was not explicitly mentioned) is the year that Rosmini wrote *The Five Wounds of Holy Church.* He published it in 1846, the first year of the reign of Pius IX who he hoped would be the nominal head of a federation of Italian states, and who appeared to Rosmini so sympathetic to libertarian principles that he published two years later his *Constitution according to Social Justice.* After Pius's return from exile and his disenchantment with republicanism, both books were placed on the index; but after a lengthy investigation of the complete works, concluded in 1854, all censures were removed.

[13] The office represents the worst form of that "priestly caste" and "medieval pageantry" which is decried by protesting "levellers"and which—as the saying goes—"drives them up the wall": but if it is the wall of the upper church at Assisi they will see there depicted by Giotto a tonsured St. Francis accompanied by friars preaching to a crowned and attentive Honorius III with his attendant cardinals: the scene representing that homeostatic balance between center and periphery which has been the leitmotiv of this book—and a "periphery" notably absent in another depiction in St. Paul's-Outside-the-Walls where this pope (albeit miniaturized) communicates directly with Christ.

relates to the "historical." Abbé Bremond in his early study of what he called "the psychology" of Newman regretted that Dr. Newman of Birmingham[14] had accepted the red hat and thus gone down in a blaze of scarlet. But for Newman personally it was the final "lifting of the cloud" that he believed had hovered over him since his conversion. So much for the personal record—which Bremond would be more cognizant of after his own scurrying to attain his "fauteuil," and thus seemingly to transcend time among the "forty immortals" of the French Academy. But in the record as it relates to the "historical," Newman was again under a cloud with Pius X, and oscillatingly tolerated and forborne under later popes, only to be finally rehabilitated under John Paul II. The paradox here is that "personal" time is closed and definitive, historical time is ever-changing like the church it measures. As Pius XII said of the latter: "The mystical body of Christ, like the members who constitute it, does not muffle itself in the abstract, outside the fluctuations of space and time."

Another lesson of that opening parable is its illustration of the fact that the "patience" extolled in Hopkins' sonnet or in Lonergan's observation is not a matter of supine acquiescence, but of creative tension between ecclesiastical authority and its critics and occasional victims. The nature of this tension is described by Cardinal Congar in his suppressed *Vraie et fausse Réforme dans l'Eglise* when he speaks of the two levels of fidelity: "Fidelity to the Christian reality may be a fidelity to the state actually attained, to the forms here and now established of this reality: in brief a fidelity to its present. It may also be a fidelity to its future, which is the equivalent of a fidelity to its principle." He then adds that "there is a communication, a continuity, and therefore a harmony" between these two fidelities. But a harmony that entails what is a dominant note in Baron von Hügel's work, a "friction," that in turn entails a struggle towards resolution.

---

[14] We have, once again, more of that contemned human ambition publicly scorned (but privately sought) by purists: the "Dr." was Rome's chary compensation for Newman's Irish years, which he had expected would result in a mitre.

— II —

If there is anything that our nineteenth-century forebears offer to the twenty-first century, it is some noteworthy examples of how people under great personal pressure responded to ecclesiastical intransigence, how they parried its blows, temporized, feinted, struck back, or maintained silence; in sum, how they expressed in their actions the realization that the church not only exists in a given space and time, but that it is constituted by Congar's two levels of fidelity which demand a varying response at each level. Thus after Archbishop Ullathorne's suggestion to Newman bidding him give up the editorship of the *Rambler,* he published as we have seen his celebrated essay "On Consulting the Faithful in Matters of Doctrine." This was the advantageous moment to strike back, not at Ullathorne but at the curialists who in his own words had been making him "fight with a chain on my arm; it is like the Persians driven to fight under the lash."[15] At other times Newman published under pseudonyms, as would the Modernists; on other more provocative occasions he governed himself by the principle, "There are truths that are inexpedient," and remained silent with other "kings of modern thought."

One might learn similar lessons in the maintenance of the tension, the friction, between the two fidelities from the response to Roman exorbitance or obstinacy made by such a theologian-historian as Döllinger or by such a social reformer as de Lamennais. Döllinger himself told Ferdinand Gregorovius that he had written *Janus* anonymously in order not to sever himself from the Roman communion.[16] One may recall as well the "appeals to Rome" that flowed incessantly, in his own name, anonymously, or pseudonymously, from the pen of de Lamennais. It is not immobility to exercise restraint, to abide by the signs of the time, to have faith in history, to say as did Döllinger to Newman: "Is it at all prudent, advisable, to write . . . and to try to shake prejudices which seem

---

[15] Wilfrid Ward, *Life,* I, p. 588.

[16] *The Roman Journals of Ferdinand Gregorovius* (London, 1911), p. 339.

so firmly rooted?"[17] Such men as these did not "reject" the church, they were as noted in the previous chapter, hounded out of it. Up to his death, Döllinger protested himself a Roman Catholic, and de Lamennais, as Willfrid Ward accurately observed, finally broke only under the personal harassment of the bishops, and this after nearly a decade of incessant persecution.

Thus one rightly regards such figures as predecessors to be honored and imitated. Döllinger's *Lectures on the Reunion of the Churches* (London, 1872) is a primer of ecumenism for our time as for his own. One cannot but applaud de Lamennais for his stimulus to creative theology[18] (though no great theologian himself, as Dru rightly observed), and one should read the quotation that follows as the direct antecedent of *Gaudium et Spes* and the ancestral manifesto of liberation theology. In this passage, however much it bespeaks nineteenth-century Catholicism, or rather precisely because of its nineteenth-century origin and flavor, we see the second and now affirmative lesson that de Lamennais has for contemporary Catholicism. But it is not the Catholicism of the technologically and industrially advanced nations, but the Catholicism adapted to nations emerging from the depths of colonialism whether in Africa or Latin America; the Catholicism that in many cases has been both the cause and the partial cure of the malaise that liberation theology was intended to alleviate; and lastly, the Catholicism which has close affinities with that of nineteenth-century France as described by de Lamennais in *Des Maux de l'Eglise et de Société*: [19]

> Our cause is that of Catholicism, that of the Church, inseparable in itself from the cause of society. To defend the Church and work to revivify its antiquated character, for too long a time enervated,

---

[17] Wilfrid Ward, *Life,* I, p. 493.

[18] "In general one is not able to deny that the School of La Chênaie, not only by its example and its exhortations, but by the very questions that it raised, has been one of the factors, and perhaps the most effective at this time, of a renewal in theological speculation." Edgar Hocédez, *Histoire de la Théologie au XIXe Siècle* (Brussels, 1948), I, p. 123.

[19] Oeuvres complètes de F. de La Mennais (Paris, 1836–1837), XII, pp. 201–202.

is therefore to defend society and work for the salvation of people who everywhere today are so suffering. . . . It is therefore the Church that it is necessary to scrutinize first, it is for its evils that it is necessary to strive to find a remedy for there are no evils that do not derive from hers.

A Segundo or a Boff could not have put it better.

And there may be a further lesson in terms of another easily dismissed prophet, haughty, unsympathetic, unintellectual, as he appeared to many contemporaries and to his first biographers, Cardinal Manning, who not only as we have seen drew nearer to Newman's position limiting the scope of papal primacy, [20] but also became the Catholic leader who reestablished—as Newman could not—Catholicism as a force in English public life. He was on royal commissions for housing and for educating the families of the poor; he influenced *Rerum Novarum*, and his support for organizing—or as we would say, "unionizing"— workers was so vigorous that it led critics to denounce him as a "socialist." Lastly, he was a leader in temperance crusades—the latter dismissed by Newman ("my brother of Birmingham," as Manning caustically referred to him) in a chilling comment to the effect that he did not know whether there were too many dram shops, or too few. (Newman rightly described himself as "living out of the world," since Gin Lane and Beer Alley were as much a part of mid-Victorian London as they had been a century before when Hogarth satirized them.)

Of the first three English cardinals since the restoration of the hierarchy, Wiseman, Manning, and Newman, it was Manning who touched the heart of the nation and who was commemorated by Francis Thompson in a then-celebrated poem, "To the Dead Cardinal of Westminster." As to the other two prelates, Cardinal Wiseman, brilliant, affable, *and* feckless, was mocked by Browning in "Bishop Blougram's Reply"—a poem almost as exaggerated as recent journalistic descriptions of Pio Nono; even as Newman's conversion was a stimulus to Browning's publishing "The Bishop Orders His Tomb at St. Praxed's Church."

---

[20] The reference in earlier chapters and again here is: Shane Leslie, *Henry Edward Manning* (New York, 1921), p. 295.

So the lesson of all these figures from a tradition which is clothed in variety is that to depict this church as one-dimensional in *any* sense—whether as hungry for domination over its members,[21] or as marked more by deceit and sin than by holiness and catholicity—is to fall victim to unmitigated narrow mindedness and narrow sightedness. It is to squint at a heritage which for all its blemishes remains . . . ¿ not that of a power-hungry dominatrix but rather that of a community so full and so polyvalent that any right-minded persons can find "places" in it that are comforting and comfortable; that, as used to be said, allow "comfortable access" to the ultimate; and a community so multifaceted that in it

---

[21] Those who might have thought Foucault as theorist of master narratives had gone the way of *le grand bricoleur,* Lévi-Strauss, into the dusty bin of history (much as Diamat went the way of Tiamat) may be surprised that among postmodernists of a "retro" orientation Foucault is still invoked, as two citations from a diligent researcher, Gary Lease, in the field of "religious studies" illustrate. The first relates—rather monitorially—to "theory," the second to its application to historical phenomena. "Religions thus become the most finely tuned examples of *power structures* [original italics], patterns of force and power which control human lives and dictate how they are to be conducted. Make no mistake about it—religions are about power, about the power to be given you and about the power which controls you" (*"Odd Fellows"in the Politics of Religion,* Hawthorne, N.Y., 1994, pp. 50–51). During the period of the Modernist crisis, and speaking of the reaction of Pius X and his Secretary of State "to the collapse of a Church State and the resultant decline in the political power and role of the Vatican," Lease observes that they decided ". . . to refocus the church's attention and energies upon the so-called inner forum. . . . If one cannot control the actions and policies of other countries and their governments, then one can at least control what their populations believe." (*Catholicism Contending with Modernity,* edited by Darrell Jodock, Cambridge, 2000, p. 48.) I have noted frequently in this and earlier chapters the vulnerability of specialists in "religious studies" to transient fads or mercurial cultural trends. It stems from the discipline itself having traditionally at least a tertiary focus on a *deus ineffabilis,* that is, a focus on a "topic" about which whatever is said is by definition merely analogous. (It was not Karl Barth, but Stéphane Mallarmé who wrote "Le Démon de l'analogie.") Add to this the trendiness to which the "soft" humanistic disciplines are subject and one has all the components of a field day for the harebrained—who, unfortunately, never seem to seek out postmodern neurologists or pathologists, much less trepanners. I redeem my earlier criticism of George Steiner by citing that same Edinburgh lecture on "the voluminous triviality of so much that is produced in humane letters, art history, musicology. . . . the jugglers' ingenuities of deconstruction and post-modernism. *I have seen scientists stare, as at lunacy, at the central deconstructive axiom that 'there is nothing outside the text'."*

any right-minded persons can find models that are inspiring, endearing, enriching— and of course occasionally mystifying and even exasperating.[22]

One understands, then, why Newman though indifferent to social issues (the year of the *Essay on the Development of Christian Doctrine* is the year of Engels' *Conditions of the Working Class in England)* could reverse his reactionary Anglican opinion of de Lamennais, and reading the signs of the time more clearly that Gregory XVI or Gregory's successor, could declare "Perhaps La Mennais will be a true prophet after all."[23] It is also why he could praise such social liberals as Montalembert and Lacordaire, and in the process describe both the drastic change time brings, and the significance of localized "space" in such a process of change. Writing as a Catholic, he said in the *Apologia,* "I do not think that it is possible for me to differ in any important matter from two men whom I so highly admire. In their general line of thought and conduct I enthusiastically concur, and consider them to be before their age." Then in a revisionary autobiographical twist—what Seán O'Faoláin called "postcogitational" rumination—Newman, looking back on his Anglican days, bemusedly explains this seeming evolution in attitude:[24]

---

[22] It is worth noting the varying views these models had of one another. William George Ward, rhino-skinned ultramontanist, and friend of Tennyson who attended Maisie's christening, described Newman as "a powerful influence, perhaps unknown, to disloyalty to the Vicar of Christ, and to *worldliness.*" Maisie Ward, *The Wilfrid Wards and the Transition* (New York, 1934), p. 11. Acton described Newman as "an *ultramontane* fanatic and genius." Ibid., p. 240; whereas Döllinger in a letter to *The Times* wrote of Newman: " . . . the most brilliant, and the most precious acquisition the Church of Rome has made since the Reformation" (Birmingham Oratory Collection, uncatalogued). Newman on Wiseman: "The only thing of course, which it is worth producing, is *fruit*—but with the Cardinal, immediate show is fruit, and conversions the sole fruit. . . . And further still, they must be splendid conversions of great men, noble men, learned men, not simply of the poor" (Ward, *Life,* I, p. 584). Manning of Newman: "Do you know what ruined that man? Temper! Temper!" Shane Leslie, *Henry Edward Manning* (New York, 1921), p. 273. Von Hügel on Newman: "I used to wonder in my intercourse with John Henry Newman, how one so good, and who had made so many sacrifices to God, could be so depressing." Michael de la Bedoyere, *The Life of Baron von Hügel,* (London, 1952), p. 32.

[23] *Unpublished Letters of Matthew Arnold* (New Haven, 1923), p. 60.

[24] *Apologia pro Vita Sua* (London, 1902), p. 286.

If I might presume to contrast Lacordaire and myself, I should say; that we had been both of us inconsistent; —he, a Catholic, in calling himself a Liberal; I, a Protestant, in being an Anti-liberal; and moreover, that the cause of this inconsistency had been in both cases one and the same. That is, we were both of us such good conservatives, as to take up with what we happened to find established in our respective countries, at the time when we came into active life. Toryism was the creed of Oxford. He inherited, and made the best of, the French Revolution.

One understands, too, why Newman in his declining years, though he was unsympathetic to Döllinger's position, wanted to minister to his spiritual needs. Both the cardinal and the outcasts, Döllinger and de Lamennais, were men who clung to the faith of the church and looked to history for their vindication.

Like so many in our own day, history has proved them prophets—much to the discomfiture of other augurs like J.-M. Paupert who wrote a few decades ago about "le Stalinisme pioduodécimal"—though from time to time the ascription did not seem too far from the mark. But like the anatomists of papal sin and deceit (and like post-Foucauldians with their accusation, "all power to the steeple"—the White Panthers¿), Paupert proved another squinting seer. *Humani Generis*, the suppression of the Mission de France, the silencing of Jesuit and Dominican theologians (ominously known at the time as *la grande purge)* were foreseen by him as engendering disenchantment and defection. What was implicitly anticipated from the "purged" was the Roman Catholic counterpart of *The God that Failed.* (Well, *that* "god" did fail and the detritus still clutters the intellectual, and the real, landscape.) But the purged, silenced, suppressed, and sometimes exiled victims of Pius XII turned to prayer when forbidden to teach; to teaching "neutral" courses rather than theology (as earlier, Loisy was warned by Duchesne to "do" history, not theology); and if allowed to teach the latter, turning to less contemporaneous and thus less controversial areas, like historical studies in Scholasticism or Patristics; and finally to writing books hitherto unimagined by the authors themselves, and inconceivable to their faithful

readers. (De Lubac writing on Proudhon was possibly understandable; but to write on Buddhism could only be compared to—what
seems not only inconceivable but impossible—Solzhenitsyn writing a novel on New England rural life.) And for several, the vindication of history came, as it came for Newman, through elevation
to the cardinalate; for several others, through elevation *in petto,* in
the core of the faithful.

— III —

But even if the lesson appears to be that patience triumphs, again,
it is not a neutral or utterly resigned capitulation. That being said,
it must also be said that neither is it a blind acceptance of what
history or fate offer. Not everything that presents itself crying
out, as it were "Lord, Lord," is necessarily a providential opportunity. Hence the importance of Ignatian "discernment," discernment of the spirit as such and discernment of the spirit of the
times. (To take an example out of the air, i.e., the internet, Hans
Küng is not cousin germane to Matthew Fox.) Early in chapter
one I criticized McInerny's book on Pius XII for being contradictory in its treatment of Maurras, and wrong about Maritain and
Action Française. In the context of "discernment," I want to revisit both criticisms. The relevant paragraph in McInerny begins:
"In France, the *submission* of Charles Maurras . . . brought the conflict with Action Française to an end." The same paragraph concludes with: "Maurras and many of his followers defied the
condemnation for years before *submitting* to it." These two sentences bracket the discussion of Maritain. (It is of no importance
here that Maurras' actual submission occurred after he had been
sentenced to life imprisonment for siding with the Vichy fascists
during the war—finally converting shortly before his death in
1952.)[25]

---

[25] It is difficult to determine whether McInerny is himself sympathetic to
Maurras. There is his expression of admiration for Franco's fascists who were
supported by Maurras, and the only previous reference to the leader of Action
Française is a curiously neutral statement regarding Benedict XV's peace overtures in World War I: "Léon Bloy . . . called him Judas XV, while Charles Maurras
of Action Française supported the papal peacemaking efforts." (*The Defamation*

As I pointed out, McInerny failed to mention the influence of Maritain's spiritual director, Humbert Clérissac, an ardent advocate of Action Française during the years of Maritain's own conversion, and instead offered as reason why the movement "attracted many Catholics" including Maritain was that "it seemed to pit the tradition of French Catholicism against the secular and anti-clerical French government." Unmentioned is that other "tradition" of French Catholicism, antisemitism, particularly repugnant to Maritain whose wife was Jewish. Equally ignored is the "royalism" which was one of the cornerstones of Maurras' social edifice, and which one finds echoed in Clérissac's aphorism: "The Church stands out as an aristocracy, and through her Catholicity she canonizes the masses."[26] But the real issue has to do with discernment where one can glimpse, once again, the not always benign influence of Clérissac. In the Preface to the latter's only book (written before the first World War), Maritain quotes Clérissac, deferentially as one would expect of so generous a spirit, as offering advice that reflects not only blurred discernment but, in the end—and not withstanding the pious jargon in which it is couched—would lead to the "impractical purism" Maritain would elsewhere condemn.

The fact that a work is quite evidently useful for the good of souls is not sufficient reason for us to rush to carry it out. It is necessary that God should wish it for this precise moment (in that case there must be no delay); and God has His own time. It must first be desired, and be enriched and purified by that desire. It will be divine at this cost. And the man who will be charged with carrying it out will not perhaps be the one who has best understood it. We should beware of a human success that is too complete and too striking; it may conceal a curse. Let us not go faster than God. It is our emptiness and our thirst that He needs, not our plenitude.

---

of Pius XII, p. 12) The definitive critique of Maurras is not Maritain's politically genteel *Primauté du spirituel*, but Julien Benda's contemporary all-out assault on Catholic clerical fascism, *Trahison des clercs*. A decade later, Maritain's "humanisme intégral" would represent his genuine response to Maurras' "réalisme intégral."

[26] *The Mystery of the Church* (New York, 1937), p. 95.

In *True Humanism* Maritain criticizes "a fidelity to principles which are all the purer in being isolated from any connection with life and action, and enthroned like idols or like theorems."[27] When Newman warned that the Catholicism of his age was "sinking into a sort of Novatianism, the heresy which the early church so strenuously resisted," he was indicting this same "purism"— Novatian was in fact the first heretic to call himself "catharist"—a purism that led to "shrinking into ourselves, narrowing the lines of communion, trembling at freedom of thought."[28]

But the young Maritain (like Maisie Ward's *Young Mr. Newman* on Montalembert) also seemed to be acting as conservatively as Père Clérissac would have wished. This is implicit in my reference earlier to the "genteel" remonstrations in *Primauté du spirituel*, of which the following are not atypical: "We should always remember that there is normally a presumption of right in favor of the superior";[29] or, "The masses can in certain forms of polity appoint men to the task of watching over the public good, but, this appointment once made, sovereignty resides in them, not in the masses, and they hold it from on high, not from below."[30] Thus discernment varies with each unique occasion of place and time, with each understanding of the phenomena presented for judgment. And this, in Maritain's case would subsequently lead to his brilliant defenses, a kind of lyric philosophy of history, of democracy and human rights, only—as the dialectic and consequently

---

[27] (New York, 1938), p. 211.

[28] Ward, *Life*, II, p. 127.

[29] (New York, 1931), p. 30.

[30] *Ibid.*, p. 146. It should be noted, however, that even so conscientious a Catholic as Bernanos—though rejecting Maurras before the papal condemnation—only cleansed himself of the last vestiges of the Action Française when witnessing the thuggery of Franco's troops on Majorca during the Spanish civil war. While still a monarchist, his humanism and his passionate Christianity confronted Catholic terrorism, sanctioned by bishops and clergy, and left him bitter at the complicity of the church in the atrocities perpetrated by what he recognized would be a totalitarian regime. It is said that his memoir, *Les Grands Cimitières sous la lune*, in which he described these atrocities escaped the *Index* only at the insistence of Pius XI—whose successor as noted earlier would lift the sanctions on the Action Française. Another instance of Newman's "do/undo" dictum.

the process of discernment shifted—in old age to adopt a stance that would, again, have pleased his early mentor. Like that great phenomenologist, Dietrich von Hildebrand,[31] Maritain too became staunchly conservative in the aftermath of Vatican II. But this also was a reversal that illustrates the inevitability of change even among the prophetic spirits of the age who manifest their variegated humanness in shifting allegiances as the spirit moves them.

To an Ignatian spirit of discernment can be added a Pascalian *attente de Dieu,* but not as it is often translated and even lived in the sense of a "waiting upon":[32]—as though passive resignation were the goal, while opportunity, like some definitions of grace, was an arbitrarily given boon entirely independent of human agency. *Attente de Dieu* here has the sense of a response to being, of an *Antwort* to a *Wort.* This *"attente"* this openness to "what is" allows one to discern whether an action is to be done. It therefore

---

[31] In *Transformation in Christ* one can see exemplified *in actu exercito*—as one cannot in Scheler on resentment or empathy, or Stein on sympathy, or Husserl himself on the key notion of "Lebenswelt"—what is of value in that latter notion particularly as it devolves into a "method" of analysis that successively and progressively reveals the home ground or concrete experience of virtuous life. Von Hildebrand's book does for spirituality what Merleau-Ponty's *Phenomenology of Perception* does for corporeality: articulates a new and fresh *experience* of what one had hitherto vaguely glimpsed or sensed about one's "inner" life (with von Hildebrand) or one's embodiedness (with Merleau-Ponty). There are those who believe *Transformation in Christ* is the most significant "pure" work of spirituality of the last century— "pure" here meaning not trammeled by historical, philosophical, or even formal theological data.

[32] The phrase evokes not the searching Demeter image of a Dorothy Day but the contradictory Persephone figure of a Simone Weil who seems to have been both a winsome seeker of the absolute and an erratically gnostic infatuate of the darkest fatalism. (Hence her unusual style of Jewish antisemitism.) It was Weil's disenchantment with the Spanish civil war that led her to turn from the totalitarian left as it had led Bernanos to turn from the totalitarian right. By an almost miraculous conjunction, she read Bernanos' memoir, embraced it as the work of a fellow idealist, and wrote him of what she viewed as their common bond in a letter which he preserved—but at her request never apparently answered. She went on to her "martyrdom"; Bernanos went into exile in South America where he continued to nurse his royalist sentiments ("totalitarianism is the offspring of democracy"), and after the war returned to France from Algeria where he had written *Les Dialogues des Carmélites.* He died in 1947—like Cardinal von Galen the year before—a man of the right to the end.

can and must be related to the interior impulse of that action since, in Maritain's happy formulation, "action is the epiphany of being." And all of this means that the "interior life"—certainly a minimalist term—has to come into play in every reformist effort.

Anyone reading the works of the major religious figures mentioned here, de Lamennais, Döllinger, Lacordaire, Newman, Wilfrid Ward, Ullathorne; and more particularly anyone reading the works of the Modernists and their heirs, including von Hügel, Tyrrell, Blondel, Huvelin, early Loisy, Bremond, Laberthonnière, Teilhard, and de Lubac—anyone reading such works cannot but be struck by their sense of living in and being part of major religious crises; nor can anyone not but be struck by their heightened sense of bringing the signs of the times—scientific, social, and psychological—to bear on their reading of all "texts" whether biblical, theological, or scientific; similarly one cannot but be struck by their intense intellectualism at once elevated and profound yet practical; and finally, by their heroic scholarly aspirations and their remarkable accomplishments. But even more than all that—and it is a shocking surprise to those habituated to conventional academicians—one cannot but be struck by their manifestly deep and authentic prayer life.[33]

In every case I am talking about a high spirituality for which the abused term "mysticism" may be too grandiose; but a spirituality that is so interiorized it seems to reflect—certainly not indifference but—a calm detachment from external achievements. Here, again, one invokes the pure-hearted reformist impulse in

---

[33] It may not appear very "ecumenical" (and indeed it may stem from restricted knowledge or experience) to note that this quality is what seems to distinguish the Modernists from most other *fin-de-siècle* non-Catholic reformers. One might even venture to say that it is what distinguishes the great Catholic theologians of the twentieth century from most of their non-Catholic counterparts. Neither may it appear very "fraternal" to note, that in all the enormous output of the critics whom I am analyzing, there is virtually nothing whatever on the life of prayer, on meditation, contemplation, whatever. It is as though that long and splendid tradition of *oraison* had been replaced either by research, e.g., that *nada* is the *différance* between *apophasis* and *negativa,* or by exercises in assorted new age yogisms. This is true oddly enough even of those who had "Catholic training"—a significant phrase that will emerge later—in seminaries or other houses of religious formation.

Newman's dictum: "And that having said my say, time will decide for me, *without my trouble*, how far it was true, and how far not." This is quite unlike *perhaps* (for who can judge?) the somewhat goal-oriented spirituality displayed by Lord Acton in a letter to Mary Gladstone:[34]

> . . . we are not considering what will suit an untutored savage or an illiterate peasant woman who would never come to an end of the *Imitation* or the *Serious Call*. Her religion may be enough for heaven, without other study. Not so with a man living in the world, in constant friction with adversaries, in constant contemplation of religious changes, sensible of the power which is exerted by strange doctrines over minds more perfect, characters that are stronger, lives that are purer than his own. He is bound to know the reason why. First, because, if he does not, his faith runs a risk of sudden ruin. Secondly, for a reason which I cannot explain without saying what you may think bad psychology or bad dogma—I think that faith implies sincerity, that it is a gift, that does not dwell in dishonest minds. To be sincere a man must battle with the causes of error that beset every mind. He must pour constant streams of electric light into the deep recesses where prejudice dwells, and passion, hasty judgments and wilful blindness deem themselves unseen.

Admirable as this certainly is, and without getting into any discussion of those multiple grades, levels, scales of ascent to the sacred empyrean that have filled "manuals of perfection" from the time of the desert fathers, it nevertheless has a ring to it which is dissonant with what I am seeking to describe in several of the figures, particularly Newman, whom I mention above. Even taking into account that the latter had described himself as one "living out of the world," Acton's spirituality, appears practical and "instrumental," as the critical theorists use that term. And, of course, the unintentional touch of *snobbisme* does run counter to the piety of Maritain, "the peasant of the Garonne," or to that of the "Breton peasantry" (from whom Bremond was proudly descended), traditionally idealized as the model of devoutness and of

---

[34] *Op. cit.,* p. 134.

living in harmony with the spirit of that unread *Imitation* (that de Lamennais definitively translated into French).

Acton's faith sounds like a means to an end for "a man of the world" or like a therapeutic devisal for correcting historical misprision. Possibly Lord Acton might have profited from the advice the great spiritual director, Abbé Huvelin, gave to Baron von Hügel, that he should pray the rosary daily to help prevent his "interior life from losing touch with the devotion of the people."[35] Of course, it must be urged: would that we could all even come close to this Actonian spirituality—but that is not the issue here. The issue is the astonishing depths (particularly among the Modernists, their predecessors, and their heirs) of what can simply be defined—and one wants to be very plain here—as a living core of interiority, a core one discerns in the writings of such speculative thinkers and spiritual masters as Blondel, von Hügel, and Newman.

— IV —

Though this relationship of the intellectual to the spiritual life is difficult to define, it can be illustrated. Everyone knows—it is another of those telling passages—Newman's comment in the *Essay in Aid of a Grammar of Assent* on the fragmented lines in the *Aeneid* which are, historically, merely the result of Vergil's early death. But mortality has little to do with the foundational insight of Newman's observation on those "pathetic half lines, giving utterance, as the voice of Nature herself, to that pain and weariness, yet hope of better things which is the experience of her children in every time." It is not the echo of Vergil's death Newman hears; it is something in those lines that elicits a deeper understanding, a deeper sense of fragmented being. The connection between that deeper understanding and such heightened piety—among people who have been, after all, academically defined as just another loosely affiliated group of "professional" intellectuals—is made by

---

[35] De la Bedoyere, *Life*, p. 60.

Aquinas following Augustine when he associates the gift of *knowledge* with the Beatitude, "Blessed are they that *weep*" (*S.T.*, II,-II, 9,2). This is certainly a most surprising if not a just plainly odd nexus; but it is made on the grounds that this gift empowers one to see more deeply the traces of being in the universe and awakens, unreflectively and unintendedly, a longing for wholeness through union with the ultimate. It is this unreflective and unthematized sigh from *el profundo centro* of the person's very selfness that constitutes the "spirituality" I am trying to show as displayed in the various figures invoked above.

Here two reservations must be entered: this consideration of the remarkable phenomenon of the most serious and even rarified intellectuals being so unreservedly pious must' be as objectively detached as possible since few can speak as experienced or versed in these matters, and thus are well-advised to write, as here, only in the role of "analyst." Second, it must be said, as I suggested earlier, that within admittedly limited experience of other Christian bodies and religious institutions, and making allowance for the best of ecumenical intentions, it seems that among nineteenth- and twentieth-century religious scholars, it is primarily within such a body of Roman Catholics that one comes across such a depth of *pietas*. This judgment is quite possibly due to a narrow range of experience, and so is offered as nothing more that one reaction among others to a phenomenon that, nevertheless, strikes one as truly extraordinary. Freely admitted is the fact that this may be bias born of a whole gamut of possible limitations (however much one seeks to overcome them), just as the equally biased notion that pride and intellectuality go hand in hand may also merely indicate an unfortunate consequence of restricted experience.

That latter bias takes the form of the cliché which encapsulates the sentiment that practitioners of the Dominican, Sertillanges' *La Vie Intellectuelle* (a book almost as nugatory as Rilke's *Letters to a Young Poet*) are out of touch with reality and victims of self-infatuation. One may cite Fernand Hayward on Döllinger: ". . . a university professor of great learning, but also of excessive pride."[36] When Hayward—who could have used some Actonian piety—goes on to indulge in biographical ultramontanism by suggesting that Döllinger's opposition to the Council resulted from disappointment at not being invited, one again—as in my first chapter—wants to cry out with Newman to Kingsley, "Why, man, you are writing a romance!" In those same stereotyping circles the comparison is of the proud de Lamennais with the humble Lacordaire, the proud Loisy with the humble Laberthonnière,[37] or the comparison is of an Abbé Bremond with the snide fictional cliché of Bernanos' haughty and unbelieving Abbé Cenabre.

The reverse of the stereotype is nearer the truth. Döllinger offered mass daily—a contradiction of the priggish Cardinal Vaughan's post-1871 recollections.[38] Tyrrell kept trying to get permission to say mass after his suspension,[39] and as late as two years before his excommunication, even Loisy asked for the renewal of his permission to celebrate in his own home.[40] Von Hügel, author of two densely learned volumes on mystical experience, nourished his own spirituality on the relatively elementary writings of Jesuit

---

[36] *The Vatican Council* (Dublin, 1951), p. 49.

[37] Typical would be the Irish bishop, MacHale, "recollecting" a meeting with de Lamennais in 1832: "Fortunately for M. De La Mennais he was then accompanied by two young friends who loved him much, but who loved truth and religion more." Ulrick J. Canon Bourke, *The Life and Times of Most Rev. John MacHale* (New York, 1883), p. 96. Similarly, "Laberthonniere never lost his faith and remained faithful to the Church, while Loisy was an apostate who often minimized, contaminated and defamed the subject of his criticism." Jean-Paul Gelinas, *The Revival of Thomism under Leo XIII and the New Philosophies* (Washington, 1959), p. 67. With reference to de Lamennais and Döllinger among others the Introduction speaks of, "The pride and sufficiency of certain minds had reached, in the middle of the past century, an extreme degree of blindness." And on Loisy from a more respectable historian: "A scholar and intellectual, proud and persistent, he had always found it very hard to bow his spirit to the daily devotional exercises required of a priest." E.E.Y. Hales, *The Catholic Church in the Modern World* (New York, 1958), p. 180.

[38] Malcolm MacColl, *Memoirs and Correspondence,* ed., George W.E. Russell (London, 1914), p. 310. J.G. Snead-Cox, *The Life of Cardinal Vaughan* (St. Louis, 1911), I, p.64.

[39] De La Bedoyere, *Life,* p. 202.

[40] Alec R. Vidler, *The Modernist Movement in the Roman Catholic Church* (Cambridge, 1934), p. 139.

popularizers of what Bremond commemorated in his *Histoire du sentiment religieux en France* (just as de Lamennais had devoted himself to translating an equally fundamental treatise of Louis de Blois). Von Hügel, the embodiment of *Wissenschaft*, exulted in such derivative and rudimentary remnants of what Bremond called "the French School" as de Caussade and Louis Lallement, and sent as a gift to Blondel a volume of the *Ecole de Jésus Christ* by "my beloved Père Grou"—all of whom (Jesuits or ex-Jesuits during the suppression of the Society) he hoped would help "minimize the unfortunate mental habit of thinking life and mystery are exhausted by the definitions of St. Thomas."[41]

Of course, it is not a matter of embracing popularizations or vulgarizations, but of avoiding the over-intellectualizing of all aspects of personal existence, of not becoming either a gradgrind or a casaubon. It was alleged by Walter Benjamin that Brecht kept on his desk a toy donkey with a sign which read, "I too must understand." And Wallace Stevens once dismissed the exotically plumaged birds of Audubon with the observation, "No back yard cheepers for that connoisseur." Well, the spiritual writers favored by von Hügel and Blondel—apart from Loisy, in many ways the two most deeply learned of the Modernists—would all fall into that category of keeping their roots planted in the common ground of the settled and tested. No vainglorious aspirations to soaring to the mystical (or ornithological) heights; no Oriental raptures or Latinate levitations, no Rhenish or Flemish apophatic ecstasies, no Bérullian *élévations* whether thematically or stylistically—indeed a spirituality more akin to the *Imitation* and the *Serious Call*, and more dependent on what Cuthbert Butler described in his *Western Mysticism* as "pre-Dionysian, pre-scholastic and non-philosophical [hence the contrast between the writings of Père Grou and the definitions of Aquinas], unaccompanied by psychophysical concomitants."

But here again a caveat must be entered. The "spirituality" that Dom Butler was distinguishing as esoteric and even alien engendered its own reforms, and ultimately found its home in the larger

---

[41] René Marlé, *Au Coeur de la Crise Moderniste* (Paris, 1960), p. 29.

tradition of Catholic prayer life. The only reason for stressing the antithesis of that spirituality here is that the conventional view of reformist efforts is their stemming from arrogant "intellectuals," from those who are out of touch with day-in and day-out existence—as though academics did not live in the pressures of the commonplace. The point of discussing in this context these nineteenth-century reformers is precisely to emphasize how their spiritual life was sustained and fostered not by other insular theoreticians, but by people whose roots were steeped in the universal heritage and life of the *ecclesia*. In another odd conjunction, to again bring up that poet who, like Blondel and Loisy, was viewed as among the most "cerebral" and "abstract" writers of his age—pejoratives by contemporary standards, as was also his designation as a "deathbed convert"—Wallace Stevens, on the lure of the *scintilla Dei*: " From whose being by starlight, on seacoast, / The innermost good of their seeking / Might come in the *simplest of speech.*"

Clearly, the tradition is too rich to be reduced to a uniform sameness; and reform too complex to be achieved by a recipe or technique whether of simplicity and earthiness or of grandeur and majesty. Still, making due allowance for individual differences across the whole spectrum of possibilities, that prayer life and the reforms it engenders, will achieve most for humankind when they stem not from an abstract idea of the church, not from a notion of the church as mere object of historical research, but as Congar says from "the concrete reality and given situation of the church in the here and now."

That reality and that situation are rich and multifarious. Critics strumming a monochord and declaiming conspicuous and transitory components to be paramount in the church today, whether sinful deceit or historical antisemitism, have simply not thought enough, looked broadly enough, or been open enough to discern the polyphonic splendor of two millennia of Catholicity. Of course there are awesome flaws, flaws that the figures discussed here all sought to correct; but not out of rancor or resentment, not out of personal passion, and certainly not through distorted scholarship, but simply out of love for the tradition, out of devotion to what it represented at its purest. And another encouraging sign which I have mentioned twice, but particularly relevant to the twenty-first century, is the rehabilitation of Antonio Rosmini, another prophet born out of due time, and author of that exemplar of true reform, *The Five Wounds of Holy Church*.[42]

---

[42] Pope John Paul I wrote his thesis at the Gregorian University on Rosmini's doctrine of the origin of the human soul. There must be a literature on this, since it would be particularly useful to know whether the issue of origin relates to the rumor that as Bishop, Albino Luciani suggested to Paul VI that approval should be given for the use of anovulants.

7

BEYOND THE POLITICS OF RANCOR II

The Vagaries of Institutional Renovation

> "Instead of aiming at being a world-wide power, we are shrinking into ourselves, narrowing the lines of communication and using the language of dismay and despair at the prospects before us."
>
> *Cardinal Newman*

Because of Rosmini's wider range of concerns than, say, Peter Damian, or the Council of Constance—both cited earlier in the history of "exceptions"—but mainly because of chronological proximity, the Founder of the Institute of Charity may provide a more useful program for reform, even as he certainly provides a better model for its advocacy.[1] His major concern was political freedom for the church and implicitly for the citizen; nevertheless the five wounds still bleed, and may be translated into today's terms as clericalism, ignorance, episcopal rivalry, secularism, and wealth. Though the curing of these sores could be achieved by the simple application of Blondel's healing compress:[2]

---

[1] There is also a Newman connection. Rosmini's earliest co-worker in the Institute of Charity, Luigi Gentili, went on the "English Mission" and proved an exceptionally forceful preacher who converted one of Newman's disciples, William Lockhart, two years before Newman himself "conformed to the Church of Rome." The conversion, against Newman's explicit wishes, led to Newman's resignation from the curacy of St. Mary's church in Oxford because, as he wrote his bishop, Lockhart's conversion would be "laid at my door." There are several pages in the *Apologia* on the incident because the Anglican Newman was very intent on not appearing and not being a "Romanizing" influence on others.

[2] *Attente du Concile* (Paris, 1964), a collection of aphorisms, p. 92.

> *The worst of aberrations*:
>   Catholicism without Christ,
>   Religion without soul,
>   Authority without heart

—nevertheless there is much value to examining Rosmini's diag-
nosis. Broadly speaking, and with some application to the English-
speaking world, the clericalism takes the form of aloofness from
the body of the faithful, symbolized by a non-vernacular liturgy;[3]
the ignorance is of theology among the clergy and as a consequence among the laity as well; the rivalry is the kind that
destroys episcopal unity; the secularism has to do with governmental interference in ecclesiastical matters; and the wealth is
more the sort that begot the image of bricks-and-mortar prelates
in the American immigrant church and less the sort that is defined
as simple greed—though in Rosmini's time he had mainly in mind
government appointments to wealthy sees. Greed, I assume, is relatively rare in the contemporary church[4] as, of course, is also political interference in religious affairs. (Rosmini himself singles out
the unique situation of bishops in the United States.) As for episcopal disunity, it would in these monolithic times be a welcome
phenomenon; while the clericalism (or as Wills and Carroll would
describe it the "priestly caste") is virtually non-existent, save as it
may relate to the current papal ban on the ordination of women.
Since that is clearly a moot issue, and one that will inevitably be

---

[3] "But if it pleased God to allow His Church to receive so deep a wound by
the separation of the Christian people from their clergy in the solemn acts of
worship, is this wound incurable? Can it be that the people, who by primitive
rule not only witnessed but took part in the services of the Lord's House, will
now be satisfied with little more than bare attendance there? Scarcely so, I think;
for it is too much to expect of an intelligent and civilized people that they will
come mechanically to attend rites in which they have no longer any share, and
which they do not understand." *The Five Wounds of Holy Church* (London, 1883),
p. 24. The editor and introducer of the volume is Henry Parry Liddon, disciple
and biographer of Pusey, and spiritual director of Hopkins during his Oxford
years.

[4] But as I noted in the first chapter, the virtue police are on the prowl seeking
out such things as expensive stereos to prove a dangerous decline in sacerdotal
asceticism.

resolved in time, the one remaining "wound" with present-day relevance has to do with theological education, whether of clergy or laity. Speaking of the theological manuals of his time (the manuals used in the schooling of Pio Nono), Rosmini rises to rare irony and anger:[5]

> By these steps [downward]—Holy Scripture, the Fathers, Schoolmen, and theologians—we have come at last to those marvelous text-books now used in our seminaries which instil so much would-be wisdom, and so poor an opinion of our predecessors. These books, I believe, will, in the more hopeful future days of the imperishable Church, be considered to be the most meagre and the feeblest that have been written during the eighteen centuries of her history. They are books without life, without principles, without eloquence and without system . . . They are the product neither of feeling, nor talent, nor imagination; they are not episcopal nor priestly, but in every sense lay; they require only masters able to read mechanically, and pupils who can listen as mechanically.
>
> If little books and little teachers go together, can a great school be formed out of such elements? Or can they aim at a dignified system of instruction? No. And this defect is the fourth and last cause of the Wound in the Church now under review.[6]

— I —

In a period of intense centralization in the church, and of friction between that centralizing impulse and the American theological community, it is still possible to take Newman's long view which,

---

[5] *Five Wounds,* pp. 66–67.

[6] Newman says it more elegantly in the third volume of *Historical Sketches* (London, 1894), short miscellaneous papers from his Dublin experience; here speaking of "religious teaching" under the heading "What Is a University?" ". . . its great instrument, or rather organ, has ever been that which nature prescribes in all education, the personal presence of a teacher or, in theological language, Oral Tradition. It is the living voice, the breathing form, the expressive countenance, which preaches, which catechises. Truth, a subtle, invisible manifold spirit, is poured into the mind of the scholar by his eyes and ears, through his affections, imagination, and reason."

in this first instance, depicts the kinds of critics castigated in the previous chapters:[7]

> . . . authoritative prohibitions may tease and irritate, but they have no bearing whatever upon the exercise of reason. . . . I will go on to say further, that, in spite of all that the *most hostile critic* may urge about the encroachments or severities of high ecclesiastics, in *times past, in the use of their power,* I think that the event has shown after all, that they were mainly in the right, and that those whom they were hard upon were mainly in the wrong. . . . it is clearly the duty of authority to act vigorously in the case. Yet the act will go down to posterity as an instance of a tyrannical interference with private judgment, and of the silencing of a reformer, and of a *base love of corruption or error.*

Then comes the second instance, with a shift to the present and by implication to Newman's own plight as a theologian. He begins by noting as a truism that, "It is individuals, and not the Holy See, that have taken the initiative, and given the lead to the Catholic mind, in theological inquiry." He then describes an ideal type of scholar, one who is totally open to having his ideas debated.[8]

> He is willing, or rather would be thankful, to give them up, if they can be proved to be erroneous or dangerous, and by means of controversy he obtains his end. He is answered, and he yields; or on the contrary he finds that he is considered safe. He *would not dare to do this*, if he knew an authority, which was supreme and final, was *watching every word* he said, and made signs of assent or dissent to each sentence, as he uttered it. Then indeed he would be fighting, as the Persian soldiers, under the lash, and the freedom of his intellect might truly be said to be beaten out of him.

That the reference to soldiers fighting under the lash is used by Newman in his correspondence to describe his own relations with

---

[7] *Apologia pro Vita Sua* (London, 1902), pp. 258–259.
[8] Ibid., pp. 265–266.

the curia makes clear that this is not, as the context might suggest, a detached description of some hypothetical condition or some idealized *persona*.[9]

After prudently suggesting that "in the general run of things" the conditions he describes have "not been so," he moves on to a treatment of what may providentially keep them from becoming *so* in the future: the interdependence of the various national episcopates. "And here again is a further shelter for the legitimate exercise of the reason:—the multitude of nations which are within the fold of the Church" which act "for its protection against any narrowness . . . in the various authorities in Rome." He then illustrates this by discussing at length the influence of "the Greek tradition" (exemplified *only* in the church Fathers); this leads, shrewdly enough, to a treatment of how "such *national* influences" have a "providential effect in moderating the bias which the local influences of Italy may exert upon the see of Peter. It stands to reason [just *as reasonable* as that "Patristic tradition" equals "national influence"] that, as the Gallican [10] Church has in it a French element, so Rome must have an element of Italy"; then to drive home as simply obvious to any "reasonable" person the importance of the Fathers and the Gallican divines vis-à-vis Rome, he concludes with seeming deference, "and it is no prejudice to the zeal and devotion with which we submit ourselves to the Holy See to admit this plainly."

This is a rhetorical *tour de force* which will only get more incisively pre-emptive of the goals of the ultramontanists in its conclusion which, apart from his thanks to personal friends—a

---

[9] Ward, *Life,* I, p. 588.

[10] The word in 1864, before Vatican I, could only evoke "the Gallican liberties" formulated, after two centuries of practice, by French ecclesiastics in 1682. Apart from political-religious issues, the liberties were conciliarist in orientation, maintaining that papal teaching must be confirmed by the universal church, and (like the English Cisalpinists a century later) that popes could not depose civil rulers. Even more striking is Newman's subtle balancing of the Gallican and the Roman church, as though Gallican views—not only abhorred by ultramontanists but generally viewed as at least incipiently unorthodox—were on a par with Roman views centered on papal primacy, papal infallibility, and papal authority. He comes close to leaving it to the reader to pick up on the implication that both are simply two national churches, reflecting their own geographical, linguistic,

passage that deeply moved George Eliot[11]—ends the *Apologia* as far as the "position of my mind since 1845" goes. It is as much an *apologia* of his life as it is of the life of every subsequent Catholic intellectual. The following was his final swipe at the curialists:

> It is a great idea [the near-colloquialism attunes the mild irony] to introduce Latin *civilization* into America, and to improve the Catholics *there* by the *energy of French devotedness* [for which he had great disdain]; but I trust that all European races will ever have a place in the Church, and assuredly I think that the loss of the English, not to say the German element, in its composition has been a most serious misfortune.

What would sound in Rome like an admirable call to convert Lutherans and Anglicans was equally if not more so, a defense of the freedom of scholars from the needless constraints of authority—of English scholars like Newman as well as Germans like Dr. Döllinger who at the Munich Congress the previous year had aroused the wrath of Pius himself by delivering a manifesto on the independence of the Catholic intellectual. The *finale*, aptly ingratiating but with a well-honed edge, thanks the pope: "And certainly, if there is one consideration more than another which should make us English grateful to Pius the Ninth, it is that, by giving us a church of our own, he has prepared the way for *our* own habits of mind, *our* own manner of reasoning, *our* own tastes, and *our* own virtues. . . ." —as opposed to those of "Latin civilization," or "the local influences of Italy."

The issue for "civilization" in Catholic America today is whether the bishops will assert their own native heritage of independence, and thereby make a contribution to the church Catholic. It is ironic in the light of Newman's words to read the ending

---

and cultural roots—not entirely unlike his earlier equation of the *motive* of Montalembert's liberalism with the *fact* of Newman's conservatism.

[11] She wrote Sarah Hennell that "the *Apologia* breathed much life in me," and showing more discernment than would Geoffrey Faber said, "Pray mark that beautiful passage in which he thanks his friend Ambrose St. John. I know hardly anything that delights me more than such evidences of sweet brotherly love being a reality in the world." J.W. Cross, *George Eliot's Life as Related in Her Letters and Journals* (London and Edinburgh, n.d.), p. 378.

of Leo XIII's letter to Cardinal Gibbons on what has somewhat inaccurately been dismissed as a "phantom heresy": "American-ism, in the bad sense of the word, leads one to conclude that there are some who seek a Church in America which will be different from the Church in the rest of the world." The irony is underlined when one reads such Americanists as Archbishop Ireland:[12]

> The supernatural rests on the natural, which it purifies and enno-bles, adding to it supernatural gifts of grace and glory. Where the natural is most carefully cultivated, there will be found the best results from the union of nature and grace. It is a time of novelties, and the religious action, to accord with the age, must take new forms and new directions.

And that irony is redoubled when one reads Blondel—since Amer-icanism was merely a local variant of Modernism—on the new theological era: "Now that dogmatic precision, unity, and author-ity are surely obtained and maintained, there is room for an expansion and for a meeting with modern aspirations which come from another direction, but from the same invisible breath of the Spirit who brings all to the same sheepfold."[13]

Ireland and Blondel were simply engaged in what would later be called discerning the signs of the times. This discernment is needed now when the intellectual life, particularly of theologians, is under siege (a Sainte Siege?) by the heirs of the ultramonta-nists—which leads to a final irony: that the theologically best trained American prelates at Vatican I were on the side of the "in-opportunists," the opponents of the decree on infallibility. The issue before the current episcopate is whether it will be true not only to its office as teacher but as successor to those bishops who up until the 1970's asserted their rightful place in the episcopal college *as* Americans and Catholics—and made some of the most significant contributions to the truly reformative decisions at Vat-ican II, decisions which helped shape an entire church.

The present episcopate has inherited a noble tradition that,

---

[12] *The Church and Modern Society* (Chicago, 1896), p. 63.
[13] *Attente du Concile,* p. 143.

under the pressure of increased conformity and centralization, now is in danger of being abandoned.[14] In the light of the possible enforcement of what has euphemistically been called "mandatum" (though certainly a *new* commandment)—and what might more accurately be called, after Blondel, *esprit de guillotine théologique*—Catholic theologians in any Catholic institution of higher education will be faced when broaching any controversial issue, exactly as Newman had put it "by an authority, which was supreme and final, was watching every word they said, and made signs of assent or dissent to each sentence. . . ." Perhaps some American bishops will hearken to these words of Newman. Or if they don't, they too may be confronted by not only "the loss of the English and German element" but also the loss of "the American element" in the church. And they too may be forced to wait for some future pontiff to give "us a Church of our own, . . . for our own habits of mind, our own manner of reasoning, our own tastes, and our own virtues, finding a place and thereby a sanctification, in the Catholic Church."

—II—

Before considering that heavy burden borne by the episcopate—which constitutes the central element in any reform effort—let me briefly try to address what a consistent, calm, and ultimately effective reformer from another tradition, the Southern Baptist, Will Campbell—who can best be described as a "commonsense moralist"—might say about the problems besetting two of the authors of the books I have been discussing. That is, "Brother Garry's" and "Brother James's" besetting concerns: endemic deceit,

---

[14] Perhaps there is a need for fewer canonists and more students of the history of their own church like the long-lamented Paul Hallinan of Atlanta. Perhaps the bishops of those dioceses whose predecessors opposed Cardinal Spellman and spoke out against threats to the principle of noncombatant immunity during the Vietnam war will study that record and be inspired to speak out against erosion of the principle of what Newman called like a true Englishman, "elbowroom for the mind." As a gentle nudge, those dioceses were: Evansville, Dodge City, Stockton, Lafayette, Reno, Bridgeport, Wichita, Richmond, Pueblo.

and antisemitism. As to the latter, viewed by Carroll as "constituent," he may want to extend his reading list. In the Introduction to the Autumn, 1966, issue of *Continuum*, after *Nostra Aetate* had appeared, one may read:

> "Bless me, Father, for I have sinned" has been the indispensable prologue to the sacrament of Penance. Without the admission of sin and plea for forgiveness there could be no re-acceptance into the household of the faith. Notwithstanding, the Catholic Church in the confessional of history has yet to acknowledge its guilt, before the common Father of church and synagogue, for its systematic persecution of Jews.
>
> The editors of this journal could not hope to imagine that what they offer here shall precipitate some vast collective metanoia. They merely seek to witness to their own concern at Christian complicity in the perennial resurgence of antisemitism. And, in analyzing its pathology, they write simply, as Robinson Jeffers said, "in dutiful hope of burning off at least the top crust of the time's uncleanness."

So be of good heart; you have predecessors, though not perhaps as autobiographically fixated; and you will undoubtedly have successors—though one might hope, less self-revelatory ones.[15]

---

[15] Contributors to that issue included Oscar Cohen, Charles Y. Glock, Rodney Stark, Michael Marrus, Robert Major, Norbert Muhlen, Eliezer Berkovits, Arthur Hertzberg, Erich Isaac, Gavin I. Langmuir, Jacob Neusner, Howard Nemerov, Leon Poliakov, Steven S. Schwarzschild, Gregory Baum, Thomas Merton, and Rosemary Ruether. The last named is certainly one of the most creative and productive theologians of the last half century, but she has had difficulty in recognizing that the state of Israel, for all its unquestioned but inevitable faults, is the "compensatory" international response to the Holocaust. Given her political views and passion for justice, it is understandable—if nor forgivable—that she would "accuse the main authors of this symposium . . . , together with the editor of *Continuum* . . . , of being party to the ongoing *ethnocide* of the Palestinian people." The symposium in question appeared in the first number of the second series of the journal, "Anti-Semitism, Middle East, Feminism," (Autumn, 1990); its contributors were, John K. Roth, Mary C. Boys, Robert Everett, John Pawlikowski, Alice and A. Roy Eckardt, Emil Fackenheim, Franklin Littell, Paul van Buren. This is mentioned not to underline an editorial position or ideological orientation, but simply as *récit* of a history of treating these issues without pursuing scapegoats. Those unaware of such a history are presumably those who are referred to in Garry Wills' lead-off blurb for *Constantine's Sword:* "This searingly

As for Wills' preoccupation with "papal sin and structural deceit," the emphasis should, by definition, be on the latter. No one can do anything about "sin" except perhaps to pray and to cast no stones—even at popes. But "structures" are, according to going postmodernist definitions, if not "invented," then "social" fabrications and as such subject to construction, reconstruction, deconstruction, etc.—depending of course on one's choice of prepositions, suppositions, compositions, or just plain, positions.[16] But the pursuit of sinners not only goes against Catholic training, it is the path of sterility. Sin itself is in the world where we live, and as Newman said in the quotation from *Anglican Difficulties* at the end of five chapters, it is manifest in the life of the church as of that world. It is not only in the Hebrew Bible but in all of history that the deity moves through time and achieves its ends through vehicles that are drawn by all "the cords of Adam" and subject to all the flaws of creaturehood. One might wish it otherwise, and strive to make it so, but those with any kind of "training" should hardly be surprised that, for example, the acts of the first Vatican Council are sometimes reminiscent of the reports in the *Congressional Record*, or that after the Council in order to force certain recalcitrant bishops[17] to make their public submission, the Roman authorities employed methods akin to those of a successful political machine. We live in time, and through temporal instruments, salvation comes. What else would redeeming the time mean?

---

honest book is Augustinian in the way Carroll searches his own soul, going down through layer after layer of instilled Catholic attitudes that demean Jews. *We who had the same Catholic training* badly need this book, to cleanse our souls, to make us all ask for forgiveness." Admirable sentiments particularly for those whose Catholic training taught them not to play fast and loose with truth, and not to be seduced by what Adorno called "the jargon of authenticity." (Maybe the Sisters of Mercy responsible for that Catholic training came from the capital of Kentucky where they maintained the Frankfort school.)

[16] The best short critique of social construction is by Paul A Boghossian, *The Times Literary Supplement*, February 23, 2001; the most devastating exemplification is Alan Sokal's well known "hoax"—garnering hundreds of entries on the internet—which Boghossian also treats in the *TLS*, December 13, 1996.

[17] It happened to Kenrick of St. Louis, who with his brother was one of the few American episcopal theologians, and Hefele of Rottenburg, protégé of J. A. Möhler and conciliar historian: "Rome was bringing silent pressure to bear by

But here a cautionary note might be appropriate. "Reformers" who recognize the human element in the church and rightly condemn its abuses, might also want to take into account when registering their complaints, grievances, accusations, denunciations—in that ascending order—the "human element" in *their targets.* To publicly deploy texts and interpretations that are clearly distorted, or to bring overcharged rhetoric to the arraignment before one's private bar of justice of bishops and popes, past and present—this does not seem the most effective mode of making one's case; particularly if one is making it not to disinterested bystanders but *to* those very bishops and popes or *about* their predecessors. It smacks less of the creation of an informed public opinion than of playing to the gallery, less of calm conversion and regeneration than of mobocracy and religious "mccarthyism"—if not of mere self-aggrandizement. *Fortiter in re; suaviter in modo* is not a social or legal axiom. It is a dictate of common sense.

And it is also a sign of authentic reform, as the following from Bernard Häring's book makes clear. After several times praising the German Episcopal authors of a detailed statement on ministering to people from broken marriages, to people who are divorced, separated, or remarried, and noting that three times the bishops had been called to Rome for questioning, only in the end to have the "Sacred Rota" reject their arguments, Father Häring interjects on the last page of *My Hope for the Church*: "At this point, readers may perhaps ask me how, despite everything, I still maintain that a turnaround for the better is in the offing. I have many reasons for my prognosis. *Above all,* I would mention *the dignified, upright, and absolutely nonviolent attitude* of the three German bishops and the encouraging echoes of their action." An echo certainly unexpected by Father Häring resounded after his death. In the year 2001, one of the rebuffed bishops, Karl Lehmann of Mainz, was made a cardinal by John Paul II.[18]

---

withholding dispensations . . . in marriage cases." Cuthbert Butler, *The Vatican Council* (London, 1938), II, p. 187.

[18] It seems not excessively optimistic to anticipate that after the "turnaround" foreseen by Father Häring, at least one American theologian will be a candidate for the purple precisely because of "the dignified, upright, and abso-

In the above quotation one term stands out, particularly in the context of attitudes toward curial decisions: "nonviolent." Certainly in response to such decisions one would not expect the kind of conduct that abortion protesters habitually engage in, and against which even Supreme Court decrees seem to provide only the thinnest of shields. What the term does suggest is the strategy of Martin Luther King which by its very mode of bearing witness won the support of the previously indifferent or even antagonistic. But with such curial decisions as the enforcement of contraception bans, as well of bans related to other aspects of *purely personal* comportment, one cannot expect marches and public demonstrations. (And it is quite certain that precisely to the degree written denunciations are condescending, strident, or hectoring—to that degree they will result in reinforcement of the original decisions, as well as further proliferation by "public relations" hacks of those ludicrous rants about "contraception and the culture of death" already emanating from epigonal curialists.) The very private nature of the matters involved entails a different mode for registering public opinion in the church; that mode takes life in what is called "voting with one's feet." In this instance, simply ignoring the ban altogether—as is of course the case with the vast majority of faithful Catholics. At some point, as Father Häring intimated, the message will get across to the episcopate which will then convey it to the "legislators" at the center who often have no idea of what is going on at the periphery.[19] All of this is a twenty-first century response to an age-old problem of redressing imbalances.

---

lutely nonviolent attitude" he has taken in pressing his reformist case and in responding to Roman censure. For one view of such "responding," cf. Charles E. Curran, *Faithful Dissent* (Kansas City, 1986), and *The Catholic Moral Tradition Today* (Washington, D.C., 1999).

[19] Father Häring has a revelatory tale of married priests about whose problems the pope didn't seem to have the slightest inkling: "I spoke with Pope Paul VI about the whole issue in the first year of his pontificate. He was full of consternation and asked me to draw up a detailed memorandum." *(My Hope for the Church,* p. 120.) This is obviously not a case of what the "priestly caste" and its aspirant, Garry Wills, would call *ignorantia affectata,* which is an intentionally willed act of nescience.

In this context, it may be pointed out that while patristic and earlier models of the episcopate may provide inspiration for contemporary reforms, it is naive to try to eradicate nearly two millennia of evolution in the hope of returning to governmental and administrative styles vaguely evident among the primitive Christian communities. The goal is not to introduce a literalist and fundamentalist reading of the most ancient "texts," nor to emulate sectaries from time immemorial in constructing idyllic—and short lived—utopias, but to build on the kind of organic development Cardinal Newman envisaged. To decry in the name of a dubious fidelity to gospel data such foundational doctrines as the apostolic succession is not to engage in renewal but in reversal. Of course, no one thinks of the apostolic succession in the mechanistic terms of the medieval and post-tridentine church. It may rightly be regarded as an unbroken metaphoric chain, but it is defined as a continuum residing in the people of God and exercised among them by their chosen leaders in union with their chief bishop.[20] The

---

[20] In chapter one I cited as the reason for "cautious optimism" about the future a sequence of historical reforms, each one affirming a kind of mechanism of equilibrium between center and periphery. James Carroll has a different view: "Again, if the long history we have seen demonstrates anything, it is that [the ideology of papal power] drives relentlessly along the unbroken shaft of *apostolic succession* [which he seems to believe relates only to the papacy], from Leo I. . . ." Then follow Gregory VII, Urban II, Innocent III, Boniface VIII, Paul IV, Pius IX, Pius XII, and John Paul II. But Leo the Great, a Doctor of the Church, is remembered mainly for his confrontation with "the scourge of God," Attila, and his central role at Chalcedon in maintaining the two natures of Christ. Of the early and medieval popes Carroll "outs," Dante criticizes only Boniface VIII (not unworthily, but largely on personal political grounds) whose jubilee year (1300) is the date of the vision of the *Commedia;* Innocent III is mentioned in Paradiso as approving the "harsh rule" of St. Francis whose followers along with those of St. Dominic and the Seven Holy Founders represented the counterweight to Innocent's excesses. Other than on church-state issues, it is difficult to condemn Gregory VII whose reforms were manifold and lasting—but after a millennium understandably somewhat outworn. Paul IV reigned only four years, was founder with St. Cajetan of the Theatines, the first modern pope to express vehement antisemitism, but also an over-zealous reformer. The ideology Carroll has in mind is not "papal power" but "antisemitism," and to include Pius XII in his true bill is to base his case on mere repetition not investigation. What John Paul II is doing at this assize is incomprehensible. The lesson here is simply that nothing in this historical sequence has to do with apostolic succession as such, while

primitive Christian communities are not a template or blue-print—they are at best an exemplary cause. Again, it is not a dictate of religion but of common sense that an institution is only the lengthened *shadow* of the original or founding group.

Wills even more enthusiastically than Carroll attacks "apostolic succession" and goes on at great length, and presumably to the mystification of his readers, about the primitive church not having bishops in any present sense of the word, not having any notion of such succession, not having ordination or consecration as currently understood—citing *passim* assorted New Testament scholars and historians. He concludes that "Ignatius of Antioch, writing in the first decade of the second century is the first author we know of to make a clear distinction between bishops and elders." Then follows a history of Ignatius's travails among Antiochenes, Smyrneans, Philippians, Magnesians, Tralians, etc.. It is an interesting excursion. Even more interesting is the absence of any reference to the views of Newman (one of Wills' "heroes") as an Anglican on Ignatius and on the episcopal office in chapter two of the *Apologia*: "My own Bishop was my Pope, . . . the successor of the Apostles, the Vicar of Christ." Nor is there any reference to the *Essay on the Development of Christian Doctrine* which certainly assumes that everything wasn't crystallized and fixed before the "first decade of the second century." And as his mockery of liturgical practice, its gestures, language, and garb, was written precisely when several Protestant groups were taking up these same rites and ceremonials, so too his denigration of the episcopate comes within the very decade when a number of Protestant bodies have chosen to be administered by bishops—those empty vessels of Romish authority.

It should go without saying that we shall have institutions as long as we live in society, that is, in habitats of order, organization, distinction of roles, and separation of functions. The present advocacy of blurring everything into one indistinguishable, ungranulated mass, however flattering to the ambitious or the rootless, can only be regarded as signifying how transitional a stage

---

much here, particularly the presence of the two twentieth-century popes, has to do with papaphobia.

we are in. Whether we call bishops or popes chief clerks, presiding officers, or chairpersons of the board, and whether we determine them by selection of a delegated few, by election of the many, or by acclamation—all that matters little. What matters is fidelity among those who inhabit this penumbral world—this lengthened shadow—to the Spirit who was sent to preserve it.

— III —

So rather than the imputation—or deputation, computation, reputation, etc.—of "sin and deceit," one has to look to the major structural reform envisioned by the opposition party at Vatican I, and recognized by the prelates and their periti at Vatican II: the still unfinished elaboration of the theology of the one group recognized from the earliest days of the church as possessing the "plenitude of the priesthood." Three times reference has been made to Cardinal Manning's regrets that the episcopate was being reduced to "the pope's vicariate," with the subsequent denigration of national bishops conferences as the most unfortunate result of this "reduction."[21] Well before Vatican I, Newman recognized what it would take Manning another thirty years to discover.[22]

> . . . I view with equanimity the prospect of a thorough routing out of things at Rome; not till some great convulsions take place (which may go on for years and years, and when I can do neither good nor harm) and religion is felt to be in the midst of trials, red-tapism will go out of Rome, and a better spirit come in, and Cardinals and Archbishops will have some of the reality they had, amid

---

[21] It was recognized by Rosmini, who also cites Ignatius: "A Bishop's zeal was not confined to his own special charge among the Churches; it was yet greater for the Church Universal. He knew that he was a Bishop of the Church Catholic." And speaking of episcopal conferences, and the appointment of other bishops, he notes: "The Bishops of a province met twice a year, as so many brothers to discuss their common interests. . . . They decided cases; they appointed successors to deceased Bishops. These successors were not only known but acceptable to them, and they thus contributed to preserve the perfect harmony of the Episcopal body." *Five Wounds,* pp. 85–86.

[22] Wilfrid Ward, *Life,* II, p. 127.

many, abuses in the Middle Ages. At present, things are in appearance as effete, though in a different way, thank God, as they were in the tenth century.

As Newman recognized and as common sense, again, would suggest, if reform is to come it will not be by application of the counsel, physician heal thyself. A doctor with herself as patient like the lawyer with herself as client—folk wisdom rightly has it—will not be particularly well-served or well-advised. If the problem is with the Roman curia, the answer can only come from the universal episcopate, as it did in the consensual decrees of Vatican II.

That even Vatican I implicitly viewed the pope as a bishop "writ large," and did not view the local bishop as a lesser pope was generally lost sight of up to the period of Vatican II. The theological interdepedence of the local bishop and of national episcopates briefly came to the fore during the period around the second World War; however, as noted in chapter four that record is checkered. But the dark spots usually represented the final gasps of the theology of Vatican I, when some national hierarchies passively waited for word from Rome before acting. The only serious argument against this position was made by John Lukacs, writing with an obvious conservative bias. "Had there been more responsibility vested in the German national hierarchy, had the Mass been offered in German for a generation wouldn't the record of German Catholicism during the war have been even more pitiful? . . . Wasn't the problem precisely that the authority of the Holy Father was not sufficiently paternal, not sufficiently authoritative, not sufficiently universal?" (*Continuum,* Autumn, 1964) But had this responsibility and authority been vested in the episcopate from the turn of that century on—as the American bishops sought in trying to frustrate the creation of an apostolic delegate and to lay to rest the charge of "Americanism"—the German hierarchy might have had a sense of its collective mission and responded vigorously and without waiting for signals from Rome.

One highly respected German theologian sought to explain the indifference of many of the German bishops to the monstrousness of the Hitler regime by the laity's failure to inform them of it:

"The laity looked to spiritual 'leaders' on whom they could lay all the burden of responsibility."[23] There may be an element of truth in this, but it is more reasonable to assume the failure was at best reciprocal. At worst, the burden fell more heavily on the episcopate, particularly given the fact that there were strong grounds in the tradition for the bishops to have acted on their own, even when there was only the most general guidance from Rome. On the other hand, there were virtually no clearly defined grounds during the war years for what would later be called a "theology of the laity," and after Vatican II, a "theology of the people of God." And this may be worth a brief examination in this context of witness bearing.

In the thirties and forties the category of "the lay" was subsumed in the narrow notion of "Catholic Action," and the extensive literature it engendered was written, first, with a view to practical programs for what were, in effect, compliant assistants to the clergy; and, second, with a view to guaranteeing that lay people did not encroach on the mission of ordained and consecrated authorities. Cardinal Congar's groundbreaking work, *Jalons pour une Théologie du Laïcat,* published by Editions du Cerf in 1952, was the first systematic theological treatment of the topic, apart from earlier sketches by the layman, Jacques Elllul, on the Protestant side and by the Jesuit, Otto von Nell-Breuning, on the Catholic—both of the latter informed by their authors' wartime experiences. Congar though of necessity devoting much discussion to an already obsolete "Catholic Action," defined as "participation of the laity in the work of the hierarchy," turned it all around through a positive and a negative critique: first, by defining the laity as "the *pleroma* of the hierarchy," and, second, by noting that "particularly in the western church the 'communal principle' [where the laity is centered] has not been unified with the 'hierarchic principle,' resulting in the isolated [*solitaire*] development of the latter" (pp. 642–644).

So, given the absence of this theological foundation for the role of the laity, and the extensive historically developed foundation

---

[23] Werner Schoellgen, *Moral Problems Today* (New York, 1963), p. 141.

(though shaken by Vatican I) for the office of the episcopate, the response to Professor Lukacs' assumption that the record of German Catholicism would have been less pitiful if the power of the pope had been more "authoritative," more "universal"—the response has to be the traditional one which affirms that ideally a monarchy may be the best form of government from the viewpoint of execution of laws, but from the viewpoint of their formulation, a democracy is preferable. One could accept Professor Lukacs' conclusions only if one were to so exaggerate the supernatural guidance of the Holy See as to view it as incapable of political error.

Since the whole of history contradicts this notion, one is compelled to repeat the truism that over the long run there is more wisdom in the collective judgment of many prudent persons than in the individual judgment of only one. If the papacy were some utterly trans-temporal, a-historical institution, if the pope were some utterly detached and objective observer without any national, racial, or personal prejudices—in other words, if he were not a being in history—then one might prefer his judgment to all the episcopates in the church universal.[24] But in fact the bishop of Rome—as was emphatically clear from Newman's texts earlier in this chapter—is as much the subject of social pressures, is as necessarily caught up in the experience of a given place and time, is as liable to succumb to cultural or other biases as any national hierarchy. (Witness below the treatment by Pius XII of Joseph Charbonneau, Archbishop of Montreal.) Given this parallel submission to historical conditions on the part of an episcopal synod and of the papacy, the only ground for preferring the judgment of the former to that of the latter in temporal affairs is the wider range of sentiment and information available to it.

---

[24] Cited earlier were the words of Pius XII on the church as an institution subject to the fluctuations of space and time. Equally relevant is the following from his address to a group of journalists: "Public opinion is the ornament of every society composed of people conscious of their personal conduct and closely involved in the community of which they are members . . . , since the church is a living body, something would be flawed in its life if public opinion were lacking, a flaw that can be blamed on pastors and the faithful." Congar, *Jalons . . . ,* p. 360.

Turning now from these practical considerations on the reform of the episcopal office, it is necessary to look at the fundamental theological doctrine that must inspire any such reform. According to one of the still most widely used commentaries in English on ecclesiastical law (Abbo and Hannan) the common opinion of canonists is that the bishop should be more skilled in canon law than learned in theology. This judgment may indicate special pleading on the part of canonists, but one suspects rather that its general acceptance is a result of that denigration of the episcopate which Newman and Manning decried. The bishop becomes in that misconception not a teacher in his own right, but merely the representative of the Pope. And through this distortion of traditional teaching, he becomes in our time the target of those arrogant attacks launched by Foucauldian critics—the linear heirs of that celebrated postmodernist, Voltaire—on the Roman curia and its appointees as the power-hungry "Vatican foreign service": that latter definition having been proffered by another postmodern ecclesiologist, the late Paul Blanshard. But these attacks may be at least in part as much the result of the failure of theologians to explicate Catholic teaching as of contamination by the kind of francophonic faddism Acton denounced in his criticism of de Lamennais' *Essay on Indifference.* For Catholic teaching affirms that the bishop is not the pope's vicar, much less his ambassador; he is the one teacher of his *ecclesia*, and as a member of the episcopal college he is a teacher of the universal church in union with its chief bishop.

Might one not further suggest that it has been this notion of the bishop as an interpreter of the law rather than as a teacher of doctrine which accounts for the not infrequent silence of some bishops on pressing social and ethical issues? If the bishop is the chief teacher of Christian truth, he is also its chief *witness*; but if he is regarded as an interpreter of the law, his proper domain is jurisprudence, not testimony to truth. It is not desirable to discount any claims of prudence; but to make them an overriding consideration, and to define the episcopal office in terms of them, may tend to induce a silence that verges on the reprehensible—as some believe it did in *Nostra Aetate,* a well-intentioned document that needed the future *corrigenda* supplied by John Paul II. The "church of silence" was not only a reality in countries behind the iron curtain; it existed quite obviously in Hitler's Germany, and exists even with regard to some socio-political issues in this country today. Certainly the end of the cold war, while obscuring the great powers' continued reliance on a massive nuclear deterrent, has not done away with the central moral crux of that military posture: the effective nullification of the principle of noncombatant immunity, of which few bishops, except the bishop of Rome, Pius XII, spoke as often and as passionately.

That precisely during the period of adoption of an international nuclear strategy of "mutually assured *destruction*," it was the shadow of *Humanae Vitae*—a document that confronted only individuals—that persisted in hovering over the Catholic laity like an incurable case of Jansenist mumps: that precisely this could happen when the papacy was reiterating its insistence on the utter evil of total war must make one wonder about putting excessive trust in the witness of the laity *or* of some bishops. (One will recall the chauvinism of the Archbishops of New York and Seattle described earlier.) But then the question arises, as it did for many in the second World War, to whom shall we go? As always one goes to the internal forum of one's own conscience. Short of that, the arguments for the collective guidance of national episcopates, exercising their traditional rights as teachers of the church, remain as persuasive as human agents can expect.

This may call for more courageous bishops—like von Galen, von Preysing, and Saliège— than we are accustomed to. There are probably—one occasionally hears—forty or so bishops in the American church who are quietly but effectively bearing witness even in these troubled times, and who recognize that an authentic witness is one who takes personal risks. This does not mean necessarily that they are suffragans. In fact, being "auxiliaries" may allow them more freedom. At Vatican II, one of the most significant interventions was that of Stephen Lefven during a heated debate:[25]

> Why not put an end, once and for all, to the scandal of our mutual recriminations? Every day it becomes clearer that we have a real

---

[25] Cf. Peter Hebblethwaite, *Paul VI: The First Modern Pope* (New York, 1993), p. 361.

need of dialogue not merely with the Protestants but among ourselves assembled in the Council. . . . Some Fathers speak as though
the only text in the whole Bible were, "Thou art Peter and upon
this rock I will build my church." And they dare to preach at us as
though we were against Peter and his successors, or as though we
wished to weaken the faith of believers or to promote indiffer-
entism.

Nor does the risk of forthright witnessing even remotely entail a
murder in the cathedral, though it may entail what curial euphemists call "involuntary resignation"; or it may take the form of
the antagonism of some of the bishop's brethren as it did with
the effective exclusion of Archbishop T.D. Roberts from anything
other than ceremonial affairs during the period leading up to Vatican II—and even at the council itself. It may take the form of re-
buke by the pope, as it did with several prelates at the time of
Vatican I, including as we have seen Archbishop Darboy, martyred
in Paris; as it did with Archbishop Mignot under Pius X; as it did
with Archbishop Charbonneau under Pius XII;[26] and finally as it
did in this country with the scandalous treatment by John Paul II
of that noble figure, Archbishop Hunthausen—while his brother
bishops, excepting only Weakland and Bernardin, stood by as
models of *neutrality*. But, one has to ask, may not all this be the
price of accepting the plenitude of the priesthood, and of being the
successor of the apostles? So to anyone's concern with structures,

---

[26] Pius figures in another drama fraught with political and religious significance, and again does not prove to be an attractive leader. John Thomas McDonough, a Dominican wrote a controversial play, *Charbonneau & Le Chef* (Toronto,
1968), in which the influence in Rome of the Premier of Quebec, Maurice Duplessis (le chef), led to the forced resignation of the Archbishop in 1950 because of
his heroic support of striking asbestos workers. The drama is certainly more intense than anything of Hochhuth's, particularly the scenes in which Duplessis
threatens Charbonneau, and the Apostolic Delegate, Antoniutti (later an ally of
Franco, and opponent of Montini in the conclave), cites the canons justifying
Pius's decision. The 1950 *Official Catholic Directory* under the entry for Victoria,
B.C. (*read:* Vatican Gulag) states: "Institutes of Women, Sisters of St. Anne";
then in the following order (an early triumph for feminism?) names the Provincial Superior, then the Mistress of Novices, then "Most Rev. J. Charbonneau,
D.D., Chaplain." No redemptive red hat here, but Charbonneau did outlive Du-
plessis—by four months. Father McDonough was censured by his superiors.

and particularly structures of governance— though by definition, not of deceit—one may say of course adjust them, update them, reform them. But do not reject the "headstone" which sustains by its very position the whole "structured" edifice, the apostolic succession—as defined above.

One final encouraging sign of the times which relates to the two poles which the episcopate, as it were, binds together: the papacy and the laity. John Lukacs whom I briefly criticized above is one of the most wide-ranging and learned historians of our time. In the aftermath of Hochhuth's drama, he made what today may seem like an extraordinary statement:[27]

> . . . the thinking that his play manifests, represents an attitude toward the Catholic Church which is curiously recent, curiously contemporary. It is an attitude of high expectations. . . . It also reflects the great rise in Papal prestige after 1945 which is one of the most remarkable developments in the postwar history of the world. Amidst the godlessness, the plasticity, the materialism, the communism, and the neo-Marxist twaddle and patter of intellectuals about a "post-Christian" world, the prestige of the Papacy during the last decade of Pius XII's reign was higher than at any time since the Middle Ages.

It would be probably less astonishing but certainly as remarkable to prophesy that the prestige of the papacy during the last decade of John Paul II's reign may be recognized as higher than that of Pius XII. Certainly, "prestige" is an intangible concept, and in many ways, like "celebrity," a hollow one. But in a world which values "the power of public opinion," and which with Father Häring sees the latter as a hopeful indication of "the turnaround" which "looms on the horizon," papal prestige is a significant factor.

The irony regarding John Paul II, if not Pius XII, is that his prestige often seems greater among those outside the church than it is among those within it—as many of these books which I have

---

[27] "The Roots of the Dilemma," *Continuum,* Summer, 1964.

discussed in detail clearly attest. Nor should this be entirely surprising; members of a family have arguments, often vigorous among themselves, while presenting to the outside world a facade of harmony. Nevertheless, papal prestige is a datum of current history. It is an incontestible phenomenon of the beginning of the twenty-first century, and as such must be viewed in the light of salvation history as significant for the church in the modern world. How that prestige is to be utilized, I will take up shortly regarding the ethical mission of the papacy; but first some words on an area crying out for reform, "Christian ethics," about which Maximos IV declared: "Our Christian morality must have a Christocentric character with the expression of love and of liberty. It must educate in each one a sense of *communal* and personal responsibility. As a consequence a profound revision of the values of present Church discipline—of its very nature *changeable*—is imposed obligatorily."[28]

— IV —

For decades in the middle of the last century there had been a debate among theologians as to whether there is such a thing as a uniquely Christian ethic. The pious and prevalent conclusion was that, yes, there is such an ethic based on the law of charity which imposes and privileges beyond the norms of a mere ethic of natural law—this was maintained even though in the practical application of that unique ethic (that is, "how to live a good life") the actions of Catholics differed little from those of their non-Catholic neighbors. Perhaps that original question was badly framed. Should it not have been: *how* does the church have an ethical mission, and if so *primarily* to whom?

Let it be postulated that the church does have a broadly conceived mission to guide individuals to follow their consciences according to the law of love. But for the most part, it must be admitted that in these times such individual guidance is rendered

---

[28] *L'Eglise Melkite au Concile* (Beirut, 1967), p. 243.

by parental, environmental, educational, and other social factors—including of course in the whole amalgam, religious—all of
which shape and guide what we think of as the well-formed conscience of each person. This explains two paradoxes brought out
earlier: first, natural law morality *is* commonsense morality; second, commonsense morality guides personal individual moral actions far more effectively, wisely, and prudently than does
"official" Christian morality.[29] Hence the commendation earlier of
Garry Wills' "pastoral" orientation in discussing almost exclusively (regardless of how rebarbatively) personal issues: abortion,
contraception, gay and lesbian rights, gender parity, masturba-
tion, divorce, celibacy—though that commendation carried with
it the implicit criticism of ignoring collective socio-political issues.
Even Father Häring in his moving testimonial, *My Hope for the
Church,* devotes only one chapter out of eighteen (three pages in
all) to such global matters as "ethic of peace," "worldwide justice," and "life on our planet." While recognizing that in many
areas and if only by sheer numbers, individual and community
morals overlap, is it not strange that for most Catholic ethicians
individual and personal morality should trump socio-political morality, particularly when it is precisely personal morality that has
proved most intractable to official ethical "guidance"? It may
even be suggested that this emphasis on individual morality—
with its attendant dependence on outside instruction and exhor-
tation—is what has kept the Catholic community both in a
permanent state of moral tutelage, and in a condition of relative
indifference to the larger ethical issues confronting a global society.[30] (It was, after all, a celebrated "convert" to Catholicism, and

---

[29] At the height of the contraception controversy in the sixties, Thomas Merton was asked if he wanted to discuss the issue in public. His response was simply that over time such matters work themselves out in practice—as in fact they
have.

[30] An important indicator of the necessary shift in perspective, and consequently in practice is the Religious Consultation on Population, Reproductive
Health and Ethics. Here we have an agenda which goes beyond the approved
environmental issues embraced by everyone except the troglodytic right. Here is
an ethic that transcends petty moral concerns about the sinfulness of individual
acts, and which focuses on a morality for humankind—and by that fact on a
morality that uplifts the individual. Directed by ethician, Daniel C. Maguire, the

the American representative to the Vatican who coined the term, "globaloney.")

But paradoxically there may be a religious significance to this emphasis, a significance which by reason of its deficient emphasis on socio-political morality opens up a unique opportunity for the only truly global religious institution in history. The conjunction of that historically grounded deficiency *and* opportunity, envisaged by Christian thought as salvation history, brings the "prestige" of the pope fully into play. Again, one must ask whether there is not a sign of the times in the manifest phenomenon that personal moral directives and counsel as dispensed by Rome are more and more ignored in precisely that era when the institutional authority of the papacy is at its highest? Certainly there is here at least a negative criterion for the direction of the future.

There is also the manifest and readily comprehensible phenomenon of the church being adamant and undeviating on issues of personal morality, while being entirely open to historical and geographical influences—those would be denounced as "relativistic" in sexual matters—on issues of social morality. Thus compared to certitude and rigidity in the ethics of the individual, we see openness to dialogue and to the recognition of ethnic, racial, and even "local" differences as factors affecting social ethics: manufacturing, trade, and labor relations; inter-area and inter-nation relations—precisely all the fields that only a world church has the "prestige" to address. In *De Locis Theologicis,* Melchior Cano lists what might well be called "sources Chrétiennes," most of which represent the rich but anticipated "fonts," the standard but occasionally static data of the past—scripture, tradition, the theological schools, the magisterium, etc.—on which theology nurtures itself. Only the tenth, history, is responsive to the present, to the realm of the contingent and temporal. But it is precisely this historical dimension of the exigent "now" which has emerged as the queen of the sciences—just as in fact it did in previous critical eras in the life of the Church. As Blondel wrote:[31]

Consultation has published three important *and* accessible books in its series Sacred Energies.

[31] *Attente du Concile,* p. 228.

Far from having to descend from the past to the present, it is by the present that we must return to the past; it is by the last link of the divine chain that we are able to grasp the whole. The first disciples saw Christ, and seeing the head they believed in the body, in the aborning Church. We see the body in the present and we believe in the head.

And it is also this historical dimension which is now central in social ethics as a true sign of the times whose proper reading will revolutionize how we look at global issues.

This church has providentially evolved into a global institution—the only religious body to have done so—with a global mission; not of course in any neocolonialist sense of mere numerical "convert making," but in the sense of social responsibilities to the whole of world society. It can take the lead as only a world organization can in vigorously and wholeheartedly fighting for real disarmament of nuclear weapons, fostering environmental protections, defending human rights, helping the helpless and the hopeless; in short, for exercising its duty, and yes, "flexing" its muscle, as only a worldwide power can. Again, Newman said it better: "the church should be going out with the high spirits of the warrior, conquering and to conquer."[32]

The record has been excellent on some issues such as peace and war and nuclear deterrence, and we all need the kinds of reminders about these issues John Paul II has over and over reiterated. It is all well and good, as well as utterly non-controversial among any thinking people, to be a defender of environmental programs— even one-time ardently convinced marxists have now embraced that cause: making the Red one Green. But the absolutely fundamental environmental issue now almost lost sight of in the aftermath of the cold war remains the astronomical number of nuclear weapons still in place. Their overkill capability goes beyond any conceivable deterrent utility by a factor in the thousands. America alone could reduce its numbers from six thousand to six hundred and still be far outside any justifiable moral limit. This is an issue

---

[32] Ward, *Life,* II, p. 127.

that ethicists—as trendy as other specialists or even other adolescents rioting over Nafta or rainforests—have given up on, even though in their blinkered way they know that nuclear weaponry still remains the greatest threat to the planet.[33] Nuclear "disarmament" is one of the farces of the twenty-first century. And only one figure of international stature, John Paul II, seems to recognize that fact.

The record has also been admirable on the kindred issue of noncombatant immunity as such; good on economic justice; less good on political justice, still threatened in residual Catholic client states in Latin America and Africa; mixed on "environmental" and human rights issues; and dismal on such issues as are raised by overpopulation and pandemic AIDS. In short, the record is utterly deplorable when this church—now in the twenty-first century—lets its secondary mission regarding personal morality encroach on its primary mission regarding social morality. We need a new global ecclesiology for a new global church, a church that welcomes the struggle against the real forces of darkness: greed that throughout the developing world makes for petty tyrants supporting death squads, and ignorance that makes for overpopulation and disease.

— V —

And here we return to the bishops. If they remain what Newman called "lackeys," given to "toadyism," ambitious not to bear witness but to rise in the petty world of church politics, there is small

---

[33] It is now nearly two decades since the publication of the American bishops' pastoral on nuclear weapons, written largely by Cardinal Bernardin. In 1983 when the cold war was in regular danger of being reignited by conservative chauvinists, the pastoral was a reasonable document which could not be undercut by Michael Novak's *Moral Clarity in the Nuclear Age* (New York, 1983). Cf. Justus George Lawler, "Moral Confusion in the Nuclear Age" (*The Christian Century,* April 4, 1984). But now that political, and ethical, attention is focused elsewhere, the issue is treated as resolved—which it plainly is not. But the focus on "Nafta or rainforests"*is* important, if motivated constructively and not rancorously. "Adolescent" agitation has proved effective when related to strikes supporting living wages for school workers or for factory workers manufacturing products for young people.

hope. The picture at turn-of-the-millennium America is *not yet* as bleak as it was in mid-nineteenth-century Ireland: "The truth is that these bishops are so accustomed to be absolute that they usurp the rights of others and roughride over their wishes and their plans quite innocently without meaning it, and are astonished, not at finding out the fact, but at its being impossible to these others."[34] In developing countries, the issues are quite different. Unless these often newly created bishops can rise above their colonialist ethnic backgrounds or their tribal prejudices *or* the individualist moral proscriptions emanating from Roman authorities and speak as masters in their own house, there is less hope. Unless they have the courage to convey to those authorities, again and again (as did the three German bishops on marriage and divorce issues), the obvious need for safeguards against the AIDS epidemic, there is even less hope of being true to their people. The coinage, "culture of death" is truly a dysphemistic masterstroke; it makes the diabolic fetishizing of condoms almost something the gates of heaven can not prevail against.[35]

But the danger in this country is that an enervated episcopate will not only appear out of touch with the faithful, but in many instances appear hypocritical. Fifteen years ago it may have been accurate for the president of the bishops conference to maintain: "There is scarcely another group in the United States which couples a horror at abortion with a preferential option for the poor, a concern for a more generous immigration policy with a recognition of what easy divorce has done to the family, the resettlement of refugees from Southeast Asia with a condemnation of military aid to the Contras" (*America,* November 29, 1986). The impression

---

[34] Ward, *Life*, I, p. 323.

[35] Another masterstroke has been the casual acceptance of "welfare reform" into the common vocabulary of North America. Persecution of the helpless is lost sight of while a battery of sociologists, social workers, statisticians parses this pleonasm which has nothing to do with either welfare or with reform. At the height of the "reformatory" crisis when the already helpless and homeless were being shed of their remnants, the newly appointed archbishop of a major see announced the official appointment of an exorcist. Thus did the possessed trump the dispossessed.

such a recitation may leave in the twenty-first century is that public concern with social issues is merely a ploy that masks the real agenda, opposition to various matters of personal and individual morality. This, as the argument above seeks to adduce, would be to get the whole ethical issue precisely and disastrously *exactly* backwards. The phenomenon of the overriding importance of the "real" agenda becomes more apparent when, under pressure from Rome, the bishops abdicate their apostolic responsibility and display all the signs of group hysteria in denouncing this or that gender or sexually rooted individual practice. The quotation from the bishops conference above ends as follows: "The church in the United States has become *something of a* sign of contradiction." Though this is intended biblically, it will be soon read as a sign of contradictoriness, a sign of collective obsession leading to *something of a* case of schizophrenia.

Nevertheless, as this entire book attests, there remains cause for hope. Though, "at this point, readers may perhaps ask me how, despite everything, I still maintain that a turnaround for the better is in the offing." Father Häring's words are worth citing again. It is not some bromide or facile nostrum to say that faith remains in the historic "exceptions." It remains in communion with the totality, in the pilgrim church in its entirety—and not only in its entirety of members but in its entirety of past and present. When Newman was asked at a crucial juncture in his own life if he regretted having put his trust in the bishops, he replied that he had not done so, but had put his trust in the whole church. Morals no less than dogma reside in that totality. Hope resides in papacy, episcopate, people of God together, focusing not on individual behavior—which grace and what used to be called "synderesis" can take care of—but engaged in what Teilhard described as "constructing the earth."

I close with another parable, and one more recent in time than that with which I opened the previous chapter. One of Cardinal Congar's "conditions" for reform-without-schism is "to remain within the communion of the whole." It was the failure to live by that condition that led to the excommunication in 1951 of a small group of French Catholics led by one Abbé Jean Massin and calling themselves "The Community of Christian Hope." Their public program has a familiar ring: ". . . to live and think along the lines of a truly evangelical Christianity which shall respond to the needs and values of our epoch. . . . to reject any moral doctrine which makes the idolatrous pretension of codifying an imitation of Jesus Christ. . . . Can I believe at once in Jesus and in Rome?"

After the condemnation Congar himself made an important statement on church reform—with which I shall end. The statement is significant because Congar at the time had himself been pilloried by clerical delators and censors for being in part responsible, through the influence of *Vraie et fausse Réforme dans l'Eglise,* for Abbé Massin's defection. The statement took on even greater weight when during the conciliar period Congar sketched in *Chrétiens en dialogue* the mistrust and even contempt shown during the fifties by Roman authorities towards himself and some of the most dedicated and saintly figures of the postwar French religious revival—*la grande purge* referred to earlier. That he and his confreres, though bending, never broke under the lash of Rome made his testimony utterly probative and persuasive.[36] This is his statement with only the least possible commentary added.[37]

One is able to leave the church. But after that, what then? I have here before me a number of manifestoes: that of the liberal Catholic Church, of the Kingdom of God, of the Evangelical Catholic Church, of the French Evangelical Church, and of many others. Several of these groups which in their time have caused much suffering and trouble to souls no longer exist. What have they achieved in the final analysis but to break with the Faith and to render more difficult the work of the Gospel in the world? Does not history cry out with all its might at the vanity of trying to purify the church against itself? In forty or fifty years [precisely

---

[36] For the Community of Christian Hope and its aftermath, there are mimeographed materials privately circulated, and printed commentaries in *Informations Catholiques* (February 14, 1952); *La Vie Intellectuelle* (February, 1952); *Life of the Spirit* (March, 1952); and in Massin's book, *Le Festin chez Levi* (Paris, 1952).

[37] *Témoinage Chrétien* (January 11, 1952).

now], when others shall overtake us on the paths of our present cares, those who today destroy and rebuild in the flower of their twenty or thirty years shall be not only ignored but forgotten [save as object lessons]. Where shall they be? What shall they believe? Reading the manifesto of their youth, I fear that they find nothing great in the profound truths which the saints have lived in the church and for which at this very moment confessors [like Congar and other victims of the "great purge"] are offering without glory before the eyes of men, their health, their liberty, and the very life of the body.

Cardinal Congar had faith in history and faith in the power of spirit ultimately to reform the distortions and errors which he saw about him. That he did not react in violation of his own principles to the suppression of *Vraie et fausse Réforme dans l'Eglise* and of many other writings by friends and colleagues has resulted in his achievements bearing now in these more propitious times— completely unforeseeable five decades ago—the richest and most lasting fruit. Paul VI and John Paul II have stated publicly that the work of Congar had nurtured their own spirit and instructed them in the ways of religious renewal. It is no small thing to be a teacher of popes.

Lastly, and fundamentally, what Congar taught in *Vraie et fausse Réforme dans l'Eglise* is that "the church must safeguard above all its very being and the integrity of its principles. An adaptation to the needs of the world, an openness to the longings of the faithful, or real improvements in the order of theological science and pastoral effort—these are certainly desirable: but they have reference to the life of the church, to her *bene esse.* The primary concern of her responsible leaders is with reference to her constitutive principles, to her *esse.*"

That, however, is not an injunction to those in authority to "just let things be."

Index of Names